Just Around the Corner

Encouragement and Challenge for Christian Dads and Moms
Volume 1

by Steven and Teri Maxwell

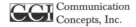

Communication Concepts, Inc.

JUST AROUND THE CORNER

Ordering information:
Managers of Their Homes
2416 South 15th Street
Leavenworth, Kansas 66048
Phone: (913) 772-0392
Web: www.Titus2.com

Published by:
Communication Concepts, Inc.
www.we-communicate.com

ACKNOWLEDGEMENTS

Scripture taken from the HOLY BIBLE, KING JAMES VERSION.

ISBN 978-0-9669107-2-8

Printed in the United States of America

1 2 3 4

This book was created in Microsoft Word. QuarkXPress 4.0 and Adobe Photoshop 5.5 were used for layout and design. All computers were Windows based systems running Windows NT/2000.

Design by Christopher Maxwell.

This book is dedicated to:

Homeschooling dads and moms–
the most dedicated, courageous,
self-sacrificing people we know!

Contents–Mom's Corners

Contents–Dad's Corners

Acknowledgments

We would like to thank those who have helped make *Just Around the Corner* a reality. Steve and Teri could not have completed this project alone–at least not for many more months or maybe even years!

We are ever praising our Lord Jesus Christ for His salvation and continuing work in our lives. Without that, we would have nothing to write about.

Teri's father, Rex Frazer, helped with editing and proofreading. Sarah, the Maxwell's oldest daughter, also edited and proofed. The Maxwell's second oldest son, Christopher, is responsible for the layout and design of *Just Around the Corner*.

Finally, we are very grateful for the homeschooling dads and moms who are on our e-mail list and read the Dad's and Mom's Corners each month. Their regular e-mails of encouragement are part of the reason we keep writing the Corners. Our readers' reoccurring suggestion to compile the Corners into a book was the impetus we needed to do just that!

Dad's and Mom's Corners

If you enjoy what you read in this book, you may want to sign up for the Dad's and Mom's Corners each month. Steve and Teri continue to write the free, monthly encouragement articles. To be on our list (which is never given away or sold–all addresses are kept strictly confidential), stop by our website, www.Titus2.com, or call us 913.772.0392.

Additional Books

Many of the subjects contained in this book are now covered in-depth by resources written since the Corners were first published. If you are interested in them, please see Additional Resources, page 381, or www.Titus2.com for more information.

A list of our current books include:

Managers of Their Homes: A Practical Guide to Daily Scheduling for Christian Homeschool Families
Managers of Their Chores: A Practical Guide to Children's Chores
Keeping Our Children's Hearts: Our Vital Priority
Homeschooling with a Meek and Quiet Spirit
Preparing Sons to Provide for a Single-Income Family
Just Around the Corner: Volume 2
Children's books:
Summer with the Moodys
Autumn with the Moodys
Winter with the Moodys
Spring with the Moodys

Preface

Five years after Steve and I began to homeschool, we were asked to lead our local homeschool support group. One facet of this job included publishing a monthly newsletter. We quickly discovered there was little to go in the newsletter aside from information on the upcoming meeting. At that point, Steve and I decided to each write a monthly article with the purpose of encouraging and challenging the dads and moms in our support group. We called these articles Dad's Corner and Mom's Corner.

When families moved away from our area, they frequently asked to continue subscribing to the newsletter so they could get the Corners. We didn't want them to have the expense of paying for the newsletter when they wouldn't be able to participate in the group. Therefore, we began offering the Corners free via e-mail.

In the past couple of years, we have been asked if we planned to put the Corners into a book. Many felt it would be easier to read in a book format than on the website or by e-mail. Therefore, this book is a compilation of several years of the monthly Corners articles. Steve and I regularly coordinate our articles so they are on the same topic but from a mom's point of view versus a dad's. However, we decided you would have less difficulty reading the book if the Mom's Corners were all together, followed by the Dad's Corners.

Moms, there is a caution we have for you concerning the Dad's Corners. Steve writes very much to a man's heart. Steve wants to "talk" man to man with your husband without setting any expectations in your heart. We would suggest that you not read the Dad's Corners unless your husband has read them first, and he encourages you to as well.

We have many on our Corners e-mail list who are not homeschooling parents. While they say they benefit from the Corners, it is important that you understand we are writing from the perspective of homeschooling.

It is truly a joy to look in our hearts each month and ask the Lord what He has taught us that we can share with other Christian parents. With three of our children now being adults, we believe we can write from the perspective of having seen the truth of God's Word put into practice. At the same time, we are still in the trenches homeschooling five children. You will have a candid vantage point as you see us fail, succeed, laugh, and cry while we endeavor to serve the Lord Jesus Christ.

We pray the articles will be a blessing to you. We think you will be encouraged and challenged as you read these pages!

Teri

School Year Planning

My summertime provides an opportunity to reflect back over our past school year and prepare for the upcoming one. New school beginnings hold the excitement, hope, and promise of significant accomplishments for each member of our household. Often, though, this promise will not come to fruition unless specific goals and direction are set for the year.

Planning with Steve for the next school year is a highlight of my summer. The two of us block out time together where we can set goals and the course of our school year. This past summer we went to the conference room at Steve's work with a nice table, chairs, and a big whiteboard. Being away where there were no interruptions had obvious advantages. One year, though, we spent Saturday morning at home working on this with nothing else scheduled "to do" and encouraged the children to play in their rooms or outside as much as possible. After our planning time we try to have a "date" with dinner out.

To prepare for our planning time, I put together some background information for Steve to review before we meet. He takes what I give him, looks at it, and prays about it for several days before we have our meeting. I start by giving him our plan or goals from the previous summer and a schedule of what we actually did during the school year. I also write out areas in which I felt we did not do what we had wanted, including difficulties with attitudes, schedules, specific schoolwork, our not keeping the children accountable or their not doing what we had wanted. I give him a list of subjects that I think we may want each child to study or work in and the number of hours we do school each day. I may write out some character concerns that specifically affect schoolwork.

When we have our planning sessions we start with prayer, since Proverbs 16:9 says, "A man's heart deviseth his way: but the LORD directeth his steps." First, we go over last year's plan to see what we achieved, what we deleted, and what did not work. Next, if we want to write out goals, we start with that. Then we look at our list of what each child could spend his school time on, and prioritize it. The big white board was great for this. We listed each child's name on the board and then underneath placed the school subjects we wanted them to pursue with a number beside it for its priority. From there, we work with the specific amount of time to spend per day or week on a particular subject. We also write down ideas on how to make sure the character deficiencies are being addressed and followed up on.

I am very grateful that Steve is willing to sit down with me and make what we consider very important decisions regarding our school direction. Although I usually put together the specifics after this major meeting, I know where we as a team are heading. If I run into further snags, Steve and I set aside more time to address the new items that come up.

I hope it is possible for each of you as couples to make time to be together and focus on your school planning for the next year. Perhaps it will be something that you can look forward to as I do to my conference with my wonderful husband.

August 1995

Children

As I write this Mom's Corner I am celebrating my 40th birthday! Birthdays have a way of causing us to reflect on life, and my heart has been filled with joy for my family today. I can't help but think about how few women, at the age of 40, have the privilege of nursing a baby and delighting in an adult son too.

Had God not changed Steve's and my heart regarding children and family planning I would have held my last baby in my arms 13 years ago. Joseph, John, Anna, and Jesse would not have been given life, and my nest would quickly be emptying. As we evaluate these past seven years of our lives, Steve and I believe that there is nothing we could have invested our lives in that would have had any more value.

After we surgically cut off the possibility of having more children for seven years, God showed us, from His Word, that closing the womb or opening it was His domain and could be trusted to Him in faith. We knew there was a great probability, even with reversing the original procedure, that we might not have more children.

With the realization of how dependent Steve and I were on the Lord for His gift of children came very different feelings in our hearts about our children. With our first three, having children was the thing to do–taken for granted–the norm for a young married couple. But with the last four we have known it was not a matter of our will that they were conceived but God's, and we have had the pleasure that comes to hearts that choose obedience to God's will.

What about those seven empty years, the gap between older children and younger ones, in our family? Did God have children for us that we refused? We think about that question from time to time and for me it usually brings tears.

What did God use to change our hearts and thinking in this area? He used His Word. Scriptures like: "Lo, children *are* an heritage of the LORD . . . Happy *is* the man that hath his quiver full of them. . ." (Psalms 127:3, 5), "And when the LORD saw that Leah *was* hated, he opened her womb: but Rachel *was* barren" (Genesis 29:31), ". . . but the LORD had shut up her womb" (1 Samuel 1:5), ". . . Be fruitful, and multiply. . ." (Genesis 1:28). Steve, home sick one day, got out his concordance and began a study on God's view of children that both broke and changed his heart. Malachi 2:15 clearly sums up God's purpose for marriage.

I share this part of our lives because my heart is so full of joy in my family. We wish someone had confronted us with this idea before we made our decision to cut off having children, challenging us to search the Bible for its truth in this area. We might not have liked what we found enough to consider obedience to it since my life was so full of three little children whom I was not dealing well with emotionally–but that is another Mom's Corner. For now, let a forty-year-old mother who is nursing her eleven-month-old baby encourage you to evaluate where you stand in relation to having children, not in light of your present circumstances or difficulties, but in the light of Scripture.

September 1995

Right Thinking

Resting in the quiet of the afternoon following a turbulent morning of peacemaking between Joseph (6), John (4), and Anna (2), I was cuddled up in my recliner chair. A heavy heart, jumbled mind, Bible, and notebook were my companions as my pen titled the page, "Thinking Right Thoughts When Discouraged and Worn Out by My Children's Unkindness to Each Other." Five "thoughts" soon filled the recently empty lines.

Number one: Every mother faces these same problems. Do you take any comfort in knowing my children fuss with each other? As I prayed about the situation, God reminded me every child is just like mine, and every mother must deal with the same things. None of us enjoys having children squabble. I need to change my mind-set to expect the unkindness and be thrilled if any kind deed comes from them, rather than expect the kindness and be discouraged when it doesn't happen.

Number two: God is developing my character as much as He is working in their lives. We say this often, but I have to keep telling it to myself. God is as much concerned with my learning to be patient, kind, loving, and gentle as He is in my children developing these qualities. What frequent opportunities He gives me to learn them, practice them, and even fail at them (thereby gaining humility and therefore God's grace through my failures).

Number three: God is developing my faith, as I trust Him to do this work since I can't myself. I can consistently train and teach my children. I can be an example to them, but it is God who works in their lives just as He works in mine. Therefore, my eyes must be on my Lord and my faith rooted in His working in their lives in His time. As a mother with both older and younger children I have proof of this as I have seen Nathan, Christopher, and Sarah develop more godly attitudes toward each other as they have grown up.

Number four: God is teaching me to rest in Him since my strength and will cannot bring it to pass. If I could, I would certainly force my children to have godly attitudes toward each other, and I do try. The truth is I can command some measure of outward conformity to the standard, but I cannot change a selfish heart. God is the One who does that, but He wants me to rest in Him as I wait for His timing. I can even trust that through the bickering He is working good in my life and theirs. We have talked about developing character in my life, but even the child who is being wronged in a disagreement is growing in character through it.

Number five: My greatest goal—even more than my goal to have a peaceful home and loving children—needs to be to teach my children to love God. Often the squabbles in our home make me focus more on peace and quiet than on the goal of turning my children's hearts toward loving their heavenly Father. As we focus on loving God, certainly a by-product of that, in time, will be children who have servant's hearts and are willing to give up their rights.

I find I can get so overpowered by thoughts and feelings of discouragement that I have to sit down and write truth out, like I did here, to bring my perspective back where it should be. Then I have to control my mind to think the truth when situations arise that trigger discouragement. In the midst of the emotions it is hard for me to do.

Usually, the change in thinking comes when I get down on my knees, cry out to God for His forgiveness for my self-focus, and ask for His help in my thinking truth. I pray each of you will use these situations you face with your children to see the benefits He is working for both you and them.

October 1995

A Controlling Wife?

The other night Steve gave Joseph, 6, and John, 4, a discipline that I didn't want them to have. In addition, the little boys were missing playtime with Dad because they were refusing to comply with their discipline. I asked Steve to let them finish their discipline later. Steve felt strongly that Joseph and John should understand there were consequences for what they had done and the discipline shouldn't be postponed. I commenced to help the boys, but this only made me unhappier with my husband. Steve could read my attitude even though I had not said anything. When he asked me what was wrong, I told him! Can you guess what the outcome was? Steve said he felt he could not please me since there are discipline issues that I want him to deal with, but when he does, I am not satisfied. He ended up unhappy with me, and I with him.

Later, as I reflected back in prayer over the situation, I was again made aware of how much I try to control what goes on in our home. Although my desire is to be a submissive wife, I am quick to jump into these situations and express myself vocally or by my attitudes and emotions. Wouldn't it have been better if I had been supportive of my husband's leadership in our home? How often I undermine him!

I see this area of supporting my husband as an opportunity to build my faith in God. Surely, God is big enough that He can influence Steve in his actions and decisions. Can I trust Him? Will I give way to fear, as 1 Peter 3:6 warns wives against, stepping in to try to take control? It is presumptive on my part to imagine that my way is God's way and my husband's is not.

1 Peter 3:3-4 says, "Whose adorning let it not be that outward *adorning* of plaiting the hair, and of wearing of gold, or of putting on of apparel; But *let it be* the hidden man of the heart, in that which is not corruptible, *even the ornament* of a meek and quiet spirit, which is in the sight of God of great price." I have found that the more I have this meek and quiet spirit, the more peace I have in my heart. I am quick to explain something, justify a child's action, or say what I think in a matter. If I will sit quietly and let my husband be in charge, I have chosen the path of submission rather than control.

The pride in my heart makes it difficult to go to Steve and ask his forgiveness when I fail in being submissive. It is much easier for me to justify myself than to admit being wrong. God's way is to break down my pride and build humility in my life. This is accomplished by my failures if I deal with them properly.

Steve is gracious and encouraging to me as God works in my life. It has taken more than twenty years of being married for me to begin to understand this vital truth in God's Word about a wife's meek and quiet spirit. I am just starting to see why He says it is precious in His sight. May we all walk in God's truth in our relationships with our husbands.

November 1995

Evaluating Reading Materials

When Nathan, Christopher, and Sarah began homeschooling in grades three, one, and preschool, we had a regular time of me reading out loud after lunch. With the coming of babies a few years later, this enjoyable time went by the wayside. Recently, I have made a bit of time to read to Joseph (6), while the other little ones nap, and then to John (4) and Anna (3), before the baby gets up.

Reading children's books to Joseph, which are more in depth than the picture books we used to read, has made me once more aware of the importance of the quality of our children's reading material. We have taken Philippians 4:8 as our gauge of what we want to read ourselves and have our children read. It says, "Finally, brethren, whatsoever things are true, whatsoever things *are* honest, whatsoever things *are* just, whatsoever things *are* pure, whatsoever things *are* lovely, whatsoever things *are* of good report; if *there be* any virtue, and if *there be* any praise, think on these things."

First, I am finding, although some of the books are interesting to Joseph, there is no value in them, no virtue. They are simply entertaining. Then other books actually have negative behaviors and attitudes. They are not just or pure. For example, one book we read talked about a person wanting to punch someone else in the nose. My little boys laughed and laughed, and it came up in conversation between them after that. They had never before heard of punching in the nose. I don't want them learning wrong behavior, thoughts, or attitudes from what they read. There are many books in which brothers and sisters have bad attitudes toward each other and say unkind things to and about each other. Is that what I want to foster in my children? Of course not!

We started reading a book from a very popular children's series. Before we had gone halfway through the first book, it had brought up Jack Frost, Santa Claus, and the need for birthday spanks if a child is to grow. None of that is true. It may have been what actually happened in the family of this story, but it becomes very confusing to Joseph as I try to explain why the book character believed in these things, and we don't.

Also, there was a whole chapter on the tediousness of Sundays because the children weren't allowed to do very much. The book did not explain why these people chose to honor God by devoting a day to Him and limiting their activities as Isaiah 58:13-14 says: "If thou turn away thy foot from the sabbath, *from* doing thy pleasure on my holy day; and call the sabbath a delight, the holy of the LORD, honourable; and shalt honour him, not doing thine own ways, nor finding thine own pleasure, nor speaking *thine own* words: Then shalt thou delight thyself in the LORD; and I will cause thee to ride upon the high places of the earth, and feed thee with the heritage of Jacob thy father: for the mouth of the LORD hath spoken *it*." Rather, they centered on the deprivation and hardship of the day for children. When we got to this part, I told Joseph we had to stop reading it. I was sad I had not stopped earlier.

Along this line, but down a slightly different path, is the choice of books for our daughters to read. Christian romance novels are very popular, but do they promote what we want our daughters to think about? It is hard enough for a young girl who is committed to waiting on God for a spouse to not think about young men, but when she is constantly immersed in romance, it becomes even harder. We have found it much better to encourage our thirteen-year-old daughter to read Christian biographies. These challenge her in her Christian walk and give true insights into the realities of love and marriage.

The tiny bit of reading time I have with Joseph is valuable for us just because we are together. However, I want to redeem every moment of the day. I don't want to waste any of our time by reading books that don't meet the test of Philippians 4:9. Reading-aloud time can be wonderful inspiration and encouragement to Joseph in the Lord. This is especially true as we find books about great Christians or stories that bring out character and right attitudes. We can have the benefits that educationalists tell us come from reading to our children, plus more, if they are inspired to godly behavior by what we read without the negative influences that come if we do not carefully screen what we read.

What about you? Have you put a high value on what your children are reading or what you are reading to them? Have you thought through what criteria reading material should pass in your home? It takes effort and sometimes means we miss out on what everyone else may say is great. I think choosing to please God in this way will have significant benefits in the lives of our children now and throughout the years.

January 1996

Cherishing Our Children

My heart is heavy as I write this Mom's Corner because Tim P. is at his earthly home, nearing his heavenly home-going. We have followed with prayers, interest, concern, and support the course of the battle this past year with Tim's brain cancer. The final chapter is now being written.

Sarah had the privilege of visiting Tim last Friday with her grandmother. When she came home she related how quick Wendy, Tim's mother, was to respond to each of Tim's calls and how patient she was with him even when it wasn't easy to determine what he needed.

What an encouragement to each of us moms to treat our children with that same love and respect. It is easy for me to fall into the trap of impatient tones, harsh words, and anger as I deal, day to day, with my children. Would I respond the same if I knew that I had only a short time left with that child? Or would I work hard to handle the situation with gentleness, love, and patience?

Surely, each day, the Lord would have me recognize the value and preciousness of the children He has given to me. I do not want to take them for granted. Despite the fact that I have a responsibility to train my children, which involves some discipline, my home should be as filled with smiles, encouragement, praise, security, and love as it would be if I knew I were spending the last few hours with my child. Even when discipline is necessary, it can be done with a quiet spirit and attitude, which will be much more effective than harshness or anger.

Sometimes I get so focused on the goals of the day and what needs to be accomplished that those God has placed me in the home to serve become no longer my ministry, but an interference. They have to be worked around so I can get done what I want to get done. I pray that as my heart has been touched by Tim and his family, God can keep my eyes on the children He has given me to minister to. Then I will interact with each one as an individual with needs that God has enabled me to help meet.

Wendy has shared with our homeschool group what home-schooling has meant to her these past two years. It gave her valuable time with a precious son. When she started homeschooling, she didn't know how little time she had left with Tim. I hope that each of us will also value the time God has given us with our children in this endeavor of homeschooling. May the educating not become so big that we lose the opportunity to cherish each precious child.

February 1996

A Tired Mama

Not long ago I had a bad week! It was especially disheartening because I had just come home from a wonderful three-and-a-half-day weekend away alone with my husband. I thought I would be skipping through the house with energy and love bubbling over onto all my family. Instead, I was dragging through each day. The children seemed very demanding and naughty, and school was long and tedious. I was disappointed in my lack of patience and the resigned attitude with which I dealt with the day's needs.

After two and a half days of feeling like crying but not being able to figure out what to cry about, I realized I was tired. My feelings and attitudes were coming from my physical lack of energy. This may not seem like a great insight to you, but for me it was. Instead of my world being bleak and forlorn, I realized I felt bleak and forlorn.

Understanding the problem didn't change my energy level, but it did allow several things to happen. First, I was able to accept my reactions to what was going on around me as coming from a physical source. Then I could treat it as I would the flu or a cold and try to get more rest. I could also work at mind control in thinking God's thoughts rather than my own thoughts. The Lord Jesus said He came to bear my burdens, so when I am worn out I need to be especially careful to cast them on Him. I also want to confess to my family each instance of my wrong attitudes and ask their forgiveness, rather than letting them pile up and make the burden of guilt even greater. I didn't have to feel guilty for being tired, but I did need to handle the tiredness in a godly manner rather than a selfish way.

It wasn't long until my normal energy level returned and I "felt" like myself again. I wished the first day I had felt "down" I had been aware of what was causing my discouragement rather than struggling with it for two and a half days.

I wonder how many difficulties, when they become mountains, actually relate more to our physical condition than to the circumstances themselves. When we get run down, behind on rest, are pushing beyond our physical limits, and maybe don't even know we are, our whole outlook changes. We can go to biblical examples to confirm this. I remember doing a Bible study one time where we read stories about godly men who became physically worn out and suddenly lost their spiritual zeal–men like Ezekiel, Jonah, and Jeremiah. But God met their needs: physical, emotional, and spiritual. He will do that for us too.

I encourage us as moms to become aware of how often our feelings and emotions are flowing from our physical state. Then we can accept them as temporary without having to be overwhelmed. We can take them to our burden bearer, Jesus Christ, and leave them with Him while we rest in Him.

May 1996

How Can We Convey the Preciousness of Our Children to Them?

Early morning walks take me past several day-care homes where I observe mommies dropping their children off. My heart is always heavy as I watch the process, but filled with gratitude that I have the privilege and make the choice to keep mine home with me. I hope that as the years go by, my children will realize their preciousness through seeing the investment God has led their dad and mom to make in them. We express to them their preciousness by giving of our time and resources to keep them in the environment where they are more loved than anywhere else in the world. But I also know how important it is for us to verbalize to them their preciousness.

Recently, in an effort to convey to two of my little boys the necessity of being kind to each other, I started by looking at each of them and telling them of their preciousness to me. Those two little boys' faces lit up. They were so happy with what I had told them. They remembered it that evening when Daddy came home and wanted to tell him at the dinner table.

That one simple situation made me see how easy it is to be at home with my children, involved with them all day long, and yet not express to them how precious they are to me. I can be so busy that my conversations with them don't even involve eye contact because I am doing another task as we talk. I need to have the Lord remind me to get eyeball to eyeball with them and let them know how much I love them, how special they are, how valuable they are, and what they mean to me.

Certainly, as we begin a new school year, our focus can be so intense on schooling that we forget our desire to value the ones in whom we are investing our lives through homeschooling. We are so close to everything that goes on with our children that our gaze often is fixed on their faults and shortcomings. We feel a responsibility to train our children in the admonition of the Lord and to build godly character in their lives, so we spend our time teaching and disciplining. Do we take an equal amount of time to bring them up in the nurture of the Lord? Can we speak words of love, encouragement, and value–building them up, looking them in the eye, and holding them close to us?

As we start a school year with the excitement of fresh beginnings, I pray each of our children will know of their preciousness to us and to the Lord. I pray that all of our teaching interactions can be without pressure and criticism, but characterized by an attitude of patience and love. This school year, may we as mothers embody the qualities we want to see grow and develop in our children.

August 1996

Waiting on the Lord

Most of our homeschool support group knows we have been, as a family, waiting; we are waiting longer for this baby to arrive than for any other birth yet. This has been good for each member of our family in developing patience. We trust completely in God's sovereignty over the timing for bringing our baby. We are daily given opportunities to be gentle and patient, to think about others' needs rather than our own, to keep murmurs and complaints to ourselves, and to keep our attitudes positive.

We don't know why this baby did not come before its due date as six of our seven children have or why it is lingering longer than the one other that went past due date. But there are some things that, from our perspective, could have played a part. The week before the baby was due our four little children came down with colds that lasted for a week and a half. Had our baby been born at that time, the sick ones would have had to look at the baby from a distance, not being allowed to touch it so it would be protected from their illness. Having the baby wait also gave me the pleasure of not missing the first homeschool meeting but getting the opportunity to see old friends and meet new ones.

As we have looked to the Lord for what He wants us to learn through waiting on a baby, I have seen how waiting applies in our homeschooling situations. There we are often waiting too: waiting for direction on a curriculum decision, waiting for a child to grasp a concept, waiting for character growth, waiting, waiting, waiting.

With a baby, as in some homeschooling waiting opportunities, we have no choice but to wait on God's timing. What we can choose in the waiting is our attitude. I can complain each time I am asked about whether the baby has come or not, or I can have a positive response. I can focus on my discomfort, lack of sleep, and impatience for a tiny baby, or I can focus on the Lord, praising Him throughout the difficulties.

During any waiting process, I want to make sure my heart is constantly on the Lord with an attitude of praise rather than murmuring. My tendency is toward self-pity and complaint during a difficult waiting situation. I want to manipulate the circumstances, force an answer or solution, and mutter my frustrations to my husband. Is that God's way or my way? God wants to use that time period to turn my heart and reliance to Him. When that happens, He receives the glory.

Recently, we had a decision to make concerning which of three phonics programs to use. I wanted the decision made quickly so I could get on with my planning for the new school year, but the decision was not an easy, cut-and-dried one. I pondered over it, poured over the programs several times, discussed the pros and cons with Steve, and complained about how hard it was to decide. Finally, Steve suggested that I start praying about it, waiting on the Lord for an answer. That was what I should have done in the first place.

I can excitedly report that when I did what God wanted me to do, the decision was not nearly as hard as I had made it to be in my own thinking. I saw God's direction and leading, but it didn't come the first time I prayed about it. Each time I started to feel anxious about no decision, that would be my signal to pray for God's will rather than worrying. As Steve and I discussed those phonics programs, it was clear to us that one of them could easily be blessed by the Lord because of the content used to teach the phonics. That was where we felt the Lord guiding. If I doubt the decision, it is an opportunity to go back to praying and put my mind on trusting God. The decision was made under His direction; it should be left in His control.

As we face these waiting situations in homeschooling, may God teach us to accept them with a positive heart and expectant attitude just as we can choose to wait with joy for the arrival of a baby. His answers to needs that involve waiting for homeschooling are just as trustworthy as His answer to when a baby is brought into the world.

P.S. Our time of waiting for Mary ended eight days after her due date. We had some challenges with the labor that we had not experienced with any of our other babies. Since she came after due date, we had many friends and family interested, concerned, and praying for her delivery. Do you think God had us wait so He could answer the prayers of His people on behalf of Mary and me? We praise our Lord Jesus, giving Him the glory for Mary's arrival.

September 1996

A Mother's Gratefulness

Having a baby creates many great topics for a Mom's Corner. What I want to share with you this month has to do with a grateful spirit versus a critical one.

My family graciously and lovingly allows me to stay in bed recovering for a week after the birth of a baby. Steve takes time off work while the rest of the family helps him run the home. Sarah especially went "extra miles" in serving and blessing. Not only did she spend her days accomplishing things that I normally would do, but she also wanted to do special things for Mom. She made my favorite candy for dessert one night and my favorite breakfast the next morning. She was careful to have a treat of some kind on my plate each meal and would often hold the baby while I ate. Sarah was the one who went through the house picking things up and putting them away so the house would stay tidy.

The week after Mary's birth gave me the perfect opportunity to work on a grateful spirit. There were times when, even though others were doing all my work for me and relieving me of almost all responsibility, I would criticize how a job was done or perhaps its timing. My heart grieved when the Lord would prompt me that I had had an ungrateful attitude. How much better to express my gratitude for what was done and let love cover over any inadequacies.

Steve has helped me see, as we discussed my desire to learn to have a grateful spirit, how just saying "thank you" is not always enough. I have felt I was grateful because I said "thank you," so I must admit, I did not receive his insight graciously at first.

I am seeing in my life that I can choose to be grateful for what my family does, or I can be critical about how it was done. Which attitude is going to generate a desire in their heart to have a servant's spirit and be willing to help? I can get so wrapped up in the job being done well that I forget to have a spirit of praise and commendation.

I have had to stop myself many times in the past three weeks to try again with what I was starting to say. I have had to go back and ask forgiveness for an ungrateful spirit. It is not easy for me to humble myself. I can usually justify any criticism that I am giving out, but I feel God is working in my life to have a grateful heart instead.

I pray that you, too, will think about how you can express your gratitude to the members of your family, not just a "thank you" but also a genuine attitude of praise. We express our love by building others up, and gratefulness will certainly do that. I hope God will continue to work a grateful spirit in each of our lives!

October 1996

Pleasant Disciplining

Recently I began to play back in my mind how I interact with my children, especially when it comes to discipline. This is an area in which the Lord has been teaching me, so I have been aware of it over the past few years. I could picture the stern look that sometimes comes to my face as I interact with an offender.

I have brought this before the Lord, asking Him to teach me how to discipline without becoming emotionally involved. Steve has likened this process to a policeman giving a speeder a ticket. This is just part of his job. The policeman isn't angry with the motorist; he isn't frustrated with having to give a ticket; he doesn't have an irritated tone in his voice; he just does his job. As a mom, that is how I have wanted to handle my discipline situations. My job is to teach and train my children. There will be times when this will involve discipline. If I expect my children to learn from training and teaching situations without ever needing discipline, then I am setting myself up for disciplining filled with negative emotions. If, on the other hand, I expect that discipline will also be a part of my mothering job, then I can have a better chance of handling it as the policeman does his job.

I have realized that I not only want to discipline without being negatively involved emotionally, but also choose to go a step further and be pleasant through the process. As I have tried this over the past two weeks, I have seen some positive results. One of my children even told me the other night that they liked it much better when I was happy when correcting them. There are some reasons why I think this may be. A pleasant attitude on my part while disciplining eases the tension of the situation. It relieves me of any negative feelings that I might take away with me and carry into the next interaction with that child. It shows honor and respect for the child. If Steve has to correct me on something, I want him to be pleasant with me; I owe my children the same courtesy.

Proverbs 16:21 says, ". . . the sweetness of the lips increaseth learning." During discipline, we want our children to learn from our instruction. Therefore, it would benefit us to heed God's Word and choose to use sweet words. Our attitude and tone can cause our words to lose their pleasantness.

We often will not feel pleasant, so we have to choose to act pleasant. The Lord has been showing me this is a choice I can make. I do not have to act according to negative feelings. This choice is a part of taking my thoughts captive to the obedience of Christ as 2 Corinthians 10:5 tells me to do. When I do make the choice to act pleasant despite feeling negative emotions, I find my feelings will begin to become positive too.

What about you? Can you think back to your recent interactions with your children? Are you looking at their faces? Are you smiling at them? Are you being pleasant with them? I pray each of us will choose to make our homes pleasant places by our pleasantness even when it is necessary to discipline. May God make us women who build our houses up rather than tearing them down with our own hands (Proverbs 14:1).

November 1996

Christmas Decorating

"If someone walked into your home this Christmas season, would they know by your decorations that you were celebrating the birth of your Savior, Jesus Christ?" This was a question asked of the congregation by our pastor during his Sunday sermon.

That question challenged us to evaluate the Christmas decorations we put up. Was the birth of Jesus the theme? Would someone else, who didn't know us, be able to see that? We began a purging of our decorations to eliminate the ones we did not feel fit with the emphasis we wanted to have–celebrating the birth of Jesus.

We also began to pray for the Lord to show us where to find decorations that would have Him be the focus. In the following years, we have been excited to see how God has answered this prayer. The weeding-out part was easy except when there was sentimental attachment to an item. Even then, I would think about what I wanted my children's hearts endeared to through the years of putting up the Christmas decorations. The items were then easier to let go.

The acquiring of replacement decorations was harder since so many Christmas decorations have nothing to do with the story of the birth of Christ. It was several years later that I saw an ad in a Christian catalog for a fireplace mantle garland with a large ornament hanging from the middle of it that said, "Name Above All Names." There were smaller, scroll-shaped ornaments hanging on the sides with words on them such as, "Truth," "Bread of Life,"

"Emmanuel." This became the focal point of our Christmas decorating, with our Nativity set sitting on the mantle right above the "Name Above All Names." My parents give us one more name to hang each year.

I go to the Christmas craft bazaar each November and ask the Lord to give me two or three new decorations to add to the collection. Every year He has done that. I rejoice in God's goodness to provide things that keep our mind on His birth during the Christmas season. This year I found a large ceramic ornament with the nativity scene painted on it that can be hung on the wall. I also found a wooden plaque with a Mary, Joseph, and baby Jesus painted on it, and the words, "Remember the reason for the season." The third item was another wooden plaque with an angel on one end and "Joy to the World" on the other. I come home from the bazaar with my purchases, hang them in my bedroom until the time to decorate the house, and delight in looking at them.

With Christmas fast approaching, may Jesus be known to our children even by the decorations we put up. May we use them to draw our children's hearts into a deeper love for Jesus as they experience the excitement year to year of getting out those Christmas decorations that remind them of His birth. May they also bring joy to our hearts as we reflect on the magnificent miracle of the birth of our Savior.

December 1996

Dealing with Daily Pressures

The sticky note was titled, "Mom's Pressure." The following items were listed on it: wrapping Toni and Nettie's gifts, making Anna's Christmas dress, John's phonics, meeting topic, Mom's Corner, Christmas letter, more Sarah school help time, Christmas gifts, clean fridge, work on baby book, spelling bee, Gram's puzzle, work on Sarah's Christmas dress. These were things that I was feeling pressure about; things that needed to be done or decisions that needed to be made.

When I expressed to Steve that I was overwhelmed with what all had to be done, he encouraged me to make a list of these things so we could sit down together and figure them out. Just making the list helped greatly because I was no longer trying to keep track of all of them in my mind. The mountain didn't look quite so high when it was written on a little sticky note.

Before Steve and I sat down to talk about the list, I had already eliminated cleaning the fridge, allotted Saturday night to wrap the presents that needed to be in the mail, decided to use my daily sewing time to work on Anna's Christmas dress, put "as time permits" beside John's phonics, and "don't worry about it" next to needing more Sarah school help time.

As Steve and I talked about the other items, we were able to make some decisions. We also agreed to pray about the ones that had no clear leading at that point. No longer was I carrying a burden of pressure.

As homeschooling moms, with the task of running our households and getting school done each day, we easily fall prey to being overwhelmed by what we have to accomplish in a normal day, not to mention when "extras" come along. When we allow our minds to dwell on these burdens, we become discouraged and lose the joy and delight in following the path God has called us to. Not only does this affect our hearts, but also our husbands' and children's.

Jesus says in Matthew 11:30, "For my yoke *is* easy, and my burden is light." Could it be that when the yoke feels hard and the burden heavy, we are carrying a burden of responsibility that we have loaded on ourselves? Before I wrote down the list of what was pressure to me, I was feeling like I had to clean the refrigerator. When I evaluated my priorities, I realized I didn't need to take on that project right before Christmas. It is now the middle of January, and I never did clean the refrigerator. It doesn't look too bad! The spelling bee was Christopher's project, not mine. I was involved in concern over it that I didn't need to have.

Sometimes the burdens are there because we allow ourselves to worry about a situation rather than taking it to the Lord in prayer right away. Worry, anxiety, and pressure should all be signals to us that in some way we are not responding to the situation properly. Without the Lord's help, the hard places will easily become burdens. We want to learn to cast all our anxiety on Him. I have often heard Elisabeth Elliot, the popular Christian writer and speaker, say she will get down on her knees in prayer to give worries to the Lord and do that as often as the worries return.

I don't want my focus to be on the things that I think I need to accomplish. Then my eyes are essentially on myself, my agenda. My family will fall victim to my frantic push to get everything done.

My "list" may grow shorter, but is it worth it if I am irritable with my children, won't sit down to talk with my husband, or skip quiet time with the Lord?

I pray that our daily pressures, that never ending "to do" list, will help us learn what it means to serve a Savior whose yoke is easy and burden is light. May we see those "to do's" as our service to the Lord, not as burdens. May they turn our eyes to Jesus, not put us into despair. May the Lord teach us how to truly rest in Him.

February 1997

Mom's Corners

A Wife's Submission

As I have shared with you in other Mom's Corners, the Lord has been working in my life in relation to my husband's leadership in our home. I have a real-life example of this to share with you.

Recently, my husband announced that he wanted to make some changes in our evening schedule. This would involve all of the children joining the little boys and him for their evening time in the Word. Wouldn't you think that would delight a mother whose greatest desire is to have godly children? Delight was not my first reaction! Not at all! I immediately thought of many reasons why Steve's plan would not work; my face told what was going on inside. When Steve questioned me, I began telling him my excuses. Before I had the last one out of my mouth, each of the older children had joined my rebellion with their own reasons.

The Lord convicted me of my lack of submission and wrong attitudes. Still, my heart was not following what I knew was right. I was selfishly hanging on to fears of what a change might mean for me. I asked Steve's forgiveness for my not having a positive response to his plan and for sharing my negative reactions. I still had a "thought" battle to wage to bring my heart to follow what I knew God wanted from me. I desired to not just grit my teeth and plaster a smile on my face. I needed to be truly willing to be a helpmeet to my husband.

45

Daily the Lord is giving me opportunities to be tested, tried, and refined in this area of submission. I have been trying an experiment in faith. When I want to remind Steve of something, I write it down in a prayer journal and pray about it. God can work in Steve's heart to deal with an issue when the time is right rather than me bringing it up. To be honest, even in this experiment I fail regularly. The other day I went to bed praying about, and determined not to bring up, my desire to have the Christmas decorations taken down. The very next morning, though, I mentioned it. Steve's response was, "Would you believe just this morning as I was praying I was thinking about that?" I saw God working but was robbed of joy. I had gone ahead and brought it up rather than waiting on the Lord.

When I think of submission to my husband, one of the things the Lord continues to show me is that I have to let my husband be the leader. I am quick to question, remind, suggest, offer opinions, and give input. As I have evaluated this behavior of mine, I have come to see that it is trying to control my husband. If I can set my pride aside long enough, I can even objectively view it as treating him like a child rather than my mature husband. If you were to ask me if I were a submissive wife through these married years, I would have said determinedly, "Yes!" However, I was living "the letter of the law" of submission. The "spirit of the law" of submission would be willingly following, without always having a better way, another idea, or a reminder.

The end of the story on evening Bible time with the little boys is that God gave me great joy. I began to lay down, before Jesus, the sacrifices that I felt might be involved for the older ones and me. I asked God to help me to creatively figure out where to fit in the things I had been doing during that time. I asked Him to give me a heart to happily support my husband–to be a helpmeet rather than a hindrance. He has! Now I get Jesse and Mary ready for bed a little bit earlier, read to Anna before teeth brushing, and brush Sarah's hair during the Bible time with Daddy. That time has become something I look forward to; it brings us all together for the most important focus we could have as a family before going to bed. Daddy is teaching us that we are men and women of God. Daddy is interested in our spiritual growth!

May we encourage one another to be wives and mothers with meek and quiet spirits, in whom our husbands can fully trust.

March 1997

Discouragement

Several years ago, I shared with you in a Mom's Corner something that always hurts my heart. When I walk in the mornings, I pass by several day-care homes. I watch mommies and daddies take little children and babies from their car seats, carrying them into a house to spend the day while they go to work. My mind quickly imagines my own little ones snug in their beds, soon to wake and spend their whole day with their mommy and family. My heart fills with sadness for those day-care children and gratitude for my own children's circumstances.

Remembering these scenes is good for me when I am tempted to complain or murmur about my situation. If I consider the alternatives to what I am doing, I know there isn't anything in the world I would rather be doing. I also don't feel there is anything else in the world of greater importance.

So why do I get discouraged? I let my thoughts dwell on the negative parts of my circumstances rather than keeping them fixed on gratefulness for them. If each time my little one's fussing began getting to me, I were to think, "Lord, I am so grateful that this child is here with me and not spending each day with someone else," rather than, "Will this child ever stop crying?"–wouldn't that give me a different perspective on the difficulty?

I can truthfully tell you I know this principle in my mind, but putting it into practice isn't something that comes naturally. As a matter of fact, I am selfish and will think "poor me" thoughts if the situation lends itself to such thoughts. I have had to see my discouragement as displeasing to my Lord and confess it as sin. In God's time, as I cry out to Him to strengthen me in this area of weakness, He has been giving me the grace to think the right thoughts in what are naturally discouraging circumstances to me. It is a process He is still taking me through.

How much am I walking consistently, day by day, in gratefulness? When was the last time I thanked my husband for his hard work out of the home that allows me to stay home? Am I regularly expressing my gratefulness to my children for being able to be home so I can homeschool them? These thoughts need to be in my mind and then shared with my family.

Last year, I would tell one of my children that my school time with him was one of the very best parts of my day. Almost every day, he would reply that it wasn't good for him. I continued day after day and eventually the closeness and expressed love for our time together overcame his dislike of the school material. He eventually stopped his negative remarks, reaching over for my hand and giving me a big smile when I shared my happiness over our school time.

Will my family think I am a content wife and mother if what they see and hear is discouragement and complaining? I can know in my heart that I am content and happy, but those around me want to hear me say it in words. Frequently, I will find if I am happy they are happy. My spirit and attitude is conveyed and transferred to them.

May we as homeschooling mothers remember to have grateful hearts for our tremendous privilege of being at home with our children. May we know that the investment of our lives in our families will count for eternity instead of being burned up as wood, hay, and stubble in an outside job. May our attitudes and faces convey to our family the contentment we find in our role as wife, mother, and teacher.

April 1997

Weariness

"Today I am weary." That was a part of a letter I recently wrote to a friend. Her response was very encouraging to me, so I asked if I could use it in a Mom's Corner. Here is what she said.

"The purpose of this fax is to encourage you to keep laying the foundation. I know that you do not want to quit; keep building. Rest, if you must, but don't you quit. These years will be over so quickly. There will be no more diapers to change (of children belonging to us); no more babies to nurse; no more toddlers to crawl into our lap or to tug at our skirts or to open the door to the bathroom when we are in there. All too soon the door will stay shut; our laps will be empty; there will be time to do all the 'things' that we think we'd like to do. But Teri, will that make us happy? No. What will bring joy to our hearts are the memories we hold of our children, and of the times we had together with them. So, let us make diaper-changing a memorable experience. Let us build memories while making supper. Let us lay the foundation for future generations, moment by moment, in the lives of our children." Sandy

This is so good for me to keep in mind. I am always having an influence on my children either for good or bad, whether I am rested or weary. When I am tired, feeling overwhelmed, can I let go of what I think I have to do? What will count for eternity? What do I want my children to remember about me? Will they remember a mom who fussed and nagged at them? Will they remember a pleasant, tender mommy who smiled at them, loved them, and encouraged them even when she was tired? Our attitude and how we approach a situation makes all the difference! Does it matter if all the schoolwork is finished, the house is tidy, and the laundry done? I don't want it to if the only way to accomplish it is with negative emotion from me. Yes, these things are goals I will work toward, but please, Lord Jesus, only when I can pursue them sweetly and patiently.

What opportunities the Lord gives us each day to learn to depend fully on Him! I am not capable of being the mother I want to be, and that I know He wants me to be, in my own strength. I am aware of that every day when I see how I react naturally to things that are difficult. I want to learn to cry out to the Lord for His strength, grace, and mercy throughout my day. I can testify that as we have hearts that desire to please the Lord, He does the work in us. He has worked many changes in my life from a mommy with three small children who could hardly wait until they were in school full time to where I am now. Was it a special formula? Seven steps to change? An overnight miracle? No, but a faithful Savior working in a sinful mother's life over the course of twenty years.

Perhaps you are caught in the middle of an overloaded schedule. If irritation is creeping into your interactions with your children, can you ask yourself, "Will this count for eternity?" When you are exhausted, will you rest and let tomorrow's worries take care of themselves? "But seek ye first the kingdom of God, and his righteousness; and all these things shall be added unto you. Take therefore no thought for the morrow: for the morrow shall take thought for the things of itself. Sufficient unto the day *is* the evil thereof" (Matthew 6:33-34). Build the foundation with your children one moment by one moment.

May 1997

Key to Time Management

Four jumpers, two culottes jumpers, two vests, two baby outfits, one skirt, putting ruffles on ten baby outfits turning them from pant sets to dresses, plus keeping current on mending projects. That is the list I came up with as I thought back over my sewing the past eight months. "How do you find time to sew?" you ask. I'd love to share the key to my treasure.

This special key is "a half hour a day." I have planned in my day a half hour of sewing every afternoon during the week. It takes time to get the project out and to put it away so sewing time is only twenty to twenty-five minutes a day. Over the course of a year, just a little bit each day adds up to—four jumpers, two culottes jumpers, two vests . . .

You might think, why bother for such a few minutes to actually sew each day? For me the slow, steady progress and accomplishment is better than not getting any sewing done at all. If I did not have this time set aside for sewing, I would not get around to it. Other, more urgent things would easily fill this time space. Therefore, if you call at 1:30 p.m., Sarah will answer the phone and tell you I am busy. You will know I am in doing my sewing.

If you call at 3:30 p.m., Sarah will also tell you I am busy. You might ask, "Now what is she doing since school is over for the day?" Once more I will share the key to my treasure. I had a desire in my heart, for a couple of years, to have reading time with my little children.

Between homeschooling, household chores, meals, babies, and toddlers there always seemed to be something to keep me from sitting down and reading to my precious children. This time the special key is fifteen minutes a day.

I scheduled a fifteen-minute reading period for Joseph and John. The next year I added another one for John and Anna, when Anna was old enough. Finally, two years later I included a separate one for Jesse. This adds up to forty-five minutes of my afternoon. Because it started with only fifteen minutes, added on a little each year, and is planned and set aside just like our morning school time, it happens every day. It is cherished time, looked forward to by both the children and by me, special close time. It is time where I am doing what I have said is my priority rather than being driven by the urgent.

Last year John, my then kindergartner, came to me begging to learn to read so he could read his Bible. With a new baby, I had not planned to teach him to read until first grade, but how could a mommy turn down such a request? Though I wanted to fulfill his desire, I could not come up with even a half-hour block of time to work with him. I prayed about it and discussed it with Steve. Then the Lord showed me I had some fifteen-minute time segments throughout my day that I could devote to phonics with John. As we got started, I found four of these times. That was probably better for his attention span than a solid hour would have been!

I will give you one more key to my treasure. This key is a half hour once or twice a week. Again, I had a yearning in my heart to have one-on-one time with my little children. However, as usual, the weeks would fly by with the normal routine and no individual time with a child. Then the Lord showed me that even if I could not spend individual playtime with each child every day, I could do it once or twice a week. So we started preschool two times a week.

Each little one takes a turn, individually, to spend time with Mom. Are they unhappy that it doesn't happen every day? No, they look forward to their preschool day. As they grow older, preschool time no longer fits the age so the title changes to fun school. I spend this time with one child where he gets to pick an activity to do with Mommy from a list of fun educational choices.

What is the treasure that I have been giving you my keys to? The treasure is time spent on the priorities God has led me to have. The Lord has given us each the same number of hours in our day and responsibilities that we must fulfill during this time. We can always be driven by the urgent, or we can take control of our days. We can set aside time for not only the responsibilities, but also those God-given heart desires.

These are examples from my life. What about you? What project have you put off because there isn't time to finish? What have you wanted to do with your children but are always too busy for? Seek the Lord to see if He would have you spend any of your time in these areas. If He directs, try planning fifteen minutes or thirty minutes each day at a set time and make those things happen. See how even a little bit, day after day, can net satisfying results at the end of a month or year. Try the key to treasure, which the Lord has given to me. Perhaps it will be a key to treasure for you too.

September 1997

Finding Quiet Time for the Lord

Last month in the Mom's Corner, I shared with you a key to the treasure of spending time on the priorities the Lord has given each of us. This month I want to give you the key to our success in life as a woman, wife, mother, home teacher, neighbor, and Christian. This key comes from the key we talked about in September, but is of vastly greater value. Despite its importance, this key is often not used because there is not time; other needs seem more pressing. This, though, signals an even greater urgency to use the key.

What is the key I am referring to? It is "time alone with Jesus Christ." There is a reason this key comes from last month's key. For us to have time alone with the Lord, we are going to find we must plan that time into our day. If we choose to take it during a free, quiet moment whenever we can, we will probably come to the end of the day and realize it has not happened. We will decide to try again tomorrow. The cycle will be repeated the next day and the next day.

We are foolish women if we think we can get through our days the way the Lord wants us to in our own energy and strength. Where does our dependence on the Lord come from? Where do we get our daily manna? Isn't it from our private time alone in the Word, in prayer, in memorizing Scripture, and meditating on it? I know how absolutely crucial this time is to me. Is my life busy and full? Could I spend this time doing something else? Absolutely! Is there anything else I could use this time for that would produce more lasting or greater benefits for my family or me? NO!

How, practically speaking, do you find time for quiet moments with the Lord in the midst of all the responsibilities and demands of a homeschooling mom? You pray, look at your day, and are creative. You make your quiet time a planned part of your day and remain faithful to it.

Does it have to be early in the morning? No, but I believe that is the best time. You start your day with your focus on the Lord, your heart seeking Him. If you have little children it is easier to not have disturbances if your quiet time is while they are still sleeping. Will it be hard to get up earlier? Probably. However, why make up your mind that you are too tired to get up and fear it rather than try it?

For years, I felt I needed eight hours of sleep to function well. I also struggled regularly with long sleepless nights. About a year ago I changed to seven hours of sleep at night with a short rest in the afternoon. It has been wonderful. I sleep great at night. Had you told me two years ago that I would have to survive on seven hours of sleep a day, I would have been sure I could never make it.

There have been times when early morning devotions did not work out for me. Did that mean I stopped having devotions? No! I planned time during the little ones' afternoon naps for that time with the Lord. It was a part of my day just like making dinner was.

Another common feeling about time with the Lord is that you barely get started with fifteen minutes or a half hour, so, why bother? Why not wait until you can find the large amount of time you really want? The reason is that day after day will go by when you never find an hour to spend with the Lord. How much better to consistently, day after day, spend a half hour with the Lord, finding it adds up to three and a half hours a week, than to always look for the hour or two that never appear.

Steve and I go to bed at 10:30 p.m., and the alarm clock goes off at 5:25 a.m. I go in to nurse Mary and then have a half-hour devotion before family morning Bible time at 6:25. I spend ten minutes reading a chapter in the Bible, picking a verse that is meaningful to me, copying it in a notebook, and writing a short prayer concerning it. Then I have the next ten minutes for memorizing Scripture and doing a study on the verse I am working on. The last ten minutes is my prayer time. Could I easily spend more time? Without a doubt! However, I am grateful to spend the time I have and offer it to the Lord for Him to use.

This summer I was battling discouragement over some issues with the children. By early afternoon, I felt like my hands were dragging on the ground. I was so worn out from dealing with these issues! As I was bemoaning my discouragement while sewing one day, the Lord showed me that I needed to spend extra time with Him. My unhappiness with the situations and stewing over them produced no benefit, only negative consequences for my family and me, as I moped around. However, turning those needs to Jesus Christ, the One Who carries our burdens, provides peace and rest through trials, and has direction for working through those difficulties, would produce benefit. I began getting out my spiritual notebook and getting on my knees at 2:00 p.m. each afternoon for another half hour. That extra time with the Lord was like a banquet to a starving person!

Here is a story I think we can all relate to. "Now it came to pass, as they went, that he entered into a certain village: and a certain woman named Martha received him into her house. And she had a sister called Mary, which also sat at Jesus' feet, and heard his word. But Martha was cumbered about much serving, and came to him, and said, Lord, dost thou not care that my sister hath left me to serve alone? bid her therefore that she help me. And Jesus answered and said unto her, Martha, Martha, thou art careful and troubled about many things: But one thing is needful: and Mary hath chosen that good part, which shall not be taken away from her" (Luke 10:38-42).

Our lives as wives, mothers, and home teachers are filled with Martha activities. Let us not give up what Jesus Himself says is better. The foundation for everything you do in and out of your home grows from your relationship with Jesus. Plan that time with Him every day. Be faithful to it. Use the key that will give you the desires of your heart.

October 1997

Child Training

"Correct thy son, and he shall give thee rest; yea, he shall give delight unto thy soul" (Proverbs 29:17). Does this characterize your children and your home? I must admit that there are times my children do not give me rest or delight my soul. When this happens, my first reaction is to groan inside with the thoughts, "Oh no, not again!" If my children are not delighting my soul or giving me rest, I have come to realize that the issue can fall back on me. I have become lax in discipline. I don't like this responsibility. I would rather have gentle reminders bring about results. "A servant will not be corrected by words: for though he understand he will not answer" (Proverbs 29:19). This can characterize my children.

Sometimes there are days when the constancy of my children's infractions has worn me out. I can become very discouraged by it. Considering our younger children, we have several we are working on such basics as: closing the bathroom door when they enter, flushing the toilet and washing hands, putting shoes or jackets in the closet when removed, brushing teeth without reminders, chewing with their mouth closed, and others. Since we begin teaching the children proper behavior in these areas as soon as a child is capable, one might think these habits would be developed by now. There is good news. These are not areas we are working on with our older children, so consistency does pay off!

I have come to see that the big picture can be overwhelming to me. By big picture, I mean tackling all the problems at once. However, if I focus in on one particular area, we often will achieve success. For example, four-year-old Anna was not putting her shoes in her bedroom when she took them off. She did this several times a day. This not only cluttered the living room and caused others to stumble over them, but sometimes it made us all have to go on a hunt for the shoes when they could not be found. We decided she needed to learn to take her shoes and socks to her bedroom and place them beside her bed whenever she took them off. First, we discussed this with her, and I showed her what I wanted her to do. Then for a few days, I would remind her if she forgot. "Oh, Anna, I am sure you are not planning to leave your shoes and socks in the living room, are you?"

I also looked for a creative consequence for failure. If I have too many creative consequences for different areas we are working on, I forget them! So again, I try to have one major focus at a time. The consequence in this case was to be practice. After the teaching and reminding, I would quietly call her back to the living room if she left her shoes there. In a sad voice, I would say, "Anna, I am so sorry you did not put your shoes where they belong. I want you to take them now and put them by your bed. Then come back and tell Mommy." When she returned I would ask her to go get the shoes and bring them back again. Next I would say, "Anna, you did not remember to put your shoes by your bed when you took them off, so I want you to practice by taking them and putting them there again. Report to me when you are done." I would have her do this two or three times.

It was amazing how much that little girl could dislike practicing putting her shoes away! I also highly praised her when she remembered to make that trip down the hallway to her bedroom. I would report her success to the other family members in front of her. She did learn to carry the shoes to her room when she took them off, although, as I write this, I think I have seen them out again lately. Maybe it is time to "practice" again.

Often to help me avoid getting frustrated over some of these discipline areas, I will write them on a list or on the whiteboard. Sometimes I do not have time to address a problem. If I write it down, I know I will not forget it, and I remember to deal with it later. For instance, when I go downstairs to put Jesse down for his nap, I might see clothes out in the bedroom or toys that have not been put away. Calling one of the three boys who share this bedroom to come pick up, when it is time for Jesse to get to sleep, is not a good option. I make a mental note about the problem and write a physical note when I get upstairs so that it can be corrected after naptime.

Another reason writing down the problem helps is that with a little time it may not be as emotional or upsetting to me. I might realize I was making a mountain out of a molehill. It will also give me time to pray and ask the Lord what to do about the situation. Sometimes frustration comes because I know we have a problem, but I am not doing anything about it. Maybe I don't know what to do. I simply need time to pray about it. With it written down, it won't be forgotten if it is important enough to need attention that can't be given or figured out at that moment.

Working on one problem area at a time helps me, too, because in order to be consistent, I must be the one who is trained. Once I made a list on the white board that said, "Train Mom to: send children to wash hands before meals and after meals, ask if they flushed the toilet, turned the light off. . . ." When we decided it would be a good idea for our children to respond to us with a, "Yes, Mom," or, "Yes, Dad," I would say something to a child and get no response. I would then say, "Yes, Mom," for that child. I laughed with Steve at how well I was trained in saying, "Yes, Mom." If I can remember to work in the weak area, or to check on it, we will usually have some measure of success. That is why keeping the number of things to focus on small helps me to be consistent. If there are too many, they all slip away from me.

Evaluate your home life for areas where peace is lacking. Do not be discouraged! Instead, be committed to working toward peace by tackling one area at a time that needs attention. Teach your children with a meek and quiet spirit. Be positive. Praise them for little successes. Look for creative, reasonable discipline for failure. God's Word is always true, "Correct thy son, and he shall give thee rest; yea, he shall give delight unto thy soul" (Proverbs 29:17).

November 1997

Review of *Shepherding a Child's Heart*

When I read a review on a new book called *Shepherding a Child's Heart*, by Tedd Tripp, I was quite interested. I purchased the book a year and a half ago and have read it through two times, planning to reread it once a year. The things Tedd Tripp said about our children's hearts made sense.

We do not deal simply with behavior issues, but rather with the heart from which the behavior comes. If, by the firmness of my discipline, I gain the compliance of my child's actions but not his heart, we still have a long way to go. Mr. Tripp says, "A change in behavior that does not stem from a change in heart is not commendable; it is condemnable. Is it not the hypocrisy that Jesus condemned in the Pharisees? In Matthew 15, Jesus denounces the Pharisees who honored Him with their lips while their hearts were far from Him. Jesus censures them as people who wash the outside of the cup while the inside is still unclean. Yet this is what we often do in child-rearing. We demand changed behavior and never address the heart that drives the behavior."

This book dealt with how we can use situations in our homes that require discipline or teaching to help our children look at their hearts. Rather than addressing a fight over a toy by trying to determine who had it first, we are encouraged to show each child the sinfulness in his heart that caused the offense. Mr. Tripp encourages us with, "Your concern is to unmask your child's sin, helping him to understand how it reflects a heart that has strayed. That leads to the cross of Christ. It underscores the need for a Savior. It provides opportunities to show the glories of God Who sent His Son to change hearts and free people enslaved to sin."

This is important to me. Although I do desire good behavior and attitudes in our home, my greater desire is for my children to learn to see their sin, ask forgiveness for it, and seek Jesus' help in forsaking it. Good behavior and attitudes will naturally result from this. My children struggle with kindness toward each other practically every day. As a mother, I would much rather have a child who humbly admits his selfishness and asks forgiveness for it than one who pridefully defends his behavior. I also tend to be more lenient with a child whom I feel has a genuinely repentant heart than with the one who cannot, or will not, admit fault.

Mr. Tripp also says, "You must understand, and help your child to understand, how his straying heart has resulted in wrong behavior. How did his heart defect to produce this behavior? In what characteristic ways has his inability or refusal to know, trust, and obey God resulted in actions and speech that are wrong? . . . You must learn to work back from the behavior you see to the heart, exposing heart issues for your children. In short, you must learn to engage them, not just reprove them. Help them see the ways that they are trying to slake their soul's thirst with that which cannot satisfy. You must help your kids gain a clear focus on the cross of Christ."

I have not found this to be easy for two reasons. First, it takes time to have these discussions with a child, and often they are needed at an inconvenient time. Second, I will sometimes not be able to convince my child that his behavior was wrong. He will strongly defend what he has done, usually based on what another did to him. Often, if I confront him with a question, which asks him if Jesus would be pleased with his behavior, the answer is rather simple. Whether it is easy, or whether the time is readily available, it is my goal to address the heart of my child. That is one of the main reasons we homeschool. What better use of the time even if it does interrupt Joseph's math or John's phonics? As a matter of fact, this year I have planned extra time into my one-on-one school with each child so that I will have time to handle interruptions when they need to be addressed.

Mr. Tripp also mentions, "Secondly, you must be actively shepherding the Godward orientation of your children. In all of this you must pray that God will work in and around your efforts and the responses of your children to make them people who know and honor God." The longer Steve and I parent, the more we see our need to be constantly crying out to the Lord for wisdom in parenting our children, for our children's hearts and attitudes, and for their future and direction. Our own efforts may produce "good" children, but we want children whose hearts are turned fully to the Lord. This will not come about if Steve and I are only faithful in our personal walk with the Lord. We must also fulfill what He has called us to as parents, being totally dependent on the Lord to work in the hearts of our children.

There is much more that this book talks about, which I do not have the space for in this Mom's Corner. I have read many Christian books on raising children. Most of them have a focus on manipulating a child's behavior but don't deal at all with the heart from which that behavior comes. I think *Shepherding a Child's Heart* is a valuable resource for our homes. I hope, if you have not read it and choose to, that it will give you encouragement and direction.

Shepherding a Child's Heart, Shepherd Press, P.O. Box 24, Wapwallopen, PA 18660 or (800) 338-1445

January 1998

A Meek and Quiet Spirit: Some Real-Life Examples and Failures!

It seems that I can't let a year go by without a Mom's Corner dealing with a wife's need for a meek and quiet spirit. 1 Peter 3:4 says, "But *let it be* the hidden man of the heart, in that which is not corruptible, *even the ornament* of a meek and quiet spirit, which is in the sight of God of great price."

I wonder how many of us were born with meek and quiet spirits. I know I was not! This is something that God began pointing out in my life several years ago. He did this in what I considered a most unusual way. He began to make me aware of my interactions with my husband, viewing them as an outsider would.

Here are some things I heard myself saying to my husband:

"Honey, who was that on the phone? What did they want? Well, what did you say?"

"Steven, did you see what Joseph just did? No matter how many times I tell him he still does it."

"Have you made a decision yet? I asked you about this on Monday, and I am feeling like I should know what we are going to do."

I needed to learn, and am still in training, to have a meek and quiet spirit. Often a meek and quiet spirit, for me, would translate into a quiet mouth. If my husband chooses to share a phone conversation with me, I am pleased to have my curiosity satisfied. If he does not, it is good for me to trust God to give me information that I am interested in or might need to know. Should Steve forget to tell me something important, it may become known at some point. Then if he feels badly about having forgotten to tell me, it is a lesson from the Lord, not a controlling wife!

When Steve was home, I wanted him to be the one to correct the children. However, I also felt it my duty to point out what the children were doing that needed his attention. How much better it is when I am quiet. It is quite presumptive of me to think I know best what the children are doing that would need correction. This has been clearly illustrated to me during our evening Bible time. I wanted to keep telling the little children to be quiet, sit still, or perhaps put down a toy. You know what? My speaking to the child was as disruptive to our Bible time as what the child was doing. I found that if I would just sit very quietly with my mouth tightly closed, Steve would take care of anything that was a distraction to him. It is a great relief to not have to be "in charge" but just to sit and let my husband do what God has called him to.

It is a relief, but it is not easy! Everything within me so often wants to push, control, and some would say, nag. Usually, if I will be quiet, all will work out just fine the way Steve does it. The times it might not, it is so much better to have that realization come from the Lord and not from me.

Another area that has been difficult for me is to learn not to correct my husband in front of others—even sweetly. What does it matter if we did this thing on Monday or Wednesday night, as I would be prone to point out if he said the wrong one? I have discovered that, even if it does matter, it is better to be quiet and maintain our testimony than to correct my husband in public. There is seldom anything that important. Truly, if misinformation was given, I believe it would be better for my husband to call the person later and correct it than for me to have spoken up publicly.

Despite knowing I do not want to do this, as recently as Saturday morning this happened. Steve was driving a group of moms and girls from our church to a baby shower because of bad road conditions. I stepped into his conversation to clarify something I thought the ladies might misunderstand. Almost as quickly as the words were out of my mouth they seemed to shout back at me in accusation. I am glad, because I do want to learn these lessons. In my pride, I do not like to continually fail in something that is pretty cut and dried–don't correct your husband in public, including in front of the children!

Something amazing has happened over these past three years that God has had me in this training course, Meek and Quiet Spirit 101. Steve's love for me has grown. It has been so exciting for me to see God use an area where He showed me I needed to become obedient. He has poured out His blessing in a way I did not foresee.

May I encourage each of you who are wives to honor, respect, and love your husband by asking the Lord to teach you to have a meek and quiet spirit, which is of great worth in His sight. May we treat our husbands as our leaders and not be controlling. May it never be said by an outsider watching our interactions with our husbands, "I know she wears the pants in that home."

February 1998

Trials

I was lying on my bed trying to do my Bible study. Instead, I couldn't keep from crying. Some difficulties with the children had discouraged me, and the tears were flowing. At 10:30 p.m. the phone rang.

"Mom, it's Nathan. My car just spun out, and I am sitting in the median. I'm not hurt, and the car isn't either. A guy stopped to help me. He's going to try to get me out. I wanted you to know so you and Dad could pray that we can get it out."

Nathan, our twenty-one-year-old son, was returning from a long weekend retreat with a friend. Driving home, he had entered into freezing rain. While driving fifty miles per hour on the interstate, he hit a patch of ice.

Suddenly, the troubles of a few minutes ago didn't seem so important any more. We now were thinking about life and death. God's hand of mercy and protection were greatly evident in the events of the accident. I continued to cry–for another reason. Steve immediately knelt down at the bed to pray. He praised the Lord, thanked the Lord, and petitioned the Lord.

The little trials God sends my way are not sent to discourage me. For me, right now, these trials usually have to do with my children. Your trials may be different. Trials are meant to get and keep my focus on the Lord. Where will that focus be? Will it be on me–my failures, my inconveniences, my feelings? Or will it be on the Lord?

Lately, too often, I have allowed my thoughts to dwell on the small, negative things happening around me. Then I am caught in a trap of discouragement. Sometimes this discouragement so overwhelms me that I can't even begin to think the right thoughts. Then I cry and feel defeated. Of course, these are the times I most need to call out to the Lord rather than allow my mind to continue to dwell on me and on what is going on. The truth is that sometimes I can't even do this. When that is the case, I have to make myself take out my spiritual notebook.

My spiritual notebook is a large three-ring notebook that I was encouraged to begin five years ago. It has ABC tabs and normal tabs. Behind the ABC tabs, I have pages of Scriptures for specific needs. As I find a verse that has special meaning to me, I will write it on a page under an appropriate topic. Verses to help with discouragement are written on a page filed after "D" and ones on discipline on another "D" page. There is a page for verses on sin, love, fear, patience, thoughts, etc.

One of the tabs has pages of special spiritual notes, book notes, and handouts. Another section has areas in which the Lord has dealt with me in the past. This includes Scripture and encouragement He has given me that I have written out. When I read through the Scripture and notes in this notebook, I begin to have the right thoughts and focus, even though I haven't been able to have them on my own. These verses are familiar ones. They are verses that have ministered to me and met my need in the past, and they continue to do so. I have to take what little steps I can, leaving the emotionally distressing situations behind as I go to be alone with the Lord to seek Him. To be honest, even this step can be difficult for me in the midst of an emotional storm. However, if I will go where I know the truth is, the Lord reaches out to meet the need.

Last night, after the call from Nathan, I realized I was allowing little things to take too much of my attention. Steve encouraged me to stop thinking negatively about things and get my focus back on the Lord. Doesn't that sound right and easy? But again, when I am allowing my emotions to run my thoughts, it is not easy. So I, a little facetiously, asked Steve exactly how I was to do this. His response was that I needed to put my energy into crying out to the Lord in prayer, expressing my concerns and inability to speak truth in my heart.

Knowing he was right, I also recalled the words of our pastor that morning. He was preaching on God's purposes for storms–physical storms–and drawing analogies to God's purposes for allowing storms in our lives. He was encouraging us not to try to hide from the storms, in storm shelters, but to let God work His purpose in us through the storm. If my heart's desire is truly to know Jesus Christ and be conformed to His image, why am I not willing to accept difficulties that will cause my heart to look to Him?

I decided one way to get my mind back on the Lord was to read in Psalms. I started reading Psalms 91. I was stopped as I read verse 4, ". . . his truth *shall be thy* shield and buckler." That verse spoke to my heart and my need at the time. To move my thinking from myself to my Lord, I needed this thought of God's faithfulness. Concentrating on Who He is and what He has done put my attention where God could use it positively. I was able to recall the verse throughout the day. It was a comfort and encouragement to me, keeping my heart on the Lord, not on myself.

Do you have times when your thinking is off track; perhaps emotions are controlling those thoughts in a negative way? Does it seem impossible to get them back on the Lord and on His truth? When this is the case, don't allow yourself to continue that way, but take one tiny step. Get out your Bible or spiritual notebook, and put God's thoughts back into your mind. Then allow those thoughts to push out the wrong ones. Let them speak truth to your heart, and believe them, whether you feel like it or not. Your heart will be at peace once more; you will be filled with true thoughts; your mind will be focused on Jesus Christ, not on your own self!

April 1998

Evaluating Your School Year

As this school year draws to a close, do you begin to think about what your children have accomplished over the past months? Does your mind fill with thoughts about what to use for school next year?

You may be excited about the academic and character growth of your children through the past nine months. Praise the Lord! This is exactly what God would have us thinking about our year. He would have us look for the growth, benefits, blessings, and anything positive that we can focus our thoughts on. He wants us to be grateful for what He has done in and through our homeschooling. Will we delight in it?

Perhaps these thoughts are far from you. You may even be thinking, as I have from time to time, that school would be a better place for your children. May I encourage you that this is not true. Sending your child out to a school will not ease whatever difficulties you are experiencing with him at home. God has placed both of you in an environment where, day in and day out, you are faced with problems and forced to work on them.

Let me share an analogy concerning character deficits that we may see in our children. I will use a specific one, but this could apply to any of them. Children do not learn their multiplication tables by reciting them one time. They learn them by repeating them over and over, day after day. In a similar way, a child who lacks self-discipline in applying himself to his schoolwork will not, with one correction or encouragement, become a diligent child. He may not become diligent even with a year, or two, or three. However, perhaps with ten, or twelve, he will.

Are we, as mothers, willing to pay the price? Will we choose not to grow weary in training up our children so that when they are old they will not depart? It is a sacrifice on our part. It takes great reliance on the Lord and the setting aside of our desires to see quick results. Be encouraged! The battle is not ours, but the Lord's!

What about next year? How would the Lord have us approach our plans? I think He would have us commit those thoughts and plans to Him in prayer. It will be of greater benefit to us, and our families, if we will keep our thinking regarding our next year's school focused on the Lord rather than on any "comparison" thinking regarding other homeschoolers. It is an easy trap to begin feeling like everyone else is doing more with their school, having better results, or using a curriculum that is more effective. However, the Lord has an individual plan for each family based on the needs that are found there. May we set our hearts to seek this plan out with our husbands, and then be committed to following it.

These past few weeks, as Steve and I were praying and discussing schoolbooks for next year, we were faced with a decision. Sarah has loved one of her school courses this year, particularly because of the self-paced, work-text format of the curriculum. She would have been very pleased to use that curriculum for all of her studies next year. In one of the workbooks of this course, though, was the summary of the story of Dracula. As we prayed about the curriculum choices for Sarah, we came down to feeling we could not go wrong by following the principles of purity and holiness the Lord has placed on our hearts. Therefore, we chose, with Sarah's wholehearted approval, a publisher whom we have not known to compromise by presenting evil in their materials.

If we do have areas of concern about our children's character or their academics, how can we best approach it? Again, seeking the Lord in prayer is always the starting place. I will frequently bring a problem to Steve. He says to me, "Let's pray about it." A few days later, after a prayer focus on the situation, we will discuss the problem when we have a quiet, talking time. We will see what the Lord is leading us to try. Even with a "plan" on how to work with the problem, we still need to be committed to keeping it as a prayer focus. Here again, the battle is not ours, but the Lord's.

May we take these last weeks of our school year as a time to rejoice in the Lord's goodness in allowing us the privilege of teaching our children at home. May we reflect on the growth and blessings that have occurred over these months. May we cry out to the Lord for His wisdom and direction for decisions regarding next year.

May 1998

Keys to Disciplining Children

It was the last day of school. Sarah had planned a highly antic-
ipated party for Joseph, John, Anna, Jesse, and Mary. There were
water balloons, a toss game, races, soda, cookies, and chips to be
enjoyed. However, before the games could begin, the bickering had
started. Children were being sent away from the party for unkind
behavior. When they were allowed to return, there would soon be
another incident. A fun-filled morning was beginning to feel like a
disaster. Determined to not let these difficulties destroy the festive
mood of our day, we continued happily through the party, dealing
with discipline issues as they arose.

Discussing the troubled last day of school with Steve on our
next date, I said I was not sure I really wanted to take the two weeks
of school vacation we had planned, if they were going to be like the
last day of school had been.

I began praying and asking the Lord how I should handle the
upcoming vacation days. I quickly realized that I was disappointed
with the children's behavior because I saw it was going to have an
impact on MY vacation. I had wanted to have two weeks off. I
wanted them to be perfect children so I could take a break. The
Lord reminded me that my expectations needed to be straightened.
I had to let go of what I thought I had to have to enjoy the vacation
days. The Lord's calling on my life to bring up my children "in the
nurture and admonition of the Lord" (Ephesians 6:4) did not end

when vacation started! As a matter of fact, this was the perfect time to really focus on some of their weak areas, since there were not the normal schooling demands on our time.

With changed expectations, we entered our vacation, and the children lived up to those new expectations. There were numerous situations calling for discipline each day. As I was working diligently at being consistent with the children's discipline, I was quickly becoming "weary in well doing," wanting to "reap" right away (Galatians 6:9).

Again, I sought the Lord for help. He brought this question to my mind. If I truly believed, "For it is God which worketh in you both to will and to do of *his* good pleasure" (Philippians 2:13), what did that mean about any discipline the children might need? I realized I was relying on my parenting, my discipline, and my consistency, but not the Lord because I was not praying with the children when they were in need of discipline. It seemed the way to rely on the Lord for this teaching time in the children's day was to spend a portion of that time in prayer.

It may be that some of you are already doing this, but I certainly was not. It took too long. I was prone to lecturing the children instead of spending that time praying with them. This prayer time became very fruitful. I was alone with one child. I would pray first. Sometimes I would need to start by asking the Lord's forgiveness for feeling frustrated or discouraged, or maybe for having an impatient or resigned spirit toward the situation. This has become a sweet time for me as it gets my focus off the problem and onto the One Who can work it out.

The next thing I would pray has proved to be much more powerful than a lecture. "Lord, this child wants to be a wise child. He could have chosen to be kind and waited for the toy rather than trying to grab it away. Lord, You want us to learn to have a servant's heart. You want us to love each other and to be patient. Please forgive this child for his unkindness. Help him to see his need to cry out to You when he is tempted to be unkind. Please give him strength to not do this again. Thank You Lord, for this opportunity to learn and to grow in You." This prayer says all I would say in a lecture, but it is strong where my lectures are weak. I am calling out to the One Who has told me, "Be careful for nothing; but in every thing by prayer and supplication with thanksgiving let your requests be made known unto God. And the peace of God, which passeth all understanding, shall keep your hearts and minds through Christ Jesus" (Philippians 4:6-7).

Then my child is given the opportunity to pray out loud with me. This child needs the peace of God to guard his heart, and I need it to guard my heart. Both of us could become discouraged if we feel we are trying to overcome these problems on our own, in our strength. If we focus on the problem, then we feel failure. If we focus on the fact "that all things work together for good to them that love God, to them who are the called according to *his* purpose" (Romans 8:28), then our hearts are right.

I can't tell you that in those two weeks my children became perfect. I still have to battle discouragement over their behavior and my expectations that they will not need any correction. However, I know we are doing what the Lord would have us to do when we pray as we face these teaching opportunities. "For though we walk in the flesh, we do not war after the flesh: (For the weapons of our warfare *are* not carnal, but mighty through God to the pulling down of strong holds;) Casting down imaginations, and every high thing that exalteth itself against the knowledge of God, and bringing into captivity every thought to the obedience of Christ" (2 Corinthians 10:3-5).

What about you? Do you take the time to pray with your children when they need correction? Are you relying on your strength as a parent to change the behavior of your children? Are you calling out to the Lord, setting the example for your children, and showing them how to rely on the One Who has numbered the hairs on their head?

October 1998

Offensive Child Training

Do you ever feel like you are always on the defensive in raising your children? Does it seem like you are forever "putting out fires," being a "referee," acting as "judge and jury," or disciplining? It can appear that way in our home, and I find it becomes very wearisome for me when this is the case. I would rather be on the offensive with my children, but how is this accomplished?

First and foremost is the area of prayer. Prayer is the arena where we truly let go of raising our children in our own strength and rely on the Lord. We will obviously be bringing our children's needs to the Lord by defensive praying, but we can also be praying positively for our children through offensive praying.

Praying Scripture is a great way to be on the offensive with our children. We can pray some of Paul's prayers, "Lord, fill Nathan with the knowledge of Your will in all wisdom and spiritual understanding; That Nathan might walk worthy of the Lord unto all pleasing, being fruitful in every good work, and increasing in the knowledge of God; Strengthened with all might, according to His glorious power, unto all patience and long-suffering with joyfulness; Giving thanks unto the Father, which hath made Nathan to be a partaker of the inheritance of the saints in light" (paraphrased from Colossians 1:9-12).

There is another way to be on the offensive concerning child training and that is through what I will call character-teaching sessions.

What would happen if you set aside fifteen minutes each day to "work" on character needs? I think this small amount of time would go a long way in helping to prevent daily problems with the children.

For example, this summer we were teaching our younger children to answer with, "Yes, Ma'am. No, Ma'am. Yes, Sir. No, Sir." This was being accomplished by dropping one M&M into a mug with their name on it each time they respond in the desired fashion. At an approved time, the children would be allowed to eat their earned M&Ms. We also made this into a game for character-teaching time.

"Jesse,"

"Yes, Ma'am."

"Please pick up the Legos."

"Yes, Ma'am." I popped two M&Ms into his mouth and another one when he returned after finishing his pick up.

"Anna,"

"Yes, Ma'am."

"Mommy wants you to take these socks and put them in the dirty clothes hamper."

"Yes, Ma'am." Again, two M&Ms were immediately given and a third one offered when she returned. We continued until all the little tasks were completed, and would you believe they didn't want to stop even when I couldn't find anything else to do?

This training was so successful that the children were saying "Yes, Sir" to Nathan, our twenty-one-year-old son. Nathan was pleased enough with this show of respect from his younger brothers and sisters that he purchased a three-pound bag of M&Ms, and another one of Skittles, to continue the character-teaching rewards.

Let me share another example that was recently sent to me by a mom who has begun setting aside a character-teaching time for her children each day. This mom says,

"I also have a half-hour block at 8:00 a.m. called 'Training Time' and so far I have taught the 4 older children (ages 7 and younger): how to wash their hands with soap in the bathroom without making a mess or pumping out half the bottle of soap; how to quickly get down from the table, put their dishes on the counter, wash their hands and face, and go into the toy room; and how to do the morning routine properly (get up, dressed, make bed, tidy room, look at a book on their bed). They actually enjoy the practice time since I am calm and not stressed, and it's fun to have everyone else watching them as they do a task right. I have seen how just this little bit of practice has gone a long way! I think I will keep a list of things I want to teach them (like where to stand when someone rings the doorbell, how to quickly get their seatbelts on, answering the phone correctly, etc.) posted on my fridge, like you suggested a while back." Tracy

I feel so much better when I am doing something constructive to help my children with their behavior. We can make it into an enjoyable time, so that they hardly even realize they are learning a beneficial character trait. The time may be devoted to issues that have to do with manners and routines. This is important when we consider how much of our nagging and reminders go toward things like, "Did you brush your teeth? Don't forget to hang up your clothes! Where do boots go when we take them off? Please wait patiently for your turn in the bathroom."

We can also use this time to discuss situations that might occur between the children and how they could deal with them in a manner that would be pleasing to the Lord. We could even play-act some typical scenarios that occur regularly and practice the right responses in them.

So, what about your home? Are you always on the defensive? Do you think it would be worth investing time in prayer and teaching to be on the offensive? May I encourage you to consider this a wise use of your time.

November 1998

Can Teen Rebellion Be Avoided? (Part 1)

Do you ever wonder what your choice to homeschool will do to your children when they are teens? Have you prayed asking the Lord to keep them from becoming rebellious teenagers? Have others told you that if you protect your children from outside influences they will rebel against your authority when they become teens?

As the parents of children ages 22, 19, and almost 17 (in addition to our five younger ones), we are asked what we have done in raising our children so that they have not rebelled as teens. Our two oldest, both adults, still choose to live at home, minister with our family, and prepare themselves for a possible future as husbands, fathers, and spiritual heads of their homes, if God so directs. This question concerning our children not rebelling has caused me to do some thinking. A simple answer has not popped into my mind, and a Mom's Corner seems like a good opportunity to reflect on this subject.

Usually I write Mom's Corners about my failures and what God has taught me through them. This Mom's Corner is along a different line. Therefore, I hesitate to share these thoughts for fear it could come across as sounding prideful, and that is not my intention. My purpose is to encourage other moms' hearts, from one who has already walked the path and discovered that teens do not have to be rebellious. I would like to relate that path the Lord has led us along, perhaps giving you some new ideas and food for thought.

The results seen in our children's lives are not because of Steve and me. We are very human, not close to perfect parents, failing in various ways, day after day. It is only the Lord's grace in our lives, and the lives of our children, that has made a difference. He is the One doing the work, "For it is God which worketh in you both to will and to do of *his* good pleasure" (Philippians 2:13). I write of these things because we are questioned on them. I see the fruit God gives of walking according to His Word, "Thy word *is* a lamp unto my feet, and a light unto my path" (Psalms 119:105). I want to counsel each of you to constantly seek the Lord as you are parenting teens or preparing to parent them.

Before reaching our children's teen years, Steve and I did not have a "seven-step, fool-proof" biblical plan to raise godly children, nor even any plan at all; we still don't! I can remember we discussed that we did not believe children had to go through a rebellious stage as teenagers. We were open to making decisions, even very difficult, unpopular decisions, for our family as the Lord led us. But that was the extent of our plan. Let me share with you, in retrospect, what I believe may have been used by the Lord to make the difference in our children's lives. We don't know for sure what the Lord Jesus has used, we can only look at where He has taken us and consider the possibilities.

Homeschooling became our choice when our oldest children were entering first and third grades. "And these words, which I command thee this day, shall be in thine heart: And thou shalt teach them diligently unto thy children, and shalt talk of them when thou sittest in thine house, and when thou walkest by the way, and when thou liest down, and when thou risest up" (Deuteronomy 6:6-7). We had the opportunity to present Christ to our children all day long.

Fourteen years later, we continue on that path. Our children have been spared from many negative influences by being at home for school! "And what agreement hath the temple of God with idols? for ye are the temple of the living God; as God hath said, I will dwell in them, and walk in *them*; and I will be their God, and they shall be my people" (2 Corinthians 6:16). Simply not being around other teens who have become rebellious has certainly spared our children from watching and observing, in their own friends, such choices.

The year after we started homeschooling, Steve began getting the children up early in the morning to have a family time reading the Bible and praying before he went to work. Reading Scripture through the years helped our children see the choices set before them of God's way versus foolishness and rebellion.

"The proverbs of Solomon the son of David, king of Israel: To know wisdom and instruction; to perceive the words of understanding; To receive the instruction of wisdom, justice, and judgment, and equity; To give subtilty to the simple, to the young man knowledge and discretion. A wise *man* will hear, and will increase learning; and a man of understanding shall attain unto wise counsels: To understand a proverb, and the interpretation; the words of the wise, and their dark sayings. The fear of the LORD *is* the beginning of knowledge: *but* fools despise wisdom and instruction" (Proverbs 1:1-7). I know Steve's spiritual leadership in our home, the importance he placed on his own personal time in the Word, and our family time in the Word has had a profound influence on our children.

When our boys were in their late elementary years, we made the decision to take them out of team sports. As we observed team sports and our sons' interactions there, we became concerned that there was more negative growing from this than positive. We saw hearts drawn to peer influences, entertainment, competition, and pride. Any one of these could lead a child toward the road of rebellion since they are at odds with God's will and parents' desires. Surely, with all of them, we placed our boys at great risk if we allowed them to continue in team sports. Matthew 6:24, "No man can serve two masters: for either he will hate the one, and love the other; or else he will hold to the one, and despise the other. . . ."

Steve prayed, sought the Lord, and knew the time had come to remove them from sports. He took each of the boys out for a soda, individually, to explain his heart in this situation. It was very difficult for us, because we all had pride and excitement in our hearts since these sons were excelling in their sport. James 4:6, ". . . God resisteth the proud, but giveth grace unto the humble." However, the boys could see their Daddy's desire was for their good, and they were willing to trust his leadership, submitting to his decision.

We have felt that if we kept our children from peer influences by homeschooling them, we would undermine this if we placed them in church youth groups (or team sports) where many of these same influences would be felt. Proverbs 10:17, ". . . but he that refuseth reproof erreth." Therefore, we have purposely looked for and chosen churches that did not have a youth group. We knew it would be hard for our teens to hear about youth activities and watch youth involved in them but be kept on the outside.

We have been so blessed these past several years to be in a church with no youth group by the church's decision. The teens are growing in wisdom and stature under their own fathers' authority, teaching, and direction. Proverbs 1:8-9, "My son, hear the instruction of thy father, and forsake not the law of thy mother: For they *shall be* an ornament of grace unto thy head, and chains about thy neck." Several families have shared how they have been drawn to this church by observing the young people and their ministries. They know in their hearts that this is the pattern they desire for their own children.

Not wanting to leave a void in the children's lives when activities were removed or prevented, we chose to replace them with our time and activities, if possible. One way this was accomplished was in Steve instituting a weekly meeting with each of the three older children. This was done on Sunday before or after church with just Steve and one child at a time. They would discuss anything on either of their hearts. These meetings still continue; they are a private matter, with me seldom knowing what was talked about during this time. Often when issues come up during the week, Steve will say, "That would be a good topic for our meeting." With a special time set aside each week to share hearts, the children have been able to approach their father with their concerns and vice versa—a certain opportunity for keeping the hearts of our children.

January 1999

Can Teen Rebellion Be Avoided? (Part 2)

Television was removed from our home over ten years ago. Psalms 101:3, "I will set no wicked thing before mine eyes. . . ." At that time the influences even "okay" shows brought into our home were often negative. Did the children treat their parents with respect? How did they interact with their siblings? What activities were they involved with? Those questions don't even take into consideration what children see on commercials or other programs that are not "okay."

Steve has been willing, as a dad, to invest time in his children's lives. He has given up the recreation he would pursue during his free time in order to be with his children. About eight years ago, when Nathan was fourteen and Christopher was twelve, Steve and the boys began to finish our basement. Could Steve have done the job faster by himself? Perhaps at first, but with a few months of teaching and training, the boys had learned many skills to make their help valuable. Not only did they learn much about construction in the process, but they also experienced wonderful, manly fellowship during those hours of working together. Ecclesiastes 4:9-12, "Two *are* better than one; because they have a good reward for their labour. For if they fall, the one will lift up his fellow: but woe to him *that is* alone when he falleth; for *he hath* not another to help him up . . . and a threefold cord is not quickly broken."

Steve has carried this policy on into car work and almost any other project or errand he does. He includes even the younger children in these activities. It would be much quicker to work alone, but he is doing more than a task. He is investing in the hearts and lives of his children. Turning the hearts of the children to their fathers and the hearts of the fathers to the children has continued to be one of our main goals in parenting children (Malachi 4:6). Proverbs 4:1-5, "Hear, ye children, the instruction of a father, and attend to know understanding. For I give you good doctrine, forsake ye not my law. For I was my father's son, tender and only *beloved* in the sight of my mother. He taught me also, and said unto me, Let thine heart retain my words: keep my commandments, and live. Get wisdom, get understanding: forget *it* not; neither decline from the words of my mouth."

Steve also will take a child with him almost any time there is a meeting or activity to attend. When he had a breakfast with our state representative, Nathan went along as a teen. Steve has made our children a part of his life. Proverbs 5:1-2, "My son, attend unto my wisdom, *and* bow thine ear to my understanding: That thou mayest regard discretion, and *that* thy lips may keep knowledge." In addition to the fellowship that the children have experienced, they have been exposed to Steve's insight and teaching on many spiritual subjects in a setting much more public than our home.

We have encouraged our children to be busy with work and ministry rather than entertainment. *"It is* good for a man that he bear the yoke in his youth" (Lamentations 3:27). Nathan and Christopher started a lawn mowing business when they were ages ten and twelve. They worked that business together until Nathan graduated from high school, whereupon Christopher continued it on his own for two more years. This work kept them profitably occupied. They worked hard in hot, uncomfortable circumstances. They learned to serve customers, to maintain their equipment, to cooperate with each other, and to manage a business.

To facilitate an appetite toward serving others, we include our children in ministry the Lord has given us. Steve and the six oldest children have ministered at the local county nursing home for seven years. Psalms 41:1 has been their ministry verse, "Blessed *is* he that considereth the poor: the LORD will deliver him in time of trouble." Also, James 1:27, "Pure religion and undefiled before God and the Father is this, To visit the fatherless and widows in their affliction, *and* to keep himself unspotted from the world." They have a "church service" every other Saturday afternoon, collecting up the residents who are interested in attending, wheeling them into the day room, and ministering to them.

Our children have helped with the homeschool group from the very beginning. One of them has always had the responsibility for the newsletter. They spend many hours preparing for the children's programs that go along with the couples' meetings. They also put on the spelling bee each year. Their hearts are being fed on the joy Jesus gives in serving Him and others, rather than self.

Nathan and Christopher each decided not to obtain a driver's license until there was a need for them to be driving. For them, this occurred around age eighteen when their work required them to have transportation. Not only did they save a considerable amount of money by not having to pay car insurance from the time they were sixteen, but also the lack of transportation may have kept them from opportunities of immorality that could have resulted in failure.

We also suggested the boys wait until the need presented itself before purchasing a car. This happened around the age of nineteen for them. Here again, they saved money by waiting and kept their focus on preparation for the future, rather than self-entertainment that can easily lead to a rebellious heart and attitude.

Steve and I encouraged our children to consider courtship rather than dating. They decided this was a biblical way and have chosen not to date. Because of this, they have been spared from situations that can lead to rebellion and immorality. Their time, money, and hearts have gone to useful occupations such as work, ministry, and family activities rather than being drained by dating.

Before our children reached their teenage years, Steve and I decided it would be good to institute a "dress policy" for how the children were to dress whenever they were in public. We shared with them that, although God judges the heart, man looks on the outward appearance. While it may be true that we don't have rebellious hearts, if the way we dress is worldly, or faddish, it can appear to others that we are. 2 Corinthians 5:20, "Now then we are ambassadors for Christ, as though God did beseech *you* by us. . . ." We wanted them to see themselves as ambassadors for Christ and suggested they choose a "classic style" of dress that would not cause others to assume they were rebellious when they were not.

Prayer has been a key factor in our children's lives for avoiding rebellion. Steve and I could always have been more consistent and diligent in our prayer time for our children, but all through their lives we have called out to the Lord. We are asking for wisdom in raising them, for guidance in decisions we must make, for strength to stand by those decisions, and for Jesus to work in the lives of our children, molding and shaping their hearts for Him.

As we think and evaluate each of these areas that I have briefly discussed, there is so much more that could be said about them, but this is an overview. Some of these may not even seem to have anything to do with rebellion versus lack of rebellion. In the ones that are less obvious, we think the children have been protected from influences and temptations that could have caused their hearts to be turned toward rebellion rather than kept with their Lord and their family.

We believe our older children have been open to these choices because the Lord has enabled us to keep their hearts. Their focus has been on the Lord, work, ministry, preparation for their futures, and family, rather than peers and fun. Therefore, they are willing to listen to our counsel and look to Scripture for their guide.

We are not saying these children are perfect, anymore than Steve and I are perfect. We have discussions where we are on different sides of the fence. There are areas of need we see in their lives where we pray for the Lord to work. However, our relationship is sweet; we delight in our adult children, seeing them as blessings and friends. We have prayed for them, protected them, taught them, and counseled them. We now enjoy watching them as they learn to seek after the Lord with all their hearts.

We give all the credit to the Lord for the work He has done in these children's lives, for the decisions He has led our family to make, and for His faithfulness to us in spite of our failures. We want to encourage other families who may struggle with some of these choices, who may feel they are too difficult and who may wonder if their children will suffer if they make them, that it is worth the sacrifices. What the world offers our young people is empty and vain, but what the Lord offers is full of riches.

As we make some of these decisions or changes, it is imperative that our hearts as parents are soft and open toward our children. We must approach the change with the right attitude. We should offer our time and ourselves to our children in return for anything we are taking from them. Our children learn from us, even what we are not aware they are learning. If our focus is on ourselves, doing what we love and serving our interests, then they learn that too. If we want to direct their hearts toward the Lord, then it must be obvious by not only our words, but also our actions, that our hearts are toward the Lord.

May we, as parents, evaluate each area that comes up with our teens and be willing to seek the Lord on it. May we make the choices the Lord directs us in even though they may be unpopular or difficult. May we continually call out to the Lord in prayer for His grace, wisdom, and strength in raising up children, who are mighty in spirit, to serve Him.

February 1999

Sheltering Our Children

The past two months' Mom's Corners have made me wonder if some of you may be thinking, "This sounds like too much sheltering to me. Shouldn't we teach our children right from wrong as they grow up, and then let them sink or swim in the real world?" With two of our children already adults (22 and 19), we have had some first-hand experience with this concept of building a strong relationship with Jesus in our children and an ability to stand alone against what they will face in the world.

Our role as parents has moved into one of counsel for our adult children, rather than directives we would give to younger children. This role is a sweet one, and we have delighted in it. This might not be the case if we had lost the hearts of our children through their teen years, which is what I addressed in those last two Mom's Corners.

How many of you have known a godly man who has fallen into immorality of some kind, perhaps adultery? It happens to pastors, deacons, elders, Sunday School teachers, even homeschooling dads. Do you think these men purposed to be unfaithful to their wives? I seriously doubt it! However, they did not heed the warning that Scripture gives us about our human, sinful condition and the need to put safeguards around ourselves. 2 Timothy 2:22 says, "Flee also youthful lusts," and 1 Thessalonians 5:22, "Abstain from all appearance of evil." If adults are susceptible to falling into immorality, aren't our young people even more at risk with their immaturity and innocence? Even Solomon, the wisest man in the world, succumbed to the lust of the flesh. David, the man after God's own heart, fell into the sin of adultery.

Shouldn't we offer our teens safeguards to help them walk the righteous path they desire? We feel the need to give boundaries that would protect them as much as possible. Not only do we want our children to be salt and light in the world, but we also want them to be holy and pure–in the world, but not of the world. While our sons are strong in their Christian faith, they are still subject to their sin nature, as are we. Therefore, we counsel our sons not to seek employment where they would be in constant, daily contact with things such as worldly music or worldly young people.

Unfortunately, the girls today are very aggressive, and while we discuss with our sons the need to guard themselves, we would not want them placed daily in the path of temptation. We do not see this as causing them to be dependent upon us. They are definitely not. We do see it as teaching them how to make wise decisions.

One of our sons has been working for large corporations in their computer service departments since he was eighteen. Here, he is in an environment where he can share his testimony when it is appropriate. However, the age group he works with is varied, not predominantly young people. Our other son is working with his dad in our business. He is often out in the world going into businesses to give computer software tutoring. He has regular contacts in the world, but they are on a professional level. As these continue, he, too, has opportunity to share his testimony.

Despite the better working environment of the corporate world, my husband has been happy to leave it, with its immodesty of dress, aggressiveness in women, and the propensity toward doing whatever is deemed necessary to get ahead. Here again, we have warned our sons of the dangers they are facing and strongly encouraged them to put "hedges of protection" around themselves.

Our twenty-two-year-old son volunteers one night a week at the City Union Mission in downtown Kansas City. In addition to being exposed to secular thinking in his work place, he is exposed to the real world at the mission. He is ready for this challenge. He has a one-on-one Bible study with one of the residents. We have encouraged him in this ministry, but have cautioned against such things as listening to details of immoral, or evil, practices.

Another example of our philosophy of "protectionism" involves not only our older children but also Steve. Steve chooses to not have lunch alone with another woman, or ride alone in a car with one, even when business related. One might ask if this means he is not strong in his faith or not independent. Of course not! It does mean that he is being wise in protecting himself from situations that have led other Christian men down a path that ends in sin, and sometimes loss of their family. My husband's standard in this area has caused inconvenience to our family at times, and has certainly given him opportunities to share, but I am pleased to have a husband who will make such choices for his family.

As far as our daughters go, I wonder how many of us developed independent spirits during our college or working days. Has this made it more difficult for us to submit to our husbands in the meek and quiet way we would like? A family shared with us their concerns for their daughter after she began working. They said, "One of our goals for our daughter is for her to have a submissive spirit to a future husband, if she marries, but we are also training her towards an independent spirit." They did ask her to stop working, sharing their heart's concerns, and she was willing.

Does this mean we keep our daughters in our house and never let them out? No, but it does mean we determine the learning, working, and ministry opportunities that will best help them toward their goals. One of our goals for all of our daughters is that they would remain holy and pure. When I hear worldly teens, and even some Christian teens, talk these days, I am very saddened by the crudeness and impurity of their conversation. I would hate to have my daughter in an environment where she was constantly exposed to that.

This may not be the way you decide to direct your teen or adult children, but it will certainly give you and your husband a great discussion topic! We do not teach our children God's Word, and then put them in the world to sink or swim. We protect them through their teen years of great vulnerability, not wanting to put them to a "test" they might easily fail and regret the rest of their lives. We counsel them as adults to be "wise as serpents," setting safeguards around themselves, as much as possible, to keep them from temptations that could result in moral failure.

We do not believe what we are doing with our children constitutes isolationism or creates dependence on us, but rather encourages them to exercise caution in the environment they place themselves in on a daily basis. I am happy when my husband makes these same choices for himself, or for me, as well as when my children do.

March 1999

Grace in the Time of Sorrow

In March, we shared with you our joy over another pregnancy and baby that was due early in November. Now we share with you our sorrow over the miscarriage we experienced this week. We have not had a miscarriage before, and each of us has had to turn to the Lord during this time of sorrow and grief. The first night we had signs of the baby's loss Steve said, "It is pretty hard to put three little boys to bed who are all crying." As these issues of life and death affect our family, I would like to share some thoughts that I see relate to our homeschooling.

First, the Lord has abundantly poured out His grace in my life. I think that some of my close friends have grieved our loss as much as, or more than, I have. Not that my heart hasn't felt sorrow upon sorrow, but the Lord is comforting me through it. This reminds me that 2 Corinthians 12:9 says, ". . . My grace is sufficient for thee: for my strength is made perfect in weakness. . . ."

I imagine you have heard, or maybe even said yourself, "I could never homeschool. I am just not cut out for it!" I have had similar thoughts about a miscarriage, "I could never handle the grief of losing a baby." When I was not facing a miscarriage myself, the Lord's grace was not there for me. I did not need it. However, in my time of need, God's grace was there, and it was sufficient. In the same way, when He calls us to homeschool, He is giving us the grace to do what He has called us to do, even in our weakness.

That first night when we were aware of the miscarriage beginning, it was very difficult to go to bed. I felt like I would cry all night long. As I settled down, though, my mind began to praise the Lord, just focusing on Him. In addition, I remembered another friend who had recently miscarried and was pregnant again, due soon after I would have been. I prayed for that other little baby in his mother's womb. With my thoughts off my own sorrow, I actually fell asleep.

How like our daily homeschooling problems this should be. But is it? What is your reaction to an attitude difficulty with a child that is ongoing, or an educational hurdle that doesn't appear to be surmountable? My reaction is often to murmur about it, to seek for an immediate solution, and to feel discouraged by it. I would be so much better off to take it to my Lord, leave it with Him, praise Him for Who He is, and focus my prayer on the need or another need altogether. My worry and my discouragement do nothing to change a situation. However, Jesus Christ can and will work on it. I wonder how often I am hindering Him by my own solutions or my anxiety over it.

Lastly, this time of grief has brought to remembrance again of the preciousness and value of each child the Lord has already given us. We watched Tim's family walk through the final months of his battle with brain cancer. We saw Larry and Wendy love Tim through those difficult last weeks with a patience and gentleness that touched all of our hearts. They allowed us to love Tim, too, during those days. Wendy shared how special that year of homeschooling had been because of the extra time it had given her with Tim.

After a loss, it is too late to express all we would like to express to that loved one. I am grateful that I had prayed for this baby's safety, that I had thanked and praised the Lord for giving him to us, and that I had prayed for each stage of his few weeks of development. In the same way, as we homeschool, we have the opportunity minute by minute and day by day to love, encourage, and praise our children. This is one of the greatest benefits of having them home with us all day. However, all too easily, we become caught up in, and focused on, the negatives of our children's behavior. Sometimes we even have trouble finding anything to praise and encourage a child about. May this never be! May our heartfelt drive be as intense to thank, praise, reward, and encourage as it is to teach, instruct, train, discipline, and correct. May we make sure that when we do teach and correct, our attitudes are sweet and pleasant. We want to truly seek our child's good, and not our own convenience!

I challenge each of us to keep our focus on our Lord and on what He has called us to do. Let's not become so wrapped up in the educational pursuits of our homes that we forget the ministry the Lord has given each of us of loving and cherishing our family members. May we delight in the grace the Lord gives us for each mountain and valley He walks us through!

April 1999

Summer Schedules

Summer is almost upon us! For many homeschoolers this means a change of pace. Some will take a total break from schoolwork, while others will have a modified school schedule. There are also those who school full time, all year long, with breaks spaced throughout the year. May I encourage you to begin to pray and plan now for those summer hours so that you can maximize them.

I love to use this month of May to occasionally close my eyes for a few moments and ask the Lord what He desires for our summer. I will make lists of things I would like to accomplish, what I could do special with the children, areas of character growth I want extra teaching time in, and new tasks that I will train the children toward. If the Lord gives me a vision and goals for our summer, how will they be managed? I find that developing a summer schedule helps me to make the most of these precious summer days, without letting them slip by.

I like to schedule one hour per summer weekday for cleaning and organizing tasks that are too large to tackle during the school year. I keep a running list of these jobs as I come across them, usually when they have bothered me in some way. During May, I will also add to this list tasks I know I do during the summer. Here are a few of mine: organize and sort school work and school boxes, organize and mount photos in albums, clean all the closets and kitchen cupboards, organize book shelves in the basement, wash walls that really need it, and plan for the next school year!

This cleaning and organizing time ends after an hour whether I feel like I want to stop or not. It is amazing how much can be completed in just one hour! Often jobs are less daunting when we know they will only last for that one hour. This helps us be willing to jump in to tackle them.

In our home, we have older children play with the younger ones during cleaning time. With only little ones, it is more difficult to make this time productive, but it can still be done. Using an evening when Dad is around to watch the children is a possibility. If not that, then try working in an area where you can directly supervise the children.

It is also a good idea to assign the children their own age-appropriate cleaning and organizing chores for summertime. I would rather have their work scheduled for a different time than mine. This way I don't have interruptions from them asking how to do the job or whether it passes inspection.

Often during the school year, I won't have time to teach a child new chores. However, scheduling a half hour a day for this through the summer months is very practical. You could rotate children through this time, as most jobs won't take more than five or ten minutes a day to learn. Usually a child is ready for new cleaning skills after a year of practicing the ones they learned the previous summer. When this is in our schedule, we are assured that the summer doesn't pass by and all of a sudden we realize there have been no new practical skills learned.

Summer also lends itself to extra playtime and one-on-one time with my children. But do you know what happens if I don't plan this into a written schedule? I will end up doing one of two things. I either keep busy with my own personal projects, or I sit and do nothing at all. This time with the children is very important to me, and when I put it into my schedule, I have the accountability of the children's enjoyment of the time to hold me to it.

For our family, summer allows us to get a jump-start on our school year. We will continue with our reading and math so that we can take those subjects off on Fridays throughout the year. This helps give the children another constructive activity for their extra time, and it keeps their reading and math skills at peak performance. Fridays are looked forward to, almost as a weekly vacation day, because of the lighter school schedule.

Another high priority for summer hours in the Maxwell home is character and habit training. Here again, if the time isn't set aside in our schedule, we will take the path of least resistance, and character won't be a focus of our summer. The month of May is when I begin seeking the Lord for the areas in which we have the greatest need, and how we could spend a half hour a day tackling them. It usually isn't difficult to come up with a character and habit training list with just a short amount of prayer. Once the list is generated, it is exciting to continue to pray about which Scripture, songs, stories, practice sessions, discipline, and reward system will best help us toward our goals.

Making a summer schedule will assure you that your summer days are maximized and that the hours are going toward the goals the Lord has called you to for this particular summer. I think you will discover your children have a more peaceful, productive summer with a schedule too. So often moms are ready for school to start again in the fall because of the chaos that results from the lack of structure without the school routine. Compensate for not having the school schedule by making and implementing a summer schedule. I think you will find it most worthwhile!

May 1999

What Is a Mother to Do?

One of the biggest mothering frustrations I face is deciding what consequences a wrong behavior in one of my children should receive. I watch an attitude or action that I know ought to be corrected, but I am at a loss as to what to do about it. I want to be consistent and have consequences standardized, but I will sometimes ignore the situation just because I don't know how to discipline for it.

For example, yesterday four-year-old Jesse came upstairs crying that eight-year-old John was wearing his hat. I had two issues to deal with. John had been unkind in wearing Jesse's hat and in keeping it when Jesse asked for it back. Jesse had also not been kind, because he wouldn't wait for John to finish with the hat, and he came whining to me. So, what is a mother to do?!

I imagine each of you faces issues like this several times a day in your home, if you have more than one child. We are able to work with these situations even more since we are homeschoolers because we have that many more hours each day with our children home. To be honest with you, I would rather avoid these sorts of interactions between my children. Wouldn't it be better, though, for me to see each one as an opportunity to teach and train my children? With these kinds of thoughts, I could actually be happy when the need for consequences arises.

A schedule gives direction for your day. In a similar way, standardizing and knowing exactly what you will do for many of the common areas that require discipline in your home gives direction to your child training. If you need help in this area, I suggest an *If/Then Chart* (www.Titus2.com) to help you work through this task of determining consequences and then writing them down to be posted in the home for easy reference. I can still remember the evening five or six years ago when two moms excitedly stood up in our homeschool support group meeting and shared this "treasure" they had discovered. I agree!

I wish I knew how many times I have said to one of my children, "If you _____ one more time, you will have to _____." By the time they do it again, I have forgotten what I said the consequence would be! If I had written it down, then I could have consulted my notes and followed through.

Recently we were working on the children becoming responsible for brushing their teeth in the morning. I spent our scheduled "training time" in the late afternoons teaching the children how to brush their teeth, how long to brush, and how to put their toothbrush away afterwards.

We still needed a consequence if the teeth weren't brushed. The decision was made to have the child lose two days' worth of dessert if he hadn't brushed his teeth. I wrote this on the white board and then kept track of any offenders there. Once the "rule" and the "consequence" were written down, I was no longer at a loss as to what to do when I noticed a toothbrush that still had toothpaste on it. I didn't have to nag, fuss, or feel frustrated. I could just call the non-toothbrusher to the bathroom, tell him to please brush his teeth, and express my sympathy that he had chosen to miss two days' worth of dessert because he hadn't brushed them!

Here are a few other examples from the Maxwell household. If a child interrupts, he is to put his hand over his mouth until Dad or Mom lets him take it off. This comes from Proverbs 30:32, "If thou hast done foolishly . . . *lay* thine hand upon thy mouth."

Certainly, a child who barges into a conversation is being foolish!

We have also "backwards" applied Proverbs 17:1, "Better *is* a dry morsel, and quietness therewith, than a house full of sacrifices *with* strife." When our children are fussing with each other, the consequence is to eat a dry crust, and we quote this particular verse with them.

May I encourage you that investing the time in determining consequences for "infractions" will be well worth the consistency you will achieve in disciplining your children. It will also remove a big area of frustration for you as the mom. This process takes thought, prayer, and consultation with your husband. Writing down the results, perhaps in a notebook, or on a chart such as the *If/Then Chart* is a necessity for remembering what you have chosen.

I plan to update our *If/Then Chart*; they do need revising, in my opinion, as the children grow. I have been dealing with times of frustration due to the uncertainty in discipline issues, because I have not been using the "tools" the Lord has given me in this area. I plan to spend time this summer regenerating my chart and then applying it! Maybe you would benefit from doing this too!

June 1999

Pleasant Words Increase Learning

"The wise in heart shall be called prudent: and the sweetness of the lips increaseth learning" (Proverbs 16:21). This is one of my favorite verses in regard to homeschooling and raising children. It is a verse I need to remind myself of daily. I also have to ask the Lord to help me see the value of sweetness of the lips or pleasant words. I need to be aware of when they can be used. It is easy for me to spot a child's infraction; that comes naturally. It takes the Lord's help to be as conscious of how to use pleasant words.

Pleasant words are appropriate in discipline situations. Sometimes I wonder what our children must think of us when we have our stern face and stern words on. Have you ever watched and listened to another mother in this mode and thought to yourself, "Look how hard and harsh she is!" Would our children have an easier time responding to our discipline if we used the same discipline, but had a sweet disposition while doing it? This is not the purpose of this Mom's Corner, though. Rather, I want us to consider the value of practicing pleasant words to praise and encourage our children.

Sometimes I am absolutely amazed, at what sounds very syrupy sweet to me when I say it, but will bring the biggest, brightest smile to my child. Right now Anna, age six, is diligently working on learning to read and write. When she makes a particular letter well, perhaps a "p," I will say, "What a great 'p' that was, Anna!" Her face immediately lights up with pleasure! I can assure you that there are many, many letters on her page that are not made nicely, and even this one I am praising is probably not perfect. I feel certain, though, that she is much more motivated to continue working to make her letters nicely by my pleasant words than she would be by my criticism of her poorly formed ones.

When we brought our oldest son, now twenty-two, home to school fifteen years ago, he was struggling with his newly acquired reading skills. I had no experience teaching reading and few resources to draw upon for the remedial help he needed. I decided that I would have him read aloud to me for fifteen minutes a day. Our initial sessions included irritation on my part when he wasn't doing well. However, the Lord soon showed me that instead I needed to praise him highly for the words he read correctly and to patiently help him sound out the words he struggled with, not allowing any criticism, or irritation, on my lips as I did so.

Unbelievably to me, within just a few short weeks, his reading skills had improved to where he could read almost anything put in front of him. He no longer dreaded reading time as he had before, but he was actually enjoying the stories he could now read for himself.

Pleasant words promote instruction. Isn't instruction our goal in homeschooling? We want our children to learn to be Christ-like; we want them to develop godly character, and we desire that they excel educationally as much as possible. Scripture says that pleasant words will help us toward these goals because they increase learning. We can say the exact same words with a sweet voice or with a hard voice, pleasant words or harsh words. What will be the outcome of each? We can also use either pleasant words or critical words in most situations. Which will promote the instruction that is the prayer of our hearts for our children?

Gratitude comes under the heading of pleasant words. How I delight in expressions of gratefulness to me, and how difficult it can be to receive criticism. I am finding this is just as true for my children. My seventeen-year-old daughter thrives on praise and gratitude, being highly motivated by it. Our children need to learn to receive criticism with a proper spirit, and I expect they will have plenty of opportunities for just that. I want to major on gratitude and praise while minoring on the reprimands that do come naturally to me.

"Whose adorning let it not be that outward *adorning* of plaiting the hair, and of wearing of gold, or of putting on of apparel; But *let it be* the hidden man of the heart, in that which is not corruptible, *even the ornament* of a meek and quiet spirit, which is in the sight of God of great price" (1 Peter 3:3-4). I wonder how much of this meek and quiet spirit is evidenced by our pleasant words. No matter how hard I try for pleasant words, it is a matter of the Lord changing my heart. ". . . for out of the abundance of the heart the mouth speaketh" (Matthew 12:34).

I must make this heart-change issue an area that I am constantly bringing before my Lord Jesus Christ in prayer and petition. Also, I want not to be satisfied with having a spirit that easily criticizes my children but has difficulty praising them. "For it is God which worketh in you both to will and to do of *his* good pleasure" (Philippians 2:13). I desire to see these negative heart attitudes as sin, confessing them to my children and to my Lord. "If we confess our sins, he is faithful and just to forgive us *our* sins, and to cleanse us from all unrighteousness" (1 John 1:9).

Yes, I have a responsibility to teach and train my children, which will involve plenty of opportunities to correct them. However, may the joy of my heart be to praise, encourage, and express gratitude to them. May I see the value in these "pleasant words." I challenge you to evaluate your day-to-day interactions with your children. Are they lopsided on the critical, hard side, or do you find frequent occasions to verbally express your pleasure with those precious children? Pleasant words promote instruction!

July 1999

A New School Year—
Introducing the Maxwell Family

Another school year is about to begin! The August Mom's Corner is the time I traditionally take to introduce my family to those of you who are new to our mailing list since last year at this time.

The Maxwell Family consists of Dad (Steve), Mom (Teri), Nathan (22), Christopher (20), Sarah (17), Joseph (10), John (8), Anna (6), Jesse (4), and Mary (2). We are beginning our fifteenth year of homeschooling, with two of our children already having graduated from our "non-accredited private school," Flowing Streams Christian School.

The Lord, two years ago, fulfilled a vision Steve has had for a long time. Steve is now working full time with Christopher in our fledgling family business, Communications Concepts, Inc. They are distributors for printed materials (letterhead, business cards, forms, etc.) and specialty items, write software manuals, and offer one-on-one software training. Nathan is doing contract computer network administration for Western Auto's corporate headquarters in Kansas City.

Sarah is in the twelfth grade, Joseph in fifth, John in third, Anna in first, and Jesse and Mary in our home preschool. We use Bob Jones University Press for high school curriculum, and ABEKA/Rod and Staff for elementary. Each year brings challenges and excitement to our home and school.

God has given us a vision for our children regarding their preparation to be self-supporting in life. We see the importance, even as young adults, of their remaining in our home where they have the counsel and guidance of their parents until they are ready for marriage. While they are living at home, working, studying, and maturing, they are saving a large portion of their earnings with the hope of being able to purchase a home debt free. We are also greatly enjoying the pleasure of having these years to enjoy our adult children as we spend our evenings and weekends together. We are constantly, as a family, seeking God's direction as they pursue a course for their future that is very non-traditional.

Ministry-wise, the children, from Anna on up, help Steve with a twice-monthly church service at the Leavenworth County Infirmary (nursing home). In addition, Steve, Christopher, Joseph, and John team up with Nathan, who has recently taken on a monthly Saturday service at the City Union Mission in downtown Kansas City. Nathan also volunteers there one night a week, leads a young men's early morning Bible study, attends our pastor's preaching class, and is head usher at our church. Christopher plans and coordinates the children's programs for our homeschool support group meetings, is the Sunday night pianist at our church, and attends Nathan's Bible study and the preaching class. Sarah helps Christopher with the children's programs for the group, edits the homeschool newsletter, and helps greatly with the workload that *Managers of Their Homes* has generated (including keeping up the Dad's and Mom's Corners e-mail list).

For many years our family had a heart's desire to be near our extended family. In 1990 God opened doors allowing us to move to Leavenworth, Kansas, where we purchased the house next door to my parents the following year. We have loved the relationships that we have been able to watch grow, develop, and change between the various members of the family: parents, daughter, son-in-law, grandparents, and grandchildren.

1999/2000 will be the tenth year Steve, with the help of the children and me, have been leading our local homeschool support group.

We know that many of you have felt God's leading to home-school your children. Most of you would tell me you feel inadequate for the task. May we encourage each other in the thought that in our own strength we are inadequate. But whom God calls He also enables. His strength is made perfect in weakness. He wants our hearts to be turned toward Him. He wants us to be truly humble. Then He can work with us and mold us as the vessels of clay we are.

Our children will learn academics this year. We will too. But, in the face of eternity, more important education will be taking place. Rough edges will rub against each other. Can I patiently instruct and train as needed? Can I admit my shortcomings to my children and seek their forgiveness? Am I willing to be consistent in working with them? Will I give and give and give of myself? It is my desire that I will. Is it your desire? Is it the constant prayer of your heart?

August 1999

Homeschooling the Dawdler

Seldom do I give a "Getting It All Done" workshop in which I do not get this question: "My child manages to draw out every school assignment he is given. This ends up making the rest of the family have to wait on him before we can go on to our next activity. I really feel like he could do the work more quickly, but he just dawdles, rather than applying himself to his task. What do I do?"

What about you? Is one of your children a classic dawdler? He sits down to do a page of math and within a minute is up sharpening his pencil. Back to the book, the child is soon noticed looking out the window while thumbing through the book. Pretty soon a drink is called for, and within minutes of returning from that, a bathroom break is taken. Sound familiar?

First, I encourage you to discern whether the fact that your child cannot complete an assignment in the allotted time is because he is incapable of doing the work, or because he is a dawdler. Here is how we made this determination. We had a son who could spend two hours or more in front of his math book without completing more than two or three problems on his two pages' worth of work. We certainly didn't want to deal with this as a character issue if it were an ability deficiency.

One evening about 5:00 p.m., after this child had sat at the table with his math book in front of him most of the afternoon, his dad announced, "I have just ordered pizza for dinner. It will be here in thirty minutes. Anyone who has all their schoolwork completed may join us for pizza. Others can have a sandwich alone when their schoolwork is finished."

Steve happened to know the current situation with this child and that the other children had long before turned in all their schoolwork. This was a test for our dawdler. You will never believe the results! Pencil went to paper, and within fifteen minutes, that child had every math problem completed on his lesson. Moreover, he had done an excellent job in terms of accuracy!

I had believed he could easily complete his math in thirty minutes, but had allowed him forty-five minutes just to be sure. It was confirmed. We had a character issue to work with, not an ability one.

This is the way we handle the dawdling situation in our home. The children are required, barring unusual circumstances, to finish any schoolwork they did not get done in their scheduled time during their free time later in the day. The more I am consistent with enforcing this, the more progress we see in our children applying themselves during their scheduled school time. It is absolutely no fun to watch your siblings out playing while you sit and complete what you could have done earlier in the day when they were working, too, and not available for play.

I can honestly tell you it is difficult for me to be consistent in this area. I want to make excuses, in my heart, for them and allow them to head out with the others for their free time. The truth, of course, is that I am not doing them any favors by not enforcing our policy, nor am I doing myself any favors!

The characteristics of a dawdler may be seen in other areas of their life, perhaps when chore time arrives. One thing that our dawdler thrives on is some motivation to get him moving, just as in the pizza story I shared with you. A time deadline that is short and immediate can help him focus on the need to keep at the task. You might try using a timer, which you or the child can set for a determined amount of time. Then the child will have a visual reminder of the need to continue with his job or schoolwork.

Here is a short testimonial I recently received on just what we are suggesting here.

> *"Our schedule has also provided an opportunity to teach them personal responsibility since they are now responsible for checking the schedule themselves to see what they should be doing, and they are also responsible for using free time to finish up anything they didn't accomplish when they were supposed to. After forfeiting part of his playtime one afternoon in order to finish math that wasn't done when it should have been, my ten-year-old son really applied himself on the other days."*

Dear Sister, if you have a dawdler in your homeschool, be encouraged! The Lord has provided you this wonderful opportunity to impact the character of your child in a needed and positive way. Be strong and courageous; take the challenge. Don't nag and fuss at your dawdler. Maintain a pleasant, matter-of-fact attitude as you enforce the consequences you have chosen. Remember to keep this need as a matter of prayer. Be consistent throughout this whole year in dealing with this issue. Look back, after the year, and check for some progress. Also, keep in mind that your child's character growth is a long-term project! Even if the progress in one year is not what you want for the finished product, know for certain that had you not worked in this area, no progress would have been realized and probably movement backward would have occurred.

September 1999

Homemade Character Training

Very frequently in the course of these Mom's Corners, I stress the importance of working on character issues with our children. We have looked at the necessity of not only being on the defensive concerning character through consistent discipline, but also being on the offensive with character training sessions. No one knows the particular needs of your children, at this moment, nearly so well as you and your husband do. Therefore, who better than the two of you to plan how this character training will take place? So often we find ourselves in search of the perfect "character curriculum," when we have the best of the best right under our noses–the Bible and our knowledge of our children.

Prayer is a key ingredient to your character training planning. Begin by praying alone and with your husband, if possible, about what character trait your family should be working on. Don't just assume that you know what it is; really seek the Lord!

Once you have decided on the character to be tackled, continue praying, asking the Lord to give you creativity in how to present this character trait to your children, and how to make it practical for their lives during your training time. You can tailor the teaching sessions to your own children to ensure that the learning and information fits their needs and learning capabilities. Your examples can be ones that come right from their daily experiences in your home. This will make your character-training time realistic and practical.

Set aside a time in which you plan for character time, and write down your ideas. I can have scheduled character training in our day, but never actually do it. Why? Because I don't have a plan for how to use that time, and it is easier just to avoid it than try to make up something when I am not prepared. On the other hand, when I know what we would like to accomplish during those minutes, then I will make the effort to be accountable to the scheduled character-training time. Our dear Pastor Anderson in Clearwater, Florida used to tell us, "Nothing becomes dynamic until it becomes specific." Making your plan isn't difficult, but having it written down is key to your success.

This process of putting together your own homemade character-training curriculum for scheduled training sessions is quite exciting. Once you get started, you will be surprised how your mind will begin "perking," and you will come up with lots and lots of ideas. Write them all down, and you are ready to go with your character-training time. Try it; I think you will like it!

October 1999

Right Timing

Have you ever been away from your children for a period of time? Were you really excited about getting back home and seeing them again? As you were nearing your arrival did you picture the perfect homecoming and reunion with your children?

Recently, Steve and I had the opportunity to go away to a cabin in Colorado for a week to celebrate our 25th anniversary. We loved our time together but were both anxious to be back with our family. We were so excited about returning home that, when we were awake at 3:30 a.m. the morning of our trip home and not sleeping well, we decided to start back then rather than waiting for the planned 5:00 a.m. wake-up time. All the way home I imagined what our evening with the children would be like.

Our homecoming was exactly what I had pictured–for the first couple of hours. Then I went downstairs into my three little boys' bedroom and playroom! Yikes! It looked like they had left everything out for the entire week I was gone, even getting into the locked storage closet of extra toys.

So what would you have done? What do you think I did? I wish I could tell you that I decided the night of my return home was the night to love and enjoy my little ones, knowing that we could tackle putting items back in place another time. Instead, I decided we had had enough homecoming time. I chose to call them downstairs to begin the task right away. The evening ended with me being frustrated with the children and myself. I was disappointed I had not let the pickup wait and unhappy with them for not keeping up with their room while I was away!

I am still learning and growing in this area of right timing. As you can see from this situation, while I may understand the need for right timing in my mind, my emotions in the heat of the moment do not always agree. Sometimes I follow those emotions rather than that still, small voice of the Lord.

Does right timing enter into our lives as homeschooling moms? I believe it is very vital and key in many areas of our homeschooling.

When we have had a night with little sleep and wake up feeling drug out, is it a good day to tackle a problem that has been looming on the horizon for months? The answer to that is an easy, "Of course not!" But what often happens? In our tired state, that problem is so discouraging and looks so big, we jump right on top of it. Usually this means we do not deal with it in a way we would have preferred if we had really thought and prayed about it.

What about right timing in teaching a child a concept in school? Have you ever been frustrated with a child who is not catching on to something–perhaps it is fractions in math? You work and work, explain and explain, search for alternative ways to demonstrate, and still the light does not come on. Finally, that section is finished, but you know very well your child has not grasped what they were to learn. You are discouraged, while at the same time relieved to be done with the struggle. Then you get into fractions again the next year, and suddenly, even at the beginning of the study, your child understands fractions!

What about right timing in working with the heart attitudes of your children? Will they respond to your discussions of the need for changes in their heart when they are angry, rebellious, or distraught?

Yet, how often do we as mothers try to reach our child's heart at exactly that moment? Then we wonder why their reaction was not what we wanted it to be. What would happen if we waited until the emotion had passed, on our part and on our child's part, and spent the ensuing time in prayer for our child's receptivity? Then we could find a non-confrontational, quiet moment to pursue the problem.

This issue of right timing affects our interactions with our husbands. Have you ever had a terrible day? Then the moment your husband walked in the door you began to dump on him all the frustrations that had built up. It wasn't just from that day, but the problems that had been hanging around for some time. Is this the best time to share these concerns and seek solutions together?

I know that although Steve is willing to listen to me, allow me to emote, and try to work through the difficulties, we are not very productive at this time. Whereas, if I will wait until our weekend date to bring up the situations from that week that are ongoing and need to be addressed, then we can discuss them in a calm, rational manner. This allows me to weed out the small issues that are not ongoing, plus I have time for prayer in the meantime.

I wonder how much better off we would be to learn, in each of these areas of right timing, to take just a moment to ask the Lord, "Lord, is this the time for me to deal with this situation or is there a better time?" If He gives the go-ahead, then the timing is right. But if He whispers to our hearts "No," then we need to let go of our agenda, lift the situation up in prayer, and listen for when the timing is right.

I have to tell you that I have a long way to go in this particular area. I know that there are victories I can point to, particularly in learning the signals my body and emotions give me when I am very tired. This is not the time to do anything except maintain the status quo and head for bed as soon as possible. Even though there is much for the Lord to teach me in the discernment of right timing, it is my heart's desire that I would be submissive and teachable.

May I encourage each of you to consider right timing. As you become more sensitive to the Lord in this, what difference will it make in your mothering? What about your effectiveness as a home-schooling mom? Could it affect your relationship with your husband? I believe the answer to each of these is a resounding "YES!"

Proverbs 25:11 says, "A word fitly spoken *is like* apples of gold in pictures of silver." May each of our words fit into this category. I know, for me, this is much more likely when my heart is attentive to the Lord for His timing.

November 1999

Tea Time with the Lord

Let me share a part of a note I received, and have permission to use, to encourage you. Marilyn writes,

> *"Something very fascinating has happened to me. I have discovered the source of my discouragement. My problem is that I was not spending any quiet time with the Lord. I haven't for years. I wasn't drawing near to Him, and I had conceded that all of my homeschooling friends had the same problems that I had. We were all just burned out and overburdened. I now have scheduled 'tea time with the Lord' in my day, first thing."*

That reminds me of how often moms tell of the excitement they have when they begin using a schedule. Once again they are having daily quiet times, those moments alone with the Lord! This pleasure is real because, sadly, time in the Word is one of the first activities to be set aside when homeschooling days become busy.

Generally, as Christians, we begin homeschooling because the Lord Jesus Christ leads us to this decision. He has first place in our lives, and when we begin to have concerns about other school options, He gently starts putting the homeschooling idea on our hearts. More often than not, we don't feel "qualified" to homeschool either in the area of patience or as an actual teacher. We know, though, that whom the Lord calls He also enables. So we step out in faith, trusting the Lord to carry out the plans He has set before us.

While this is the way we head into homeschooling, it isn't long until the demands of school, laundry, meals, cleaning, ministry, and life in general begin to wear on us, and somehow, we give up our personal time with the Lord. We allow the busyness of our days and weeks to drive the way we use our time. Then we wonder why we are discouraged, frustrated, irritable with the children, and short tempered in general.

Consider, for a moment, a few Scriptures with me. Psalms 119:105, "Thy word *is* a lamp unto my feet, and a light unto my path." Don't we desire to know the way the Lord has prepared for us personally, and for each of our children? Have you heard, or even said yourself, "If the Lord would just send a letter telling me what to do in this situation, I would be so happy to obey!" God has sent us much more than a letter; He has given us a whole book! The more we root and ground ourselves in His Word, the more we will understand His will in choices we must make. "And be not conformed to this world: but be ye transformed by the renewing of your mind, that ye may prove what *is* that good, and acceptable, and perfect, will of God" (Romans 12:2).

"But we have this treasure in earthen vessels, that the excellency of the power may be of God, and not of us. *We are* troubled on every side, yet not distressed; *we are* perplexed, but not in despair; Persecuted, but not forsaken; cast down, but not destroyed" (2 Corinthians 4:7-9). Does this describe the way you feel some days? So how is it that we "show that the excellency of the power may be of God, and not of us," if we don't have time in our day to spend with God? Without daily reliance on Jesus Christ, aren't we working through our day in our own power and strength?

"My voice shalt thou hear in the morning, O LORD; in the morning will I direct *my prayer* unto thee, and will look up" (Psalms 5:3). Do you? Do I? Or do we only take the time to shoot up arrow prayers during each crisis that occurs throughout the day? Is this truly laying our requests before God, or is it asking Him to be a firefighter for us? Can you keep a record of God's answers to prayers in your life, and your family's lives, if you don't have a consistent time to spend in prayer alone with Him?

"All scripture *is* given by inspiration of God, and *is* profitable for doctrine, for reproof, for correction, for instruction in righteousness: That the man of God may be perfect, throughly furnished unto all good works" (2 Timothy 3:16-17). Isn't this another of our hearts' desires, to be thoroughly equipped for every good work the Lord has for us to do, and especially in the teaching and training of our children? If we don't spend time daily with the Lord, in His Word, will this be possible?

My heart desperately needs the Word of God every single day! I have a scheduled forty-five minutes early in the morning to have a quiet time. For the most part, this keeps me consistent, but sometimes we are up quite late at night and that impacts my time with the Lord the next morning. I wonder if my family can tell the days I have really met with Him, versus the ones I hurry through my reading, prayer, and memory time, or skip it altogether. They don't ask me that question, but perhaps on days when my irritation is quick to show through, it would be good accountability for me if they did.

When my youngest child, now three, was a baby, she went through a stage when she wasn't nursing well at her breakfast time feeding. We decided that I should quit waking her up at 5:30 a.m. to nurse so she would be hungrier at 8:30 a.m. As we began doing this, I found I became very nervous from 6:45 until 7:45, because I would not be available if she happened to wake up and be hungry. I was out of the house walking and someone at home would have to pacify her if she awakened. That time became miserable for me because of my anxiety over the baby. I asked Steve and he agreed that we could go back to me waking the baby up early in the morning. Do you know what happened? Rather than dreading having to get up at 5:30 every morning to nurse the baby, I loved it. I was so happy to again have a peaceful heart during that hour I was out walking, that I didn't mind in the least the early morning nursing time.

In a similar way, our time feasting on the Word should be so important to us that we don't care a bit that we are rising earlier than we might otherwise, or that we are taking quiet afternoon time when the children sleep to meet with the Lord.

My husband and I are "best friends," and we love to talk with each other. Frequently, I gain insight into my own life by discovering what he thinks about various situations that don't even involve us personally. Recently I found out what he believes a wife who wants to encourage her husband to be the spiritual head of her home should do. Have you ever wondered about this or perhaps discussed it with some of your friends? What did you come up with? Do you know how a man might respond to this?

Steve says the place for a woman to begin helping her husband in his spiritual headship of their home is with her own personal time in the Word with the Lord! Her husband will observe peace, contentment, joy, gratitude, and other fruit of the Spirit that will emanate from her life when she is spending time reading her Bible and praying. He will also be drawn to the Lord and the Word.

Do we want our husbands to be the spiritual leaders of our homes? Could it really be that this begins with our personal time with the Lord in His Word? Remember, this time is for our own personal growth in the Lord. It is not to be used in a "look what I am doing" kind of attitude with our husbands. What fruit will develop in our lives as a result of our investment of this time with the Lord? Am I considering the widespread effect, within my family and ministry circle, that my devotions will have?

How much of what our hearts yearn for in our homes is tied back to this very special time? If you have felt the Lord's call to homeschool, but have been neglecting to seek Him daily by setting aside a time to spend alone with Him, may I strongly encourage you to not let another day go by before you remedy this situation. May we each follow Marilyn's example and begin our day with "tea time with the Lord"!

December 1999

How Long Does Character Growth Take?

Are you ever disheartened because your children aren't making the progress you desire, particularly in an area of character growth? Does this cause you to want to give up working on it? The Lord has been showing Steve and me some new insights concerning this that I believe are worthy of discussing in a Mom's Corner.

Do you remember when I shared with you last summer about our work on teaching our younger children to say, "Yes, Ma'am" and, "No, Ma'am?" Let me reprint that part of the Mom's Corner here to refresh your memory.

For example, this summer we were teaching our younger children to answer with, "Yes, Ma'am. No, Ma'am. Yes, Sir. No, Sir." This was being accomplished by dropping one M&M into a mug with their name on it each time they respond in the desired fashion. At an approved time they would be allowed to eat their M&Ms. We also made this into a game for character teaching time when there was a major cleanup to be done.

"Jesse,"

"Yes, Ma'am."

"Please pick up the Legos."

"Yes, Ma'am." Two M&Ms are popped into his mouth and another one when he returns after finishing his pickup.

"Anna,"

"Yes, Ma'am."

"Mommy wants you to take these socks and put them in the dirty clothes hamper."

"Yes, Ma'am." Again, two M&Ms are immediately eaten and a third one offered when she returns. We continued until all the little tasks were completed, and would you believe they didn't want to stop even when I couldn't find anything else to do?

This training was so successful that the children were saying "Yes, Sir" to Nathan, our twenty-one-year-old son. Nathan was pleased enough with this show of respect from his younger brothers and sisters that he purchased a three-pound bag of M&Ms and another one of Skittles to continue the character-teaching rewards.

I wrote that Mom's Corner a little over a year ago. At the time this was written, it sounded greatly successful, but it was short term! However, guess who, in the long run, was trained to say, "Yes, Ma'am"? It was Mom! After the newness of our project wore off, I was constantly reminding the children how they were to respond, and M&Ms were being handed out infrequently.

I was disheartened and took the situation to Steve. He encouraged me to keep working with the children on their "Yes, Ma'ams," and to wait patiently for the results. So we continued.

Do you know that a year and a half after we began this character project with our children, they are finally consistently responding the way we want them to? Our ten-year-old son, the oldest of the children who are learning this, is the "king" of "Yes, Ma'ams" in our family. It goes down the age line as to how well each child is doing with answering properly.

Does a year and a half sound like a long time to learn to say, "Yes, Ma'am?" It sure does to me! To be honest with you, if I had known a year and a half ago that it would take my children this long to learn it, I am not sure I would have undertaken the job. At least, I would have begun with different expectations. This has brought a new perspective on the reality of what character teaching really means!

I like quick results! I am willing to put forth effort in a certain direction with my children's character growth, but I want to see immediate, lasting results. I am slowly learning character development is not always an instant outcome kind of project! As a matter of fact, it is likely to take weeks, months, and even years.

A year ago September, we purchased a chore assignment and tracking system. This was to be a part of teaching the children responsibility and diligence. About two months later, I was ready to admit our money had been wasted because we could not even remember to use the system, let alone make it work for us. Once again, Steve counseled me to "hang in there" and keeping trying. A year later, we are consistently using the chore program!

This has been so amazing to me. These are two dramatic examples of where I know exactly when we began the project, and now the results are coming in—a whole year later!

What I am continually learning through these last twenty-three years of parenthood is that God has called me, as a mom, to be faithful to Him. Ephesians 6:4 says, "And, ye fathers, provoke not your children to wrath: but bring them up in the nurture and admonition of the Lord." Therefore, I am to be obedient and consistent in teaching my children the ways of the Lord. I am to teach, train, discipline, encourage, and praise. I am to pray diligently concerning the specific area we are working toward. However, the results are the Lord's; "For it is God which worketh in you both to will and to do of *his* good pleasure" (Philippians 2:13). Whether it takes a week, a month, a year, or ten years does not matter.

How freeing this can be for us, as moms, to not have to shoulder the responsibility for the outcome. On the other hand, the responsibility of remaining consistent in focusing on the teaching and training is tremendous. It can become wearisome, at times, if our eyes come off the Lord and onto ourselves. Galatians 6:9 is a familiar verse to us. It says, "And let us not be weary in well doing: for in due season we shall reap, if we faint not." What better good is there for us to do than to teach our children to grow in Christ-likeness?

It is easy for us mothers to wonder if we are ruining our children when we don't see the development of character that we believe should be there. My prayer is that we can let go of these negative thoughts and feelings while dedicating ourselves to fulfilling the calling the Lord has given us.

It should not be surprising that it would take our children time to develop godly character. Look at our own personal struggles with character as adults. For example, how often do you respond to your children with a slight tone of irritation in your voice? Is that the way you want to answer them? Have you prayed and worked toward not letting this happen? Do you still do it?

Hebrews 5:14 says, "But strong meat belongeth to them that are of full age, *even* those who by reason of use have their senses exercised to discern both good and evil." If, "by reason of use," we come to discern both good and evil, it makes sense to me that "by reason of use" is also an integral part of learning to do good. "Character" doesn't happen overnight!

I so much want to encourage each of you to expect the development of godly character to be a long, continuing, ongoing process worthy of the pouring out of your very life! Don't look at the short-range progress but at the long-term goals. Set your heart, prayers, and consistent teaching on the Lord's desire for your child to grow in Christ-likeness. Then patiently, day by day, teach, train, and love your children toward their character growth, knowing that the Lord Who has called you is faithful. "Let us hold fast the profession of *our* faith without wavering; (for he *is* faithful that promised;)" (Hebrews 10:23).

My heart rejoices when I hear my children answer with sweet, positive "Yes, Ma'ams." I am grateful Steve encouraged me to not give up when I was ready to do so a year ago. The fruit truly is worth the continuing efforts that were put forth.

What about you? Have you been discouraged lately over a lack of character growth in your children? Have you become weary in your well doing? May I encourage you to step back, take a deep breath, lift your heart to the Lord, and continue on. Be ready for the long haul, not looking for immediate results but trusting the Lord for the long-term ones.

January 2000

No Condemnation

It was the week to write a Mom's Corner, but the Lord had not been revealing to me what He wanted me to write on. I presently have my scheduled writing time after my early morning devotions. This particular morning, I lingered in bed doing some extra praying before my scheduled prayer and Bible-reading time. I knew I had nothing yet to write and would spend my writing time praying. The basis for writing is prayer, so I was continuing to ask the Lord for His direction.

My time in Romans 8 that morning was so fruitful and encouraging that I felt strongly the Lord gave it to me for the Mom's Corner. Let me share a verse I believe is especially applicable to us as homeschooling moms, and one that has personally helped me.

Romans 8:1 says, *"There is* therefore now no condemnation to them which are in Christ Jesus, who walk not after the flesh, but after the Spirit." I wonder if this is how we, as homeschooling moms, live–with no condemnation. It seems so easy to fall into the trap of self-condemnation.

One of my personal areas of greatest struggle is with my attitude and voice. If I am involved in a task and one of the children interrupts me, it is natural for me to respond to them with a short tone and an edge of irritation in my voice. My heart's desire is to do as Titus 2:4 says, "to love their children" in all my interactions with my children. Am I demonstrating love by being unhappy with a child who interrupts? Of course not! If the child was being rude in interrupting, he may need training or correcting, but that should still involve a neutral tone of voice, or a pleasant one.

When I fail, what do I think? Usually it is one of two things. I can follow the path of least resistance, and this is what goes through my mind, "There I go again. I was irritated over such a small thing. Won't I ever learn to handle these little frustrations with gentleness and kindness? I am such a failure. I don't ever change!" Self-condemnation, lots of it!

My other choice of thoughts comes from focusing on the Lord. These verses in 2 Corinthians 7:9-10 have greatly changed my thinking and dealing with my sin. "Now I rejoice, not that ye were made sorry, but that ye sorrowed to repentance: for ye were made sorry after a godly manner, that ye might receive damage by us in nothing. For godly sorrow worketh repentance to salvation not to be repented of: but the sorrow of the world worketh death." While these verses may be dealing with salvation, I have found personal application in them to my walk as a believer.

My thoughts of guilt and self-condemnation are the "sorrow of the world" that worketh "death." What benefit is there to my family, or to me, in those kinds of thoughts? Do they bring about change in my life? Do they encourage me to depend on the Lord Jesus Christ? Absolutely not! They actually keep my focus on myself and allow me to wallow in self-pity.

On the other hand, there is "sorrow to repentance." This is the sorrow that is fruitful and productive. It puts these thoughts into my mind: "Lord, You are surely not pleased when my words do not show the fruit of Your Spirit: love, joy, peace, longsuffering, gentleness, goodness, faith. My irritation and anger is sin, Lord. I confess to You my wrongdoing and ask You to forgive me." No condemnation!

What benefits are there to me and to my family with these thoughts? First, it is the reality of the joy of "no condemnation." It is the truth of 1 John 1:9, "If we confess our sins, he is faithful and just to forgive us *our* sins, and to cleanse us from all unrighteousness." Here is freedom and joy rather than guilt and self-pity. The Lord is freed to work in my heart. He is the One Who will do the changing in my life. "For it is God which worketh in you both to will and to do of *his* good pleasure" (Philippians 2:13).

I know that I am more able to love my family, if, when I sin, I confess and repent of it, and ask for the Lord's help to overcome it, than when I head in the direction of "poor me, here I go again." Confession and repentance relieves the burden of trying to be the one to bring about a change in this area of my life where I am prone to failure. I can't do it anyway, but when my thoughts are wrong, it makes me feel like it is my responsibility.

How often does self-condemnation take this form in our thoughts? "I am ruining my children by this homeschooling. Look at what a bad example I am to them. They are learning all my negative traits and following in my areas of sin. I just don't have the patience to deal with them twenty-four hours a day."

Yes, there have been times I have thought these thoughts, although not for the past several years. Is this the way God would have us think? I am sure you would agree; it is not. If we are a bad example, we need to be confessing–never excusing or justifying–each incidence of sin in our lives before the Lord and our children. We must repent of it and prayerfully submit to the Lord. If we lack patience, we should look for the benefits the Lord has for our children and for us by allowing a "furnace" in which to learn patience. Can we ruin our children if we are following the Lord in obedience to what He has called us to do, and we are walking faithfully with Him? No, of course not!

All of the negative thoughts are self-focused. We have to set them aside and take them captive to the truth the Lord gives us in His Word. "Casting down imaginations, and every high thing that exalteth itself against the knowledge of God, and bringing into captivity every thought to the obedience of Christ" (2 Corinthians 10:5).

As I walk in the Lord's path of "no condemnation," my children learn how to deal with the sin in their lives. They see a humbled mother coming to them and confessing the irritation in her heart and the negative tone in her voice. There are no excuses, simply repentance. These children will battle sin throughout their lives. If I were ruining them, it would be from teaching them to look at self and feel self-condemnation for sin, rather than to look at the Lord, repent over sin, and be grateful for forgiveness. I would be failing my children by modeling worldly sorrow, rather than sorrow to repentance.

I challenge you to take a critical look at your heart and thoughts when you fail. What are you thinking? Is there self-condemnation, or are you confessing and repenting? Are you falling into self-pity, or are you experiencing the joy of walking with the Lord Jesus in "no condemnation"? May we encourage each other to not follow what comes naturally, but to walk in the truth the Lord has given us of "no condemnation."

February 2000

Little "Nags," or Are They "Promptings"?

I had two small areas in my life that were bothering me recently. When you read about them, you may even chuckle and think, "Why would those create a problem for her? They are so insignificant." For me, these are issues that just "nag" at my mind. They are things that I have felt led by the Lord to do and have planned into my daily schedule.

The first "nag" is my writing time for Mom's Corners. I have this time set aside in my day, but often I will allow myself to be drawn into answering e-mails rather than writing an article. My scheduled Corner writing time is quiet, early in the morning, before the little children are up and interruptions begin.

The second "nag" has to do with a timeline and a set of wall maps that go with our school Bible time. We just haven't been doing them lately. Our Bible time is held in the living room, but our time-line and wall maps are located in the dining room. Therefore, we must move into the dining room for this part of our Bible time, get out our materials, sort them, and figure out which ones go up for the current lesson.

Neither of these problems is very big. Solving them has been simple. However, I allowed them to "nag" at me for several weeks, even months. I let myself follow my way rather than the way the Lord had led me in these two areas. They were small things, but left alone, they grew in their "nagging" potential in my mind. It really would have been much better for me to have addressed these difficulties early on and dealt with them, rather than to let them drag on and on.

My problem in staying on task with the Mom's Corner writing was a character issue. It is one faced by many as they implement and use a schedule. The schedule calls for a particular activity, but we are drawn away by something else to take that scheduled time. How do I feel when I allow this to happen? I am discouraged and disgruntled with myself.

Why does this involve character? It is because the Lord has directed me to use my time in this particular way. When I allow myself to be pulled to other uses for that time, uses that He has not led me to for that hour, I am choosing disobedience to my Lord Jesus Christ. It is as simple as that! Do I usually view it that way? Of course not! I rationalize in my thoughts, "This e-mail answer will only take a minute or two. It will be out of the way and off my mind. Then I will get right back to the Mom's Corner." Whether it is two minutes or the fifteen it usually turns into does not matter, it is still disobedience to what the Lord has called me to do.

What is the solution? Prayer. Begin with, "Lord, You have put on my heart the writing of Mom's Corners. You have even given me the time to spend on them. I have been allowing myself to be drawn into other tasks at the computer rather than keeping my focus on the Corner. Lord, because I know You have directed me to write the Corners, I am really choosing disobedience by doing other things. It is no different from when I tell my children to pick up the toys in their room, but find them playing with those toys instead. They went down to pick up toys; however, they became distracted with the exact thing they were sent to do. Please forgive me, Lord, for following my own way, rather than Your way. Help me to stick with the job You have assigned!"

Then I must look for ways to limit the distractions that pull me away. Just realizing it was disobedience not to spend my time as the Lord had directed was an immense help. Next, I set a specific time in my schedule for doing what was distracting me from my task at hand. In this case, I decided to use the half hour after the little ones were in bed for answering e-mails, rather than fitting them haphazardly in through the day and disrupting other scheduled activities. It really is a perfect time because I am tired by then and don't have much energy. I am motivated to not let the e-mails pile up so I won't want to head for bed without addressing them.

My second irritation that "bugged" me, of not keeping up with our Bible timeline and maps, was just as simple to relieve. All I had to do was commit to going into the dining room for part of Bible time whenever we were ready to work on the timeline or map. Doesn't that sound easy? Why was it such an effort to do this? I think it just shows the depths of my own laziness and enjoyment of comfort. After all, sitting in my living room recliner is much more pleasant than being on the hard dining room chair. Since some of our materials needed to be sorted before we could use them, I took one of our Bible times, gathered the children at the dining room table, handed out the little pieces of numbered paper, and we began to put them in order. We worked together, and it took less than fifteen minutes. Because my supplies weren't readily available, I kept putting off and putting off this part of our Bible time that really was important to me.

What about you? Are there issues that just "nag" at your mind and heart? Have you taken the time to pray about solutions? "For it is God which worketh in you both to will and to do of *his* good pleasure" (Philippians 2:13). Are you ready to seek the answer in order to be rid of the discouraging thoughts? "If any of you lack wisdom, let him ask of God, that giveth to all *men* liberally, and upbraideth not; and it shall be given him" (James 1:5).

Remember to first determine whether your "nags" are of the Lord. If they are not what the Lord would have you do, find that out so you can let go of the negative emotions that accompany your perceived failures. Pray about these areas, and consult with your husband before you assume they are from the Lord. If they are from the Lord, deal with them as He directs. Perhaps, rather than naming these areas "nags," it would be better to perceive them as the promptings of the Holy Spirit. Would we more quickly face the issues if we recognized them as the promptings of the Holy Spirit? I would! A "nag" is something that harasses you into doing what it wants you to do. A prompting of the Holy Spirit is something to follow in joyful obedience.

I expect your little areas that "prompt" you are individual to your circumstances and personality but not that much different than mine. They are small issues. Someone from the outside could look at them and be surprised that you struggle with them or haven't found a solution for them. However, for me and for you, our personal little "prompts" build and grow daily when they aren't addressed. Despite this, they truly are insignificant enough that we feel we can continue to ignore them, while their "prompting" pressure discourages us.

The solution may be setting aside time in your schedule to do what has been bothering you. It could be needing to prepare the materials for a specific activity. It may mean writing something on a list that needs to be purchased when errands are run. Perhaps it is writing down an issue that should be discussed with your husband so that a direction is reached. For some reason, these small things can be the ones that undermine us through our day.

Remember Jesus' parable of the talents? Here is His final word, "His lord said unto him, Well done, *thou* good and faithful servant: thou hast been faithful over a few things, I will make thee ruler over many things: enter thou into the joy of thy lord" (Matthew 25:21). How we respond to these "few things" in our lives is the basis for how our children will deal with similar areas of their lives. When character issues are important to our hearts for our children, shouldn't they begin with us? Each of my little "prompts" had to do with character, but because they were so insignificant, they were easy to excuse and ignore. However, I wasn't fooling the Lord, was I? Had these not been significant to Him, I believe I could be sure they wouldn't have remained on my mind.

May I encourage each of us to not allow these small "prompts" to go unaddressed and unresolved? If they are "nags," and not from the Lord, may we learn to discern that and refuse to listen to their "nagging." If they are His leading and the promptings of the Holy Spirit, then may we learn the character, through Him, to move us into joyful obedience.

March 2000

A "Wifely" Victory

Recently I had a wonderful victory in the area of reverencing my husband. I am sure you will laugh at it because it seems such a small thing. To me it was monumental even though I have been growing greatly in reverencing and submitting to my husband, particularly through the last five years.

My parents were coming over with my ninety-one-year-old grandmother. They were treating our family to ordered-in pizza. We had set a time for them to come and for the pizza to arrive. So, exactly what was my victory in the midst of this small celebration? It was pretty simple. I didn't remind Steve to call early for the pizza to arrive at the designated time! Doesn't that sound silly? Why would this be a victory for me? It is because I think Steve won't remember such things unless I remind him.

This victory did not come without a battle. I thought about reminding him. I even considered how I might do this without it seeming like I was. As it neared time for our guests to arrive, I so wanted to ask him if he had ordered the pizza. When this thought popped up into my mind, I had to take it to the Lord. 2 Corinthians 10:5, "Casting down imaginations, and every high thing that exalteth itself against the knowledge of God, and bringing into captivity every thought to the obedience of Christ." I prayed that the Lord would help me hold my tongue and that reverencing Steve would be more important than having the pizza arrive on time.

I realized that even if Steve did forget to order the pizza, the worst that would happen is he would realize this when my folks arrived, order it, and we would wait a while for dinner. Guess what? He didn't forget! Not only did he not forget, I didn't have to remind him!

Do you realize what small victories like this do for my future in reverencing my husband? Each one grows my faith in my Lord and my husband. Next time I will not have such a battle with my thoughts over whether to remind or not. It will be easier to rest, having the meek and quiet spirit I so desire (1 Peter 3:4)!

What if Steve had forgotten to order the pizza? I would still have had the peace in my heart that reverencing my husband was more important than when the food arrived. What a petty issue to be concerned about—timing of food delivery! In this particular case, it would have been just fine for the pizza to be late. My parents, due to a small emergency before they left home, were not able to arrive at the agreed-upon time. It could have been the Lord's plan not to have the timing for the pizza arrival be our timing.

I wonder if you have begun thinking about the reverencing of your husband. Ephesians 5:33 ends with, "and the wife *see* that she reverence *her* husband." I have always thought of reverencing as respecting. However, no matter how I turned the definition of reverencing around, it came back to me as a much deeper relationship than just respect. Respect takes us a long way, but where do we go with reverencing?

I have become aware, through the Holy Spirit's promptings in my life, of ways I don't reverence or even respect my husband. Much of it comes from me wanting to control and conform Steve to what I think he should be. This would not be overt to an outside observer. Nor do I feel like I purpose to do this; it just seems to be ingrained in my nature! It is so important that I see and evaluate these controlling behaviors realistically. I am talking about things like this: reminding so that he doesn't forget something important, having a better idea when he brings up a suggestion, giving him "direction" for what he should or should not do or say, always asking where he is going and what he is doing, requesting the details of his phone conversations. I can put on a sweet voice and a smile thinking that will make my controlling ways acceptable. The truth is it doesn't. Part of reverencing Steve is being under his authority without trying to manipulate him to my wishes.

Please understand this doesn't mean I never do any of these things. They just aren't the overriding characteristics of our relationship. As Steve and I have discussed these issues, he has decided that he would like me to ask if he wants reminders about certain areas that need addressing. We freely discuss, as husband and wife, what is going on in our lives. This gives the proper platform for me to give "wifely" input. How much better in our private discussion of a problem concerning the children to offer a suggestion than to raise my eyebrows at him in front of the children or speak a critical word to him! Usually Steve tells me where he is going, what he is doing, and shares details of phone conversations I would be interested in. So what does it matter if, on occasion, he doesn't do this? Do I need to jump on it and ask him? Can I rest in the Lord knowing that if I need to know the Lord will prompt Steve to tell me?

To be honest with you, this is a struggle for me. I don't want to have to watch my words or tone of voice with my husband. I don't care for needing to wait on him to ask for my opinion or counsel on a subject. I want to know all about his phone conversation with a mutual friend. These limitations frustrate me.

1 Peter 3:4 says in relation to wives, "But *let it be* the hidden man of the heart, in that which is not corruptible, *even the ornament* of a meek and quiet spirit, which is in the sight of God of great price." I am learning that the Lord is more concerned about the meek and quiet spirit He desires of me than that everything is the

way I want it. When I consider it, do I truly want to be a control-ling, nagging, "always have a better idea" wife?

The Lord has been giving me another thought in this area. How can I possibly know that what I believe is right in a given sit-uation is actually the way to go? After all, Scripture does say, "For the husband is the head of the wife, even as Christ is the head of the church: and he is the saviour of the body" (Ephesians 5:23). I am convinced that Christ, as the head of the church, is always right! While my husband is a fallible, sinful human, this word picture in Ephesians puts him in the same position in relation to me as that of Christ and the church. It is something for me to seriously consider when everything within me wants to have a situation go "my way"! Romans 8:28 says, "And we know that all things work together for good to them that love God, to them who are the called according to *his* purpose." Perhaps God has a purpose for the times Steve fails that is greater than if he did exactly what I thought he should!

I see that a part of reverencing my husband is truly trusting in his decisions, not only when they match my own. Choosing to do this puts him in a position of being responsible to the Lord, not to me. Obviously, there will be times of failure on my husband's part. For some husbands it may be a whole lifetime of failure. Will I com-pound this by my own discontent, nagging, and controlling? Will I choose to reverence my husband, trusting and obeying my Lord's command?

What about you? I expect there are areas in your relationship with your husband where you can begin to pray about and learn to let go of controlling. Will you be more concerned with following the Lord, in obedience to His Word to you as a wife, than you are about having things go the way you think they should? May the Lord encourage our hearts as we seek Him in our quest to be the wives He has called us to be.

April 2000

Time for Summer Schedule Planning

One of my children asked me this week if they would be doing math over the summer. That question prompted me to begin praying about and planning our summer schedule. We have four more weeks of school left as I write this plus a week of standardized testing; then it is summer for us. What about you? Have you considered the use of a daily schedule during the summer? Since I am beginning to think about our summer schedule, I felt like it was time for me to encourage you to begin on yours!

I was amazed by the reports of several of the moms who tested our book on scheduling for homeschool families before it was printed. After they had been on their schedules for a school year, some decided not to make and use a summer schedule. Their feedback was that they would not make that choice again. Their summer had rushed away without getting to the activities they had wanted to accomplish, and there was a greater level of disharmony among the children.

Summer is perfect for catching up on organizational and cleaning projects that the school year does not allow time for. I schedule one hour a day for these kinds of projects, and I am always surprised and delighted at how much I can do during this hour through the course of the summer.

The temptation is to continue working on the project past the allotted hour. However, this then undermines the rest of my summer schedule because I will have other priorities scheduled for the rest of the day.

I keep a running list of projects I would like to get done during that organizational hour, prioritize it, and jump in when summer begins. I also like to look back over what I have done previous summers to help me know what to tackle this year.

This is my list right now, but I will come up with other projects as the summer progresses: pack away and label children's winter clothes, box this year's school books, create a school portfolio for each child, clean kitchen cupboards, clean and organize closets, put photos in albums, and plan 2000/2001 school schedule.

I will schedule Sarah, our eighteen-year-old daughter, to spend my organizational hour taking the younger children for a walk and playing with them. This way I will have fewer interruptions during that time, and the children will be getting some exercise. Because it is hot in Kansas in the summer, this hour is scheduled for right after breakfast before it becomes unbearably hot.

Planning for a summer schedule is a great time to pray about whether year-round schooling would benefit your family. This is one way to eliminate some of the time pressures faced during the school year. When you spend a couple of hours schooling each day through the summer, you free up that time through your normal school year. It also gives your children something constructive to do with their summer days and keeps their skills fresh. We have found that we can skip the first quarter of a math book when we move into it right after finishing the previous one, because that first part is all review. We purchased an art course for our children. I am going to look at my schedule and the materials to decide if I want to give a half hour a day to beginning this course. I will find it easier to prepare for it during the summer because I have more time available.

I will also be praying about how much school to continue through the summer. Usually I schedule math that will necessitate my involvement. I try to make the other school time self-instructional and self-correcting so that as much of my time is freed up in the summer as possible.

I want to spend more time playing with the children during the summer. I put this in my schedule as well because it gives me needed accountability. I am likely to find something I feel I need to do or want to do rather than go outside with the children–especially when it is hot!–if that time isn't scheduled. When they are looking forward to it, I don't want to disappoint them.

Summer is a perfect time to teach your children new chore skills. You can revise your chore schedule during this time, moving jobs from child to child, training them on new ones, and making sure they can do them well.

We want our summers to involve a change of pace. However, we don't want to lose the direction, productivity, and peace the schedule lends to our home. Therefore, we simply pray about a summer schedule, seeking the Lord for His priorities for our summer days. Then we are ready to put together the summer schedule and look forward to what we can enjoy and accomplish.

Ephesians 5:16 and Colossians 4:5 both mention "redeeming the time." May we see the productive possibilities for a summer schedule to help us in this important directive of "redeeming the time." May I encourage you to consider a summer schedule if you have not used one before? If you already believe in the importance of a summer schedule, may I suggest you begin now to pray about and plan for the details of that schedule?

May 2000

Training Children for Church

Eleven years ago, we had four children from age twelve down to a baby. We sent these children to children's church and Sunday School but were never very excited about the outcome. Frequently, the children picked up an illness because of their close contact with other sick children. This meant the next several weeks many of us were home from church as the virus spread through the family. Our children also had a propensity for picking up every negative word or action they observed in another child. Even in a Christian church setting, they managed to discover words, attitudes, and actions of which we did not approve.

One Sunday morning a friend of Steve's visited our church. They had four children about ages six on down. I was stunned as I observed this family sit through ALL of church with ALL of those children. In addition, the children were well behaved. You had better believe the first thing I asked that mom after church was, "How do you get your children to sit so nicely through church?" Her response was very simple, but it revolutionized our family's future church attendance. We began to practice what she suggested with wonderful results. I want to share this idea in case you are in the stage of life with young children whom you would like to have with you in church, or perhaps know other families with this desire.

We began to train our children to sit in church by practicing during the week at home. We found this method to work amazingly well. It was so simple, yet very effective. Here is how we implemented it in our family.

I held the youngest child, who was still a baby, on my lap during our family Bible time. If he started to try to wiggle down, I held him firmly and said quietly, "No." If the baby began to make noise, scream, or cry (this is a baby old enough to sit up), I would gently put my finger on his mouth and say, "Shhh." I did this several times, but if the crying didn't stop, I would carry the baby to his crib and say, "You must be quiet during devotion time. Mommy will come back to get you when you stop crying." When the baby was quiet, I would bring him out to the family again and onto my lap. Consistently, we would do this repeatedly as needed. It did produce some interruptions to the devotion time, but if Mom is quietly doing this while Dad continues the Bible time, the distractions are kept to a minimum. We believed the investment was worth the hoped-for outcome.

We also required the other children to sit quietly and attentively during devotions, as we would like them to sit in church. Not only did this help their church behavior, but it also helped them during home Bible time. Because we are not currently training a baby to be quiet and sit on Mama or Papa's lap in church, we have not maintained the same high standards of behavior during our family devotions, and it has had a negative impact on the children's attentiveness.

When we were actually at church and the youngest child would not be quiet, either Steve or I would take him out and sit with him where he would not be a distraction. We would be careful not to let him down to crawl or run around because we didn't want him to learn that if he was noisy he could leave church and have fun. We would do as we did at home, holding him firmly on our lap, putting a finger on his mouth and saying, "Shhh." Since there was no place to put the baby if he kept on making noise, we would just hold him firmly, praising him anytime he was quiet. If it seemed he was going to stay quiet, we would take him back into the service, leaving again if his noise level rose. There were many services a member of our family missed sitting in the hall at church with a child between nine and eighteen months of age. That was also the age Steve's friend said was the hardest. However, the fruit of being able to sit through two-hour church services with five young children has been worth those few missed services. We never have to take our children out of church for being disruptive anymore, although there are times when they have some "practice" to do when we get home from church.

We have helped our children toward quiet, respectful behavior in church by giving them an environment to encourage their success. They don't get to eat, read, or have toys. This makes church a different place from home or another play area. They do have notebooks to scribble in or take notes in if they remember to bring them to church.

Our little ones are not "perfect" in church. They sometimes whisper to each other and to us. Their eyes can wander here and there. They will get off their seat from time to time to pick up a Bible or change laps. They don't sit like statutes through the service. This is within our level of tolerance of a child's behavior in church. Others must agree with us because we regularly receive comments on how good the little children are in church. If our children cross the boundaries for church behavior we have set, they will again find they have some practice time at home after church.

It is a joy for us to have our family worshipping all together. We don't feel our younger children are missing out on anything by being with us. They receive spiritual training on their level at home. They enjoy going to church with their family. They learn to listen, pray, and worship by watching their parents, older siblings, and other church members. It is a delight for Steve and me. We are most indebted to the Hunsburger family, whom we knew in Kent, Washington eleven years ago, for showing us that it was possible to attend a corporate worship service as a family even with little children!

June 2000

God Is Faithful

I'd like to share with you a section from my prayer journal I recently reread.

October 26, 1997

Lord, I feel hard pressed on every side—Steve's job situation, the request for him to take on additional, outside-the-family responsibilities, the homeschool support group, the children's illnesses, and Steve's magazine decision.

2 Corinthians 4:7-12, "But we have this treasure in earthen vessels, that the excellency of the power may be of God, and not of us. We are troubled on every side, yet not distressed; we are perplexed, but not in despair; Persecuted, but not forsaken; cast down, but not destroyed; Always bearing about in the body the dying of the Lord Jesus, that the life also of Jesus might be made manifest in our body. For we which live are alway delivered unto death for Jesus' sake, that the life also of Jesus might be made manifest in our mortal flesh. So then death worketh in us, but life in you."

Lord, may this time of pressing be a time of my faith being rooted and grounded in Jesus Christ—no matter what happens. May the life of Jesus Christ be revealed in my life. Lord, I feel afraid of the unknown—of what the changes may bring.

Isaiah 43:18-19, "Remember ye not the former things, neither consider the things of old. Behold, I will do a new thing; now it shall spring forth; shall ye not know it? I will even make a way in the wilderness, and rivers in the desert."

2 Timothy 1:7, "For God hath not given us the spirit of fear; but of power, and of love, and of a sound mind."

Psalms 46:1-3, "God is our refuge and strength, a very present help in trouble. Therefore will not we fear, though the earth be removed, and though the mountains be carried into the midst of the sea; Though the waters thereof roar and be troubled, though the mountains shake with the swelling thereof. Selah."

Sunday morning, Lord, and I am home alone with Jesse and Mary sick. It is the day before Steve's lay-off. I feel hard-pressed and fearful, but You sent snow, my very favorite thing—pretty, white, peaceful, quiet. Lord, was it for me? A sign that You are in the midst of the pressure and fear?

I had completely forgotten that particular morning. Even the details of what was pressing on my heart had vanished from my memory until I read them on another quite recent Sunday morning when I was home from church with sick children.

I was so encouraged when I did read this, though, because I saw clearly God's hand of faithfulness. Almost four years later, none of those pressures are a part of my life any more. The Lord walked us through each decision. The unknowns are now known and there was absolutely nothing to fear. The Lord was faithful to use His

Word to comfort my heart then and now in reading back over what He gave me that one Sunday morning.

I don't journal often, mostly when I am discouraged or feeling pressure from life in some way. At those times, it helps me to write out my struggles and to also put on paper Scriptures that apply to the emotions I am battling. Often, when I don't write them down, God's truth is pushed behind the force of my own thinking. When that Scripture is in front of me for me to read and meditate on, it helps me to take captive my thoughts and bring them into the obedience of Christ.

What about you? Are you struggling with keeping God's truth in your mind? Perhaps you could take some time to search out applicable Scriptures and then write them out. You could keep them someplace where you can actually read them to yourself over and over.

Maybe you are finding yourself in the midst of decisions and other pressures. Can you look back and give God glory for His faithfulness to you in the past rather than dwelling on the uncertainties of today? As I look at other decisions and pressures Steve and I are faced with right now, this small page from my prayer journal four years ago shows me that another four years from now I probably won't even remember what I am facing at this moment. Each difficulty and decision, taken to the Lord, is worked out in His timing with His plan.

May we, as Christian women, truly live out in our daily lives the truths of God's Word that are so dear to our hearts. May we be encouraged as we look back on God's faithfulness through the past week, month, year, four years, and more.

July 2000

School Year Preparations

For many homeschooling moms, the beginning of a new school year is just ahead! In this Mom's Corner, I would like to share with you three suggestions for making the coming school year the success that you want it to be.

As I approached the first day of school last year, I was dreading it! I wasn't ready for the changes full-time school would bring. I knew that if my spirit wasn't right, my children's wouldn't be either. I cried out to the Lord concerning the state of my heart, and He answered me.

The Lord encouraged me to set aside the Saturday night before our first day of school as a time to dedicate the school year to Him. I worked on Friday and Saturday to complete all the practical, weekend tasks I had to do so that my Saturday evening would be free. I shared with my family what I was planning and received my husband's blessing. As I waited for my evening with the Lord, I jotted down areas that I wanted to pray about.

After dinner that evening, I gathered up schoolbooks, schedules, assignments–anything that had to do with our school. I carried them into my bedroom and stacked them in piles. I pulled out my prayer notes and started praying for our school, for Steve, and for myself.

Then, child by child, I placed their school materials in front of me. I thumbed through them and made notes as to what I thought might be difficult areas for the child. I noted that on my prayer list. Then I prayed for each child and their school year. If the Lord brought ideas to mind during the prayer time, I paused, made a note, and then continued on.

I had such a sweet, sweet time with the Lord that it completely transformed my heart toward beginning school again. I would counsel any homeschooling mom, whether she is excited about her school year or dreading it, to set aside a special time to pray about and dedicate her school to the Lord. This might even be something a husband and wife could do together in addition to Mom having a prayer time alone.

Psalms 37:5 says, "Commit thy way unto the LORD; trust also in him; and he shall bring *it* to pass." I certainly saw the fruit of this as I purposed, in a different way than I ever had in the past, to commit my school year to Him. I am planning to do this every year!

The second area I would like to encourage you in is chore assignments. This would include making a list of each child's chores, scheduling a time for them to accomplish the chores, setting aside time for you to check their chores, and agreeing upon consequences when the chores aren't done properly. I have found that one of the most draining aspects of homeschooling is not the schooling itself, but getting children to fulfill their household responsibilities before and after school.

What do you do if the child assigned to wash breakfast dishes doesn't do them or takes five times longer than he should? You need to have thought through the possibilities and have consequences in place so that you aren't frustrated when this occurs. We can handle failure in our children calmly when the consequences have been planned out for future use.

When assigning chores and consequences, try to keep personalities in mind. Don't give your dawdler a mission-critical chore that must be accomplished before school can start. If he is the only choice for the job, try giving him a "first school activity" that can easily be made up in his free time later in the day, since some days he might have to spend that slot of school time doing his chore.

The last area I would like address has to do with curriculum. Having prayed about what to use for school this year, be wary of any dissatisfaction you might experience toward your curriculum. The Lord may have a different purpose for those materials that don't seem to be working out as you expected.

When something isn't going well, we are very quick to desire a curriculum change. I know, because I have "been there" many times during the past sixteen years of homeschooling! Perhaps your six-year-old's phonics program isn't working out the way you envisioned. It may be that you should lead your child through at a much, much slower pace while he matures and gradually grasps the material. Could it be your child needs to learn, even at six, to push himself beyond his comfort zone? Maybe you are to learn an extra measure of patience. We can rob our children, and ourselves, of these valuable lessons by "jumping" curriculum too quickly.

I pray that as we enter a new homeschooling year we will seek the Lord on our knees before we ever start the first day of school. May we look for His solutions in helping our children learn responsibility. May we also rest in His purposes for the curriculum choices He has led us to make.

August 2000

Depression

In one of Steve's monthly homeschooling articles for dads (www.Titus2.com; July 2000), he mentioned that my bouts with depression were part of the reason we decided, at one point, to limit our family size. We were amazed at how many people e-mailed us, after that one sentence in his article, to ask how we had dealt with the problem of depression. It seemed fitting to put together our thoughts on a subject we would be just as happy to shove into the closet and forget was ever a part of our lives. However, there is the possibility that our experience and the changes the Lord has brought in this area might be helpful to others.[1] Certainly, depression plays a huge role in the stealing of a meek and quiet spirit.

It has only been eight years since the Lord has given me freedom from the at-times-devastating depression with which I had struggled. It was usually worst during the year I nursed a baby. My pain through those difficult years was very real and is not that distant. I can fully understand the concerned feelings of a mom who is struggling with times of depression, and the worry of her husband, because that was our experience too.

I can't point to a miracle cure, nor did I discover a twelve-step program to overcome depression. This is probably so I can take no pride in what I did but always know it was the Lord's work. I will share what we see, in retrospect, about things that helped move me away from depression, and perhaps there will be something here that the Lord can use in another's life.

One of my first lessons to learn was that the Lord works in His time. I wanted to be over the emotional downs right away. I didn't want it to be "in process," and sometimes I was even angry with God because He wasn't helping me to be better right away. If He was the One to work in my life and I was still depressed, angry, and struggling, then it was His fault! That thinking was totally wrong, but that was how far off my ability to think truth had moved. I had to learn to accept my failings and sinfulness and wait on the Lord for what He would do in my life. It was not my timetable. Philippians 2:13, "For it is God which worketh in you both to will and to do of *his* good pleasure."

My depression was humbling because I knew I wasn't what I should be or what He wanted me to be. I even confessed to my church family what was going on in my life. That was a start towards the healing process for me. The depression was no longer something I had hidden away in my private life. Rather, now the Lord could use the prayers of my church family to help me.

I stayed faithful to daily Bible reading and prayed through those dark times, even though I might feel distant from and forgotten by the Lord. However, in the midst of those black days, I was sometimes closer to the Lord than I have ever been. This was because I was totally helpless and needy, not knowing where to turn or what to do.

We discovered that there were very real hormonal imbalances that affected my emotions. I would do everything I could to deny this, but it was obvious to everyone except me. What I could normally handle one day would send me into tears another day. To combat this physical imbalance, I used the natural progesterone cream for a time.[2] In addition, I followed a vitamin regime suggested by our naturopathic doctor friend.[3] I eliminated caffeine as well.

Daily exercise was critical at this time. I know daily exercise sounds impossible to an already depressed, overwhelmed, terribly tired mom. My walks were about the only time I was away from home. When I began to feel myself spiraling down, getting out would sometimes be the single thing that would change the course of my emotions. Just being away from the environment I was struggling with for a short period each day, plus the effect of the exercise itself, was very helpful.

Being tired was sure to put me off balance. I am a light sleeper, often being awakened in the night by a noise or perhaps the need to nurse a baby. After that, I wouldn't be able to go back to sleep. For eight years now, I have worn earplugs when I sleep.[4] They have transformed my nights! I thought not being able to sleep was just a part of my physical makeup. Not so! Since I began wearing earplugs, I hardly ever have a sleepless night. Steve became the "ears" for our family. I know he will wake me up if the children need me. (Earplugs may not be an option for a mom whose husband can't do this.)

If you want to see what being tired does to even the most "spiritual" of people, look at Scripture. The story of Elijah running from Jezebel after the Mt. Carmel experience is a great example. Elijah was tired, and 1 Kings 19:3-5 tells us what happened: "And when he saw *that*, he arose, and went for his life, and came to Beersheba, which *belongeth* to Judah, and left his servant there. But he himself went a day's journey into the wilderness, and came and sat down under a juniper tree: and he requested for himself that he might die; and said, It is enough; now, O LORD, take away my life; for I *am* not better than my fathers. And as he lay and slept under a juniper tree, behold, then an angel touched him, and said unto him, Arise *and* eat."

Sisters, guard sufficient sleep in your life very carefully. Don't trade it for quiet, late nights when the children are asleep, and you can have some peace. It isn't worth it!

I discovered I made it best through a time of depression when I didn't try to analyze what was causing it. It was better to accept my feelings–as Steve would encourage me to do–like a physical ailment to be patiently waited out. The more I ferreted for the causes, the more discouraged and upset I would become.

However, the times I accepted the feelings and said, "Lord, I don't like this, but I'm going to focus on You and not on me. I am not going to make any major decisions or search for the cause. I will just wait. If I do that, it will pass with no damage except for feeling down. If I think about being depressed, and talk to Steve about it, it will pull me further down, resulting in wrong thoughts and words."

When Steve had run out of ideas for how to help me on his own, he found a pastor's wife who agreed to counsel with me. Janice and I met in person one time for an afternoon. She started by making sure that I knew I was saved.[5] With that assurance, she then gave me a couple of tangible projects to put my focus on the Lord rather than on myself. I called her a few times on the phone–at Steve's insistence–and the path she set me on was exactly what I needed.

Here are two of her projects. Perhaps they will be helpful to you as well. The first project involved learning to take captive my wrong thoughts–thoughts of being depressed, thoughts that I was going to ruin my children, thoughts that I would never feel normal, thoughts of anger, bitterness, or defeat, and thoughts of being overwhelmed. Those thoughts were all lies! 2 Corinthians 10:5 is now one of my favorite verses. It says, "Casting down imaginations, and every high thing that exalteth itself against the knowledge of God, and bringing into captivity every thought to the obedience of Christ." I was to take my thoughts captive to the obedience of

Christ! For example, the truth concerning the feeling of being overwhelmed is that the Lord hasn't given me one more thing than there is time to do. If there isn't time to do it, then He doesn't expect it of me. My family was better off with next to nothing being done than with my trying to do everything my expectations said needed to be done while I was depressed, with my mind running in circles and unable to concentrate.

The pastor's wife encouraged me to begin a notebook. She showed me hers. It was a simple 8½-by-11-inch three-ring binder with "ABC" tabs in it. Behind the tabs she had notebook paper, each with a topic on it, such as "Anger," "Discouragement," "Discipline," etc. When she had her Bible reading time, she would take verses that applied to her and copy them down in her notebook under an appropriate heading. Then, when she needed to think "truth," she could open her notebook and read it.

I would suggest that moms who are prone to depression do this kind of evaluation of what you are thinking and replace any lies with God's truth. Begin a notebook such as I have described. If you can't think of God's truth–I know there were many times when I couldn't–get your Bible or notebook out and find that truth. Speak it aloud if necessary! Sometimes, I would have to say words of truth aloud because my thinking was so muddled and twisted. I could not concentrate on or accept the truth when it remained only in my mind. However, when I spoke the words, my heart would grab hold of them!

For the second project, I was to have another section of the notebook titled "Sin List." Every time I sinned, I was to write it in the notebook. I was then to confess the sin to the Lord, repent of it, and ask His forgiveness. In my notebook, I would write "FORGIVEN" over that sin. This helped me to let go of my failures rather than letting them overwhelm me.

How do you handle it when you are depressed? Do you become increasingly unhappy with yourself for being depressed, making the downward cycle even worse? I would do that, or I would end up becoming angry with the children and "beat" myself up about that. In my Mom's Corner from February 2000, called "No Condemnation" (www.Titus2.com), I share how the Lord gave me victory over that cycle, although I write of it in terms of the struggles I have now. However, the truths I apply with my current problems are the ones the Lord taught me in the depths of my need. Learning "no condemnation" came from the "Sin List" project Janice gave me.

I believe a most powerful change came when I made a decision before the Lord one morning. I remember thinking, "Lord, I just feel like crying all the time. I am miserable. My family is miserable. I can't seem to do anything about how I feel, but I can do something about how my family feels. I can act like I am happy whether I feel like it or not. My emotions don't have to drive my behavior, and I can make that choice because of my love for my family." Those reading this who are living with depression may think this would be impossible for you to do. I encourage you to test yourself. When you are down and go to church, can others tell by looking at you and talking to you that you are depressed? If you can make this choice to act differently from how you feel there, you can do it at home!

I think if depression-prone moms could figure out a way to work on even a skeleton of a schedule, it would help. I have had moms write to me that when they are depressed, brain dead, or just overwhelmed, their schedule directed them through the day. This was especially helpful because they couldn't make decisions themselves. If you have somewhat of a schedule in place, despite tiredness or feelings, many things would be accomplished because it is the easiest path to take–just do what the schedule says! Without my schedule on those bad days, I would have simply sat and cried. That would have made everything even worse because then I would have been a day behind! In addition, you can let your schedule direct your children when you don't have the energy to keep up with what you would like to be doing. At least they are accomplishing things rather than just undoing everything.

If it is any encouragement, I asked my older children if they remembered the struggles I had during those early, difficult days of their lives. My two oldest boys, who are now adults, recall nothing negative. Can you believe the Lord might blind our children to what is going on inside of us especially when so much of it is easily visible? My adult daughter only remembers one time I was really struggling. I don't share that as a license to allow hormones or depression to control your life and emotions. Rather, I tell it to help you not feel that it is ever hopeless, even if you think there is too much emotional damage already done to the children and to you.

Twenty-three years ago I would never have believed where the Lord would bring me in relation to depression. I thought it was impossible to be free of it, but I am! The process was gradual. I wanted it to happen right away. Looking back, fifteen years isn't all that long of a wait to lose what was such a devastating, negative part of my life.

As women, God created us such that there are emotions and hormones to be coped with. That is still true in my life. However, a disappointment, a "down" day, a discouraging situation is nothing more than that. These no longer send me spiraling through depression. They are simply normal burdens to be left with my Lord Jesus while I rest in Him.

I pray the Lord will give each mom who needs help in the area of depression insight into what will make a difference. Steve always encouraged me that as long as my heart's desire was to please the Lord, He would answer that heart's cry.

Somehow, these words don't come close to describing what those years were like. My prayer is that you will sense in my heart a deep desire to be able to encourage moms that it can be better. This is true even if you are homeschooling, if there are more pregnancies and babies, or if there are more challenges of any kind. My growing out of the depressions was a result, I believe, of a process the Lord brought me through in the midst of homeschooling, pregnancies, and babies. Seek the Lord!

September 2000

Notes:

1. I am not a doctor; I cannot make medical recommendations. I am only sharing my own personal experiences. I encourage each of you to pray and research as you look for your solutions to depression.

2. Natural progesterone cream can be found in most health food stores. The progesterone cream I used is called ProGest and can be purchased from Emerita: 1-800-888-6814 or www.emerita.com

3. You would need to research the vitamins on your own, because I no longer have that list.

4. I use foam ear plugs. They are called "Classic" by Aearo Technologies, 1-800-225-9038.

5. Romans 3:23, "For all have sinned, and come short of the glory of God."

   Romans 6:23, "For the wages of sin *is* death; but the gift of God *is* eternal life through Jesus Christ our Lord."

   Romans 5:8-10, "But God commendeth his love toward us, in that, while we were yet sinners, Christ died for us. Much more then, being now justified by his blood, we shall be saved from wrath through him. For if, when we were enemies, we were reconciled to God by the death of his Son, much more, being reconciled, we shall be saved by his life."

Romans 10:9-10, "That if thou shalt confess with thy mouth the Lord Jesus, and shalt believe in thine heart that God hath raised him from the dead, thou shalt be saved. For with the heart man believeth unto righteousness; and with the mouth confession is made unto salvation."

Ephesians 2:8-9, "For by grace are ye saved through faith; and that not of yourselves: *it is* the gift of God: Not of works, lest any man should boast."

Expect Children to Be Children!

Very regularly, through responses to Mom's Corners and message board posts (www.Titus2.com), I read of moms who are discouraged by character struggles in their young children. They wonder whether a child with a particular problem at age 4, 6, or 10 will still have it as an adult. They ask why their child doesn't have a repentant heart, is selfish, or still bickers with his siblings, even when the parents have been consistent in disciplining. They feel they are somehow missing their child's heart issues.

This topic is dear to me because I expect it is something that most, if not all, moms struggle with. I have had these same feelings, and asked these same questions. However, after twenty-three years of mothering, I now have the perspective of viewing both my three adult and five younger children. I can look back and evaluate the spiritual maturing process of the older children's hearts.

I have finally come to realize a profound truth—we must expect children to be children (1 Corinthians 13:11)! They simply do not yet have hearts that can respond to the Lord with the same maturity that adults do. The growth will come, but it is a process of the Lord that continues throughout childhood.

My expectation for an encounter with one of my children was often this: I would sit with him and explain his sin, he would be filled with remorse, confess, repent, and then go off to "sin no more." This is a mature biblical response that might sometimes be found in my dealings with a child. The more common occurrence, though, was as follows: I would sit with him and explain his sin, he would be filled with excuses and justification, and he would respond negatively. Then he might do the same wrong thing, which he had just been disciplined for, the very next hour (or even minute)! However, the older the children became, the more they were able to see their sin and deal with it properly. This spiritual maturity grew in relation to their advancing age and has been even greater upon their adulthood!

The feeling I get from some of the rather optimistic Christian child-training materials is that if you follow the "plan" your child will very soon be "perfect." They often don't stress, or completely leave out, the fact that it also takes time, consistency in disciplining, and prayer. In the meantime, moms are discouraged because they faithfully follow the "plan" for a month, a year, or even more, but they still don't have a child who acts and responds as an adult. While years seems like a terribly long time to be heading toward the goal, it is a slow, step-by-step process.

God calls us to our responsibilities as mothers, such as loving our children (Titus 2:4), praying for and with them (Philippians 4:6), teaching them (Deuteronomy 6:7), training them (Proverbs 22:6), correcting them (Proverbs 29:17), and disciplining them (Proverbs 19:18). Let's not forget, though, that He is the One Who works in hearts and also the One Who designed the growth and maturity process of a child. I believe getting at a child's heart issues is a constant, daily process; we must continue (over and over) to repeat God's truth to our children in a sweet and winsome way—year after year after year! When two children are fighting over a toy, both are at fault. Scripture must be shared that applies (Ephesians 4:32, "And be ye kind one to another . . ."), and discipline administered if necessary. When a child is grumbling, there is Scripture that relates, such as Philippians 2:14, "Do all things without murmurings and disputings." Knowing that God's results in the hearts of our children will likely come in a slow, gradual way can help us, as moms, to be encouraged rather than discouraged throughout the process.

Moms in the midst of child rearing have to remind themselves frequently of Galatians 6:9, "And let us not be weary in well doing: for in due season we shall reap, if we faint not." Another verse that has greatly ministered to me through my years of mothering is 2 Corinthians 4:1, "Therefore seeing we have this ministry, as we have received mercy, we faint not." Keeping up with all the "heart issues" of our children can cause us to feel like we are growing weary and faint! After all, there may be several of "them" and only one of us! Years of consistency in loving, praying, teaching, training, correcting, and disciplining children can seem like a very long time! However, remember 2 Corinthians 12:9, "And he said unto me, My grace is sufficient for thee: for my strength is made perfect in weakness. Most gladly therefore will I rather glory in my infirmities, that the power of Christ may rest upon me."

For me, while waiting to "reap in due season" in a child's life, the bottom line between a positive attitude and discouragement is my own heart. How am I viewing the situations my children present to me? Am I accepting them as opportunities to teach my children? Do I resent them as intrusions on my time? Am I discouraged because they show me what I perceive to be failures in my children? Am I more concerned about their behavior or their heart? Do I want them to act and respond as an adult would because it makes my life easier and more pleasant?

Be encouraged, Sisters! Take heart! I expect you are likely doing what you should be doing to deal with your children's hearts. Keep it up! Discouragement comes because we are immersed in the daily happenings. Instead, we have to focus on the Lord and the end goal, not the day-to-day behaviors. We can't expect our children to be adults before they actually are. Find the benefit and joy in our time with them as we teach, train, correct, and discipline, rather than being defeated by an apparent lack of results. Perhaps there are results–great results–for the age of the child you are working with, but the wrong expectation is robbing you of seeing those results.

I have the advantage of looking at my older children and seeing that where they are now has been a process that has occurred over years and years. As the children have been growing and maturing, Steve and I have been praying, teaching, training, correcting, and disciplining, and the Lord has been working. My two oldest sons, whose childhood bickering would drive me to tears, are now, as adults, best friends! My little kindergartner–the one who held the sixth grader's papers out the school bus window (and got his ankle broken)–is now a godly, responsible man. Steve and I rejoice as we watch our older children in their adult years, but it has been a long, sometimes grueling, yet truly joyful and very rewarding journey!

October 2000

Halloween

As this time of year rolls around, it brings back memories of the journey the Lord has led Steve and I on concerning Halloween. I thought it might be appropriate to tell you this story. Hopefully, it will encourage those of you facing decisions in this area, and bless those who have already made them.

As a young mother, I wanted my children to enjoy the same positive Halloween experiences and memories that I treasured from my past. However, since accepting Jesus Christ as my Savior toward the end of my college days, some doubts began to creep into my mind as I viewed Halloween decorations with a new perspective. I discounted those doubts, though, being sure we could keep our children dressed appropriately and apply our own values to this particular night.

The first Halloween our little ones were of an age to trick-or-treat (back in the early 1980s) I had made them very cute costumes. Out we trooped on Halloween night to the "safe" close neighbors, determined to make memories as we went. It wasn't long until I had one child in my arms and two more clinging to my leg begging to return home. The lure of free candy did not overpower the fear in their hearts as they looked at the other trick-or-treaters.

Steve and I began to wonder if childhood Halloween memories were worth what was beginning, in our hearts, to feel like compromise. What kind of memories were we building anyway? The Lord used the children's fears, as well as much discussion and prayer between Steve and me, to convict us. We decided that it wasn't right for our children to be out trick-or-treating–participating in a "holiday" that focuses on evil. Verses such as the following would stand out to us as we were praying about this decision. Romans 12:9, "*Let* love be without dissimulation. Abhor that which is evil; cleave to that which is good." Romans 16:19, "For your obedience is come abroad unto all *men*. I am glad therefore on your behalf: but yet I would have you wise unto that which is good, and simple concerning evil." 1 Thessalonians 5:22, "Abstain from all appearance of evil."

Once we made the "no trick-or-treating" decision, we still had to deal with children who would come to the door on Halloween. Surely, this would be an opportunity to witness to them by handing out tracts along with the candy. We could involve our children in choosing tracts. Plus, we would still be building warm, childhood memories by letting them hand out the goodies and tracts.

The year was now 1983, and Halloween had once again rolled around. The doorbell rang. Excitedly, I asked Nathan (who was six years old at the time) if he would like to open the door and give the children outside each a piece of candy and a tract. After opening the door, he quickly handed the container back to me and ran to his Daddy. It didn't take long to figure out why. The "characters" facing me were frightful looking at best.

Despite our realization of the evil focus of Halloween and our own children's innocent hearts' response to all of this, Steve and I continued to look for ways not to have Halloween be a disappointment to our children. We didn't want them to miss out on anything that the other children were doing that was fun and exciting.

Our next attempts revolved around getting together with like-minded families and going out for dinner on Halloween. The first time we did this, the waitress was dressed up like a witch! The next year we phoned ahead requesting that our waitress not be dressed up as anything evil, but of course that couldn't change what other customers and waitresses were wearing. Nor could we avoid our children seeing the trick-or-treaters on the streets as we went to and from the restaurant.

Finally, the Lord got our full attention. He gave us a birthday on the 31st! About this same time, Steve and I were realizing that we wanted to completely and fully shelter our children and ourselves from the "evil" sights that permeated Halloween. From 1992 on, we have been happily content closing the blinds, turning off the porch lights, and having a birthday party every October 31st!

Our younger children didn't even know the word "Halloween" for many years. When the now-popular Halloween lights began to go up, they thought they were Christmas lights. Steve does not take the younger children with him to do the nursing home ministry during the month of October because they would have to stare at evil figures hung on the curtains behind him for an entire hour. We encourage the children to look away from the grotesque and evil.

We no longer feel our children are missing out on anything. We don't discuss and pray about ways to make it work for our children to participate in any aspect of Halloween. We are happy to shelter them from as many of the sights and influences of Halloween as we possibly can. We don't mind them associating Halloween with Satan and having a disdain for it. When asked by a neighbor or a store clerk what a child was going to be for Halloween, we haven't received negative feedback as the children say, "We don't do Halloween." We feel secure in our Halloween decisions. However, it did take us about fifteen years of Halloween experiences, conviction, prayer, and discussion to come to this point!

Perhaps the Lord is taking you along a similar path concerning Halloween as He has our family. I want to encourage you not to feel strange or alone if you decide to spend that night in your house making it look from the outside like no one is at home. Even though you likely won't have a birthday to celebrate, it can still be an evening of family togetherness. Stand firm on being separate if that is what the Lord has put on your heart. Your children aren't missing out on special memories. Instead, you are building other memories that will be just as strong and of much more positive eternal value!

November 2000

Chores

It is Friday cleaning morning at the Maxwell house! Eleven-year-old Joseph busily oils our oak dining-room table while Anna, age eight, runs the hand-held vacuum over the throw rugs. John, our nine-year-old, is singing as he pushes the vacuum, and Mom is mopping the kitchen and bathroom floor. These are a few of our weekly chores.

I would love for my children to have lots of free time. Unfortunately, the more hours they are on their own, the more likely they are to fuss and squabble with each other. We have found schoolwork and housework are very helpful in giving the children positive direction for their time. Then they are able to comfortably handle the free hours they have left. They greatly enjoy their personal time, and the children don't complain of being bored!

Steve and I want our children to learn to work. We desire for them to have a healthy attitude toward responsibilities, approaching them with diligence and initiative. Having the children help with the daily workload in our home is a part of their training to eventually become good husbands, wives, homemakers, employees, and employers.

I need the help of my children to keep up with housework. I would not physically have the time to do it all myself in addition to homeschooling. I remind the children regularly of how much they contribute to the family and lighten my workload. Children love to please their mommies, and usually, mine love to do anything that visibly makes me happy. Much of their attitude toward their work stems from how diligent I am to praise them for help and to encourage them that they are needed members of the family.

Chores can present challenges to homeschooling moms. They wonder how much they should expect of their children as far as chores are concerned. Are they giving the children too many or too few jobs? What kind of work is a child capable of and at what age? How do you equitably divide the tasks? When can a child do his chores without being reminded? What consequences are reasonable for not doing an assigned job or for doing it poorly?

As you are considering chores for your children, I have a starting place. It is often helpful to see how other families structure their chore assignments. While your chore chart won't be identical to another mom's, you can glean ideas. You could evaluate what is expected of her children at various ages and determine how the chores are divided among the family members. You will get a picture of how long the chores are probably taking plus how often certain jobs are being done.

We have begun a section on our website (www.Titus2.com) where you can see real-life chore charts of homeschooling families. (2006 update: We now have a book on chores. See Additional Resources, page 384.) When we announced to the MOTHBoard that these chores charts were available to look at, we received some interesting feedback.

"Teri, an unexpected plus to the charts . . .

"I looked at the charts for the chores. I have to tell you what happened. I printed them out to do some comparing with the charts we use. Well, our nine-year-old son saw me looking at the charts and noticed that compared to other nine- and ten-year-old boys, he has it pretty easy. 'WOW, Mom, look at all they have to do!'

"Needless to say, after a conversation our son did come to the realization that he could be doing more. Then, of course, so could his sister! So this morning we made new charts with some more involved chores! Just by seeing what other children are doing, our son was convicted! Today the new chores begin! It looks like Mom is going to get more help!" Janice

"Same here! My almost nine-year-old son, who moans and groans when asked to fold a pile of towels, which is one of about four or five chores, was amazed at the work that children younger than himself were capable of. A six-year-old clean the bathroom? Even he agreed that he could easily handle more work, and that's exactly what I'm going to give him!" Amanda

As I was writing this Mom's Corner, I realized something amazing. We have virtually eliminated grumbling about chores in our family! I am pleased this is the case; however, it happened unintentionally. It appears, though, there may be several factors as to why we have moved past chore complaints.

First, we begin assigning regular chores (beyond picking up after himself) around the time a child starts school. Second, the chores are written down. The child knows what is expected of him and so do I. Each child keeps the same chores for at least a year. We also have accountability to ensure the jobs are accomplished. Lastly, the child has a set time each day to do his work. I believe because chores have become so much a part of their daily routine, the children don't grumble.

If I were always to call the children at random times from their play to do this job or that one, they might respond differently. However, even when I need to do this, the response is generally good. Perhaps it is because they have their assigned, scheduled tasks, and I don't ask for "over and above" help very often. Just tonight I needed extra hands to get dinner on the table. Steve asked two of the children who were not my normal Thursday dinner helpers to pitch in. They did so with sweet, willing attitudes. They were happily surprised to receive an extra portion of dessert as a reward from their daddy for their cooperation!

The responsibility of whether chores are being done, and being done well, falls squarely back on me. I find it is important to take adequate time to train each child in what he is expected to do. It is all too easy to tell my son to vacuum the floor and then be unhappy with a poor job. However, I can't assume a child knows how to do a task properly until I have taught him.

Also important, in addition to chore training, are regular inspections to check on the work. My children become sloppy in their jobs if I am not frequently looking at them. In the past two years we have had periods of time when I am intensely busy for several weeks. The children's thoroughness in their chores slips greatly because I am not checking their work.

I encourage you to have consequences in place for failure to do a job or for not doing it well. The children and I have decided upon a consequence for this in our family. They made the suggestion, and I approved it. For each chore that isn't done, or is poorly done, they have to sit on a chair for fifteen minutes. This discipline was decided upon because most of our chores take five minutes or less. The children thought that sitting on the chair for fifteen minutes would motivate them to do their jobs since the jobs take much less time than chair sitting would. Whatever consequences you and your husband decide upon, make sure you consistently use them.

I suggest you view your children's chores as a great learning tool. See the benefits in teaching them to work diligently at their chores with a good attitude. Not only is this a help to you now, but you are also training your children for the lifetime of serving and ministering that the Lord Jesus has called them to.

December 2000

Love Your Wife

"Husbands, love your wives, even as Christ also loved the church, and gave himself for it" (Ephesians 5:25).

I have asked many men over the years if they loved their wife enough to die for her. Christ was our example and we are to love our wives in the same way. Most dads have quickly replied, "Yes I would." Certainly, I have placed myself in that category.

The next question is usually more difficult to answer. Would you wash dishes every evening (or some other task you might not care to do) for the rest of your married life? That is where we often take longer to answer. Again, I've proudly thought to myself, "Yes, I'd gladly do that for my wife." God recently provided me with an opportunity to see just how deep my commitment was.

Teri, the four little ones, and I were at Wal-Mart early on a Saturday evening while the older ones were with Grandma and Grandad. We finished shopping and had just returned to the car when the familiar refrain of, "I've got to go potty," was heard. After making sure it was a serious, high-priority request, I was to be the one to return to the store with the little one and take care of the matter.

I gave the keys to Teri so she could get the others settled while I was taking the child and cart back in the store. Teri unlocked the van, tossed the keys on the seat and turned to pick a little one up. Just then the door swung closed, and she realized she had pushed the power lock button instead of unlock! She looked at me with the most innocent expression and said the keys were locked inside.

At that moment, I had one of those rare opportunities to prove how much I loved Teri and that she was more important than circumstances. My unbelief was quickly replaced with anger. Of course, I retained my outward composure, but inside I was a very unhappy camper.

How Teri needed me to put my arm around her and tell her it was okay. I failed! I asked her to go inside and wait while I tried to get in. I figured I wasn't very creative if I couldn't get in the car with a whole store of resources at my disposal. But God had a lesson for me. Fifteen dollars later, I knew it was hopeless.

By the way, have you ever noticed how people snicker in a parking lot when they see someone trying to get into their locked vehicle? I deserved it and more. I even tried to be a little spiritual and thank God for the situation.

However, I really didn't mean it, and so back in the store I went to sit with Teri and the children until her parents came to rescue us. Notice, I wasn't blaming myself for not having hidden another key or carrying one in my wallet. I was feeling sorry for myself.

For the rest of my life I will deeply grieve every time I remember that day. How easy it is to prove our wives and families actually aren't first in our lives and how difficult it is to demonstrate true love.

As we begin the new school year, we will have many, if not daily, opportunities to put our families first. When we come home we can spend time with our wives, see how their day went, and how we can support and encourage them. We can take the time to have the children show us their work and tell us what they learned. We can deal with the character issues that surfaced and need to be addressed. The list goes on and on.

Hopefully, you will not fail like I did. I know I'm praying that I will set my priorities properly and be the loving husband and dad that my Lord Jesus Christ would have me to be.

September 1995

Shepherding Away from Wrong Influences

A short time ago I was speaking with a co-worker, whom I'll call Bob, about his son who is involved in a very serious problem. He said his son was saddened by a family who wouldn't let their son associate with his son anymore because of this problem. Bob said he understood how the other parents felt, and he didn't hold it against them. However, his son might not be in trouble now, had Bob exercised the same judgment at a previous point in time.

You see, Bob's son's trouble stemmed from his friendship with a fourteen-year-old young man. This young man had a history of this kind of problem, and yet Bob didn't discourage his son from the friendship. Now, as Bob looks back, he can see how costly his lack of protecting his son will be.

Proverbs 22:24 says, "Make no friendship with an angry man; and with a furious man thou shalt not go." Otherwise we will learn his ways. We are also not to join with the rebellious, or we too will pay the consequences. Proverbs 24:21, "My son, fear thou the LORD and the king: *and* meddle not with them that are given to change." These principles hold true for us as parents and certainly even more for our children. Children are extremely impressionable, and that is why negative peer pressure and other wrong influences are very dangerous.

I know some will say that young people have to learn to deal with the world; you can't shelter them forever. However, aren't our children more precious than young, tender plants that are raised in a greenhouse until they are mature and able to stand the environment? We don't put a plant out in a violent thunderstorm for just a little while so it can get used to the wind and hail. It would be permanently injured. The same is true for our children. They must be protected until they have a strong foundation and have matured.

God's role is for the father to be the protector of the family. We must be on guard for all types of threats. Certainly, the top of the list is wrong friends. They often appear to be nice and well behaved. Do you remember Eddy from "Leave It to Beaver"? He was nice while he was around the parents, but was a terrible influence the rest of the time. Your children may have friends who sow seeds of discontent with home education. Is it any wonder when your children then become discontented?

There are problems with wrong books, TV, and computer games. I am incredulous to find fathers who let their sons play the latest popular computer games. Some are very hideous and violent. Are we so naïve as to believe our children won't be affected? Do we forget that companies spend millions of dollars for sixty-second commercials to influence people's buying habits?

So, dads, are we being the shepherds that God has called us to be? Are we aware of what our children are reading, playing, watching, and who they are playing with? If so, are we certain that these influences will be for our children's good? We will all give an accounting to the Lord someday for what kind of stewards we have been with these treasures God has entrusted us with.

October 1995

Finding Causes for Character Problems

Here is a test. Can you quickly write down what the major character needs are of each of your children? As dads we are not only responsible for the education of our children, but also their character. Any character issue that is left unresolved in our children becomes a future spouse or employer's problem. If our children get by with laziness, lying, stealing, disrespect, or disobedience, they will only get worse once they are out of our homes.

I spoke to a saleswoman just yesterday who said she and her husband had decided to tell their twenty-three-year-old "dead-beat son" not to contact them ever again. That will not solve anything. Hopefully, none of us will ever experience a situation as grave as the one they are in, but the principle that we will reap what we sow is an iron-clad guarantee. The doubly sad part of their situation is that these parents view themselves as ideal role models and poor, innocent parties. Therefore, they will probably never humble themselves sufficiently to resolve the breach. They are not willing to accept responsibility for what they have created.

So, does that mean there is no hope since none of us are perfect? Certainly not! God's grace is sufficient and in our weakness He is made strong. However, we must humble ourselves and be willing to admit our failures. We need to seek God's answers to the problems. We must cry out to God for insight into the problems as we look past the surface issues to the real root causes. We must accept the possibility that we dads may have a significant part in the solution. Then we must commit to do whatever is necessary.

There is one area I encourage you not to overlook as you search for causes. I am convinced one of the biggest contributors to much of the difficulty in homes is the TV. I could write pages about TV and what it is teaching anyone watching it. I believe none of it is of value. Some might say, "Wait a minute, sometimes we watch educational shows." Yes, but aren't most of them humanistic and teach evolution? Wouldn't it be much better if our children were reading the information out of a godly textbook? They would still receive the knowledge while improving their reading skills at the same time. I used to justify watching TV, when in actuality it was my own laziness and desire to be entertained that kept us watching it. It is a mistake to confuse entertainment with rest. One day of rest is good, more than that is likely slothfulness.

Others may say TV is great entertainment. Entertainment it is, but certainly not great or profitable. Could it be responsible for a generation that is entertainment starved? There is never enough. Children show up at youth groups looking to be "wowed" and to spend each moment having fun. There is no concept of serving or spending time profitably.

I'm told there are many programs that teach rebellion, disrespect for parents, laziness (that we must be entertained), and unhealthy sexual ideals. I'm sure the list could be much longer, but if there is a grain of truth in what I've heard about TV these days, then why keep it in the home?

Certainly there are many other areas that should not be overlooked. Unfortunately, most require difficult decisions to be made. We have all made a very tough one in deciding to home educate. Now the question is: Are there other difficult ones that could help to solve character issues while there is still time?

November 1995

Where Is Your Treasure?

This is my absolute favorite time of the year. I enjoy Christmas immensely, but that is not the primary reason for preferring this above all other seasons. Our company gives us fewer holidays off during the year, so we can have the days off between Christmas and New Year's. I rejoice in being home with my family!

Teri is truly my best friend. There is no one I would rather be with and do things with than her. During workweeks I get up early enough that I also have to go to bed early. That schedule precludes staying up after the little ones are down, so we don't get as much talking time as we would like. During the holiday week, though, we can stay up a bit later and talk. Additional little errands, etc., that come up over this holiday week give us even more time together.

After Teri, our children are my next best friends. What a joy they are to be with. When we are all together, something is usually going on, and we are often laughing. I enjoy the individual time with them that the vacation allows.

However, this year is better than the last two years because in December I resigned a ministry position that was taking my time and attention away from my family. It has been such a relief to not have something major competing with the family. I had not realized how heavily this ministry had weighed on me. I believe God was telling me Kansas City is full of men He could use to fill my previous ministry position, but I was the only one He had called to be my children's Daddy.

Jesus said, "For where your treasure is, there will your heart be also." Next to the Lord, may our hearts be consumed with our families. May we cast off the myth of "quality time versus quantity time." The only way to imprint on another life is through time. Please don't let others rob your family of your time. Lavish it on them; they need you.

January 1996

A Man's True Identity

Have you noticed that as men, we can often relate to others only in terms of what each does for a living? Our job becomes our identity, who we truly are. Isn't that why the loss of a job can create such a crisis in a man's life? Certainly, the issue of providing for our family is one that shouldn't be ignored, but this seems to go beyond that.

Often I hear about divorces that are due to the father being more married to his work than to his wife. Could it be that his identity was wrapped up in his job and not in what it should be? Each one of us might do well to ask the question, "Who am I, really?" If everything I have and currently know is taken from me, am I still someone, or nothing?

There have been times in my life that I have unknowingly had my identity in other things. In Florida I was working eleven hours a day to get ahead in my job. The result was a neglected wife struggling with three young children and a gold (actually solid bronze) bar with the words "Outstanding Performance" on it. Is that something to be proud of or what? Now it is easy to see what a fool I was as I daily see that bar sitting in front of me on my desk. It isn't displayed as a trophy, but as a sad reminder to prevent me from losing my priorities again. Jobs come and go, but a family is eternal! The precious souls that God entrusts to our care are eternity bound, and as fathers we are powerful influences in their lives.

But the answer is not to have our identity in our family either. Then what happens when there is not peace in the home or a loved one is lost? It is only when our identity is in the Lord Jesus Christ that all these other areas come into proper perspective. You see, I'm the adopted son of God the Father through the blood of the Lord Jesus Christ. "According as he hath chosen us in him before the foundation of the world, that we should be holy and without blame before him in love: Having predestinated us unto the adoption of children by Jesus Christ to himself, according to the good pleasure of his will" (Ephesians 1:4-5).

If my identity is in the Lord Jesus Christ, then my identity is steadfast, since nothing can sever my relationship with my Lord (Romans 8). No matter what the circumstances, there can be peace when I am in Christ Jesus. "Peace I leave with you, my peace I give unto you: not as the world giveth, give I unto you. Let not your heart be troubled, neither let it be afraid" (John 14:27).

May 1996

Training Our Children?

There is a lot of talk about the Olympics these days. Certainly, national pride and world competition has much to do with it, but I wonder if there isn't more than that.

How impressive would those teams be if they were comprised of contestants who had been selected by lottery? I believe we are impressed because the athletes had superior training and they perform flawlessly.

Isn't that why our military is so good? They have first been instructed in what, when, and how; then they are drilled repeatedly to perfect the performance. I believe that is why those who have been home educated are doing so well. Not only are they being educated, but also they are disciplined in the application of that knowledge.

So what does that have to do with us dads? Maybe not a lot, but I did want to make a point. Quality training is respected by almost everyone, and it is no accident. It takes a concerted, organized effort, usually by more than one individual.

We are training this country's leaders of tomorrow. They will be the ones whose performance is admired. Even now, compliments on a child's behavior, attitude, and academic performance are not foreign to parents of home-educated children.

In most of your homes, Mom is the day-to-day coach, and Dad keeps things on track for the long run. Dad is the one who holds the children ultimately responsible for learning what Mom is teaching.

I have found that as I'm spending time with a child, something will come up that is an excellent chance to apply what they are learning. I suppose most often they ask a question. The solution will involve a math problem that I help them work in their minds. When I was a child, I disliked word problems in school; they revealed I didn't know how to apply what I was learning.

Dad's interest shows the children how important it is to him that they are learning. His encouragement will challenge his children and bless their mother.

August 1996

How Our Words Can Be Like Rocks

What is it about boys and rocks? You know what I mean. There is just something innate in a boy! When he sees a rock, he wants to throw it! It is simply the way boys are made. Ohhhhhhhh, and what consequences there can be. When I was four or five, I caught a rock with my forehead and immediately was covered with blood. Two little boys had some consequences. Mine was the stitches. The other boy's was courtesy of his parents.

Unfortunately, I feel our words are often like rocks in the hands of boys. We carelessly give them a good toss, and thereafter they are out of reach. We desperately wish we could take them back. But once they are in motion, there is nothing that can be done. It is so easy to think I can apologize, and it will be okay. Ever throw a rock through a window? All of the "I'm sorry's" in the world will not put that window back together like new. Even with painstaking gluing, the cracks will be seen forever.

I can remember something I said to Teri over fifteen years ago, which can bring tears to her eyes even now at the mention of it. More recently, there was an incident when I said something harshly to one of my children. It breaks my heart as I recollect the hurt expression that enveloped their face, almost a look of betrayal. I wish I could take it back, but it's too late. With both of those incidents, I have humbled myself and asked forgiveness. Asking forgiveness is a critical step as it stops bitterness from growing and destroying a relationship, but it does not eliminate the pain. The only way to avoid others' pain is not to hurt them in the first place.

As dads, we are called to nurture and encourage those entrusted to our care. Yet careless, angry words can tear down, in a minute, what has taken weeks to build up. May our words be filled with praise as we train up these precious souls God has given us.

September 1996

Communicating with Our Families

As I watched, Jesse, my next to youngest, pointed down the hallway and excitedly said, "beedsbuks." However, as many times as he repeated it, I still didn't understand what he meant. Then, finally, one of the older children translated it for me and said, "Dad, he wants you to read him some books."

Soon thereafter, I had a conversation with Teri. She revealed that she thought I did not value her organizational abilities. I was truly shocked. I have been so appreciative of them and felt I conveyed that to her through the years. I was saddened at the idea she had not known of my sincere appreciation for her abilities in that area. What we have here is a failure to communicate.

As a husband and father, I often think of English as my "second language." It's not that I have some other language that I speak as my fluent native tongue (English actually is), but I can have such difficulty communicating what is on my heart. Is that ever a problem for you? It can be a real source of frustration for me, just like poor Jesse when he was doing his best to ask me to read him a book. He was giving it his all, but he was unsuccessful. The other children understood, even though I had not. So why not me?

I'm sure one reason is I don't spend as much time around him as the others do. Sheer quantity of time around the people you want to communicate with is important. As dads, we are away from our families much of the time during the week. We miss a lot that goes on in the home, and as such, we are not as well "tuned in." That affects both how effective we are in getting our message across and how well we hear what someone is really trying to tell us. I think the best cure for that is large doses of time. Not the lie of quality time, but time. I've known dads who say they have to go for quality, since quantity isn't an option. I believe that is just an excuse to pacify their conscience. What our wives and children want is US to spend time with them. The less time we spend with them the more difficult it is to truly communicate, soul to soul, with them. There may be pleasant conversations, but they won't be on a level that is necessary to keep a healthy marriage or strong bond with your children.

I'm sure another hindrance to communicating effectively is how observant I am. Am I really listening intently to what they are saying? Am I concentrating on what is being said, or am I thinking about some other project and giving only half-hearted attention? I'm guilty of that. I can look at them and even nod appropriately, giving the pretense of interest. God hates pretense, and it seems like I am always caught when I try it. It's a good thing, too, or I would probably do it more often. In one passage in Jeremiah, God told him how He prefers unfaithful Israel over pretending Judah. "And yet for all this her treacherous sister Judah hath not turned unto me with her whole heart, but feignedly, saith the LORD. And the LORD said unto me, The backsliding Israel hath justified herself more than treacherous Judah" (Jeremiah 3:10-11). What a sobering thought when I am tempted to pretend.

Another problem is that often I don't try to compensate for the differences. We are aware there are many differences between us, our wives, and our children. The politically correct will insist there are no differences between men and women. I wonder if "they" ever tried to discuss financial issues with someone of the opposite sex. Teri and I approach money matters from different perspectives. It's difficult to explain, but somehow we can both arrive at the same conclusion from opposite directions.

Let either of us try to explain the route we took to get to the conclusion, and the other one is totally confused. I am not saying her route is wrong; it is just a different approach to getting there. I feel what is needed is understanding and patience: understanding in how we approach things differently and patience to be willing to answer questions and kindly explain.

The bottom line is that communication can be hard work. It takes time and effort. That is why Teri's and my weekly dates are critical to avoiding roadblocks and helping her be most efficient in home educating. If you don't have the weekly date habit (movies don't count since talking through them would be difficult and certainly viewed as rude by others), I strongly encourage you to begin it. In regard to the children I think it is like the rules for locating a business. There the formula is location, location, location. With our children, I believe it to be time, time, and more time.

October 1996

Fathers in America

I am amazed that we could be at a turning point in the history of our country. If Bill Clinton is re-elected, he stands to have appointed over 50 percent of all the Federal judges in our country, not to mention the ones on the Supreme Court. In addition to the appointments are the ideologies that he appears to stand for and will push to implement.

What is most incredible about this situation is what it reveals about the soul of our nation. A salesman I was speaking with the other day very honestly summed it up. He said, "All I care about is what he (the President) is going to do for me and my family." Honest, yes, but what an indictment. It appears the average person is most interested in how big the handout is going to be for him. What has failed in our country?

Instead of people being horrified over the multitude of allegations of wrongdoing, they accept them as normal, or part of one's private life, and not important. If even 5 percent of them are true, this president would make Nixon appear "squeaky clean." Does character not count anymore?

There may not be a group of people more passionate in caring about these issues than the home-educating community. One of the top reasons for home educating is that we can raise children of godly character who know how to work. To us, the consequences of the current direction are only too obvious, but it does not ease the anguish of our souls as we observe the slide. But what can be learned from this situation?

I feel the lesson is for us dads. You see, I believe the failure can be placed squarely on the backs of dads in our nation, fathers who did not seek God. Fathers who believed money was more important than time with their children. Fathers who valued their wives more when they were earning a paycheck than raising children. Fathers who wanted their own entertainment, relaxation, and pleasure more than they wanted godly children. I don't believe God will listen to excuses when fathers are held accountable for the lives they were entrusted with.

Is there anything we can glean from this mess our country is in? YES!! May we bless and appreciate our wives for the daily sacrifices they make for us. May we be zealous for being the godly fathers we are called to be. May we purpose to use every last bit of energy to train up children who love the Lord and want to serve Him, children of godly character who know how to work and enjoy it. I believe the children who are raised according to this recipe will be tomorrow's leaders.

November 1996

Gratefulness

What is "music to your ears?" I mean, what do you really enjoy hearing others say to you? I expect almost universally we love to hear expressions of gratefulness to us for something we have done. Not only is gratefulness an essential character quality, but also it does so much for producing a spirit of harmony in a home. It can't be overstated.

When I've taken the children somewhere I thought they would enjoy, I'm very pleased if I hear them thank me. However, I feel wonderful if they go on to say how much they enjoyed it and what fun it was. I don't think I've ever said to them, "Please stop, you're being too grateful." There is something about gratitude that just, well, it delights my heart!

Now the question comes up, How grateful am I? Since I am the leader in the home, just what sort of example am I setting? Am I quick to recognize the acts of kindness that are done for me and tell that person how much I appreciate them? Do I thank my sons for mowing, yard work, or cleaning the garage? Do I thank Sarah for all the baking she does? Do I thank Teri for dinner, for washing my clothes, or for the nightly neck and shoulder massage I receive while we have a session of geography immediately following our evening meal? (I wonder if that is why I have had this new-found love for geography lately. If you haven't tried this approach to geography, I guarantee you'll like it.)

However, most of all, I'm eternally grateful to Teri for her ministry of love in teaching the children at home. She has chosen a much more difficult route than to send them off to school. She appreciates how I feel about her efforts, but that alone isn't enough. She wants to hear me express it to her in words and not just once a year. Phone calls, letters, email notes, or gifts—you name it, she loves it. I have yet to come close to being too grateful, but I need to purpose anew to try.

December 1996

A Dad's Power and Authority

There probably aren't too many situations that will call a father to "arms" quicker than when his child is being picked on by a bully. I have only had it happen a few times to one of my children, but it really got my blood boiling.

What is it about power and authority? Those that have it tend to use it. That is why someone once said, "Absolute power corrupts absolutely." If the quote isn't exact, it is close enough for you to get the point. Those who have power, over time, will tend to use it for their own advantage.

Look at Solomon; he was the wisest man in the whole world. No king had the wisdom that he possessed. You would expect his reign to be picture perfect. Yet that was not the case. He failed to obey God's Word and then used his power to satisfy his lusts. However, his lusts led his heart toward worshipping false gods.

The power of Solomon's position allowed him to acquire 700 wives and 300 concubines. Can you imagine that? He used his power to indulge in pleasure against the warning of God's Word. It was the ruin of his kingdom.

What about dads? As leaders of our families, we have the power and authority to make the decisions. Certainly, we may be tempted to make decisions for our own selfish ends.

Christ, as our example, had absolute power, but He used it only to serve others as directed by the Father. He did not use it for His own selfish pleasure.

It is easy for us dads to be bullies in our own homes. I know we don't see it that way, but isn't it possible? Just like the bully, we can have what we want. We can have our way all the time if we so choose. The possibilities are endless: dad's favorite meals, more money for dad's clothes, dad's hobbies, dad's entertainment, dad's sports, dad's choice of restaurant, and on and on it goes.

However, just like Solomon, if we neglect to follow the leading of God's Word and choose to use our power and authority for our benefit, the consequences will be far reaching in our family.

May we be careful to follow Christ's example and use our authority to serve and minister to our families. We have been entrusted with the care and nurturing of our families; may we, by God's grace, be faithful stewards.

January 1997

Sin in the Children; Sin in the Father

Recently, Teri and I were surprised when two of our boys did not seem to recognize something as sin. To us it was black and white, but they just couldn't see it. How could that be? They had been taught the right things, yet their conclusion was wrong.

Last week God revealed what had happened. He convicted me that there was an area in my life of significant compromise. I couldn't believe I had not seen it sooner, but God used a situation and a verse I had just read in my devotion to point it out. Then it was as if a giant spotlight was focused on it, and all doubt was removed. Ugh, I now had to deal with the situation.

While working to set right this area of deceit, I thought about Exodus 20:5, "Thou shalt not bow down thyself to them, nor serve them: for I the LORD thy God *am* a jealous God, visiting the iniquity of the fathers upon the children unto the third and fourth *generation* of them that hate me." When I looked up "visiting," it seemed to carry more than just the consequences of the sin, but the sin itself. When I rebel against God by choosing sin, I open the door for my children to embrace this sin as well. Now my secret sin is not so secret. Unfortunately, I have seen this demonstrated clearly in our family more times than I wish to think about.

As a way of getting our attention, God allows our sin to be visible in the lives of our children. How this gets my attention! I dislike the sin in my life so much, and then, when confronted with it in my children's lives, it can be almost unbearable. What a gracious God we serve in that He will do whatever is necessary to prod us away from our sin.

How about you? What sins in your children are particularly annoying to you? Could it be that they are reflecting a sin in your life that hasn't been dealt with? I have found it is extremely difficult to remove the sin from the life of my child before I have addressed it in my life.

1 Corinthians 11:28, "But let a man examine himself, and so let him eat of *that* bread, and drink of *that* cup."

February 1997

Fathers' Decisions

Surely every one of us dads desire to make good decisions that are best for our family. We are called to be leaders. To be a good leader, we must make good decisions. I expect we have all made some choices we wish we hadn't made, but what is one of the more important aspects of any decision?

Let's take a look at Hezekiah, King of Judah. Now here is a man! He became king at age twenty-five, "And he did *that which was* right in the sight of the LORD, according to all that David his father did" (2 Kings 18:3). It continues in verse 4, "He removed the high places, and brake the images, and cut down the groves, and brake in pieces the brasen serpent that Moses had made. . . ." It says God blessed everything Hezekiah set his hand to do. He was making some very good decisions.

God waited fourteen years before He brought a significant test into Hezekiah's life. Ten years after Hezekiah rebelled from the control of Assyria, the king of Assyria mobilized his army against the towns of Judah. King Hezekiah sent word to the king of Assyria and confessed his error for rebelling. He said he would pay any sum the king of Assyria demanded. Hezekiah then had to give all the silver from his treasuries and from the temple of the Lord. Plus, he stripped the gold off of the temple doors to satisfy the Assyrian request.

To many, this would seem like a great decision on Hezekiah's part. The towns of Judah had already been conquered, and it would have seemed like a horrible disaster was about to take place had he resisted the Assyrian king. He averted a terrible situation and kept the peace. What a guy!

But wait! Next we read that the King of Assyria marches against Jerusalem. He tells them his intention is to deport them all to a very nice land with plenty of food. No talk of forced labor, but the evil one never highlights the truth. This time, however, we are told Hezekiah cries out to the Lord. God says He will take care of the situation. Overnight the Angel of the Lord proceeds to completely destroy the Assyrian army without Hezekiah doing anything.

Hezekiah has now made one good and one horrible decision. The first decision was trusting in himself. I'm sure it made good sense to him. Unfortunately, God's glory on earth was diminished by the treasures being taken and by the gold scraped off the doors. As they entered the temple, the marred surfaces would be a reminder to those worshipping the Lord of the consequences of not seeking God's will. Man's solutions are never permanent, as demonstrated by the king of Assyria's return. The second crisis resulted in God's glory and praise. As Hezekiah called on the Lord, Judah was delivered, and 185,000 Assyrians were slaughtered.

I think back to decisions I've made over the years; there have been some good ones and some bad ones. I don't recall ever feeling I made a bad decision after carefully seeking God's will. However, I can give you many examples of bad decisions I made when I did not seek the Lord's direction. May we put our will aside and seek God's will for our families. May we avoid the marred doors that remind us of trying to raise godly children in our own strength. May we be the leaders God would have us to be.

March 1997

The Cost of Training Our Children

What does it cost you to train your children? If asked that, I imagine we would most often think of what our curriculum costs us per year. Certainly, there is a financial aspect to home education, but I'm wondering how much we dads are investing personally in our children. If money is our main investment, will our influence be any greater than a dad whose children go to the government schools? Might our children turn out as bankrupt in character and training as most children these days who are educated outside the home?

In my work, I will encounter many fathers who love their children and yet send them off to school. They feel that is the American way; the job of the schools is to educate the children; dads provide the money and the home. Unfortunately, even if the school is successful in teaching the children facts, that is a far cry from preparing them for life.

Will the memorization of facts prepare a person for life and parenting? I think we would agree it wouldn't. That is where training comes in, first teaching pertinent facts and then practicing them. We dads have many opportunities to work with our children to reinforce, by practice, the application of what they are learning.

However, all of that takes time. Most of us have heard others recite the popular, self-consoling lie, "I have to give my children quality time, since my job doesn't allow quantity time." From what I've observed, additional work hours are usually a result of the dad's desire to get ahead. The extra time is not required. It also can be that there is trouble at home, and it is a convenient escape for Dad to bury himself in his work. It is a matter of priority. Is the proper training of the children most important to the dad, or is it his job? If the job is so demanding on its own, then it's time to get a new job. God will bless proper priorities, and wrong ones won't be blessed. Simple!*

Jesus said in John 10:11, "I am the good shepherd: the good shepherd giveth his life for the sheep." That is a constant challenge to me. As the shepherd of my family, am I laying aside my pleasures for the needs of my family? Am I willing to sacrifice my time for myself if there are needs in the family that haven't been met yet? Do I set the example for my wife in serving my family? For most, work is the easy part, but serving at home and working on character issues are much harder.

I am ashamed of how often I fail regarding the right response to the above questions. However, I serve a God Who daily gives grace. May we be like the Lord Jesus and daily lay down our lives for our families.

*(I'm not referring to families where the dad has to work longer hours just so the mom can stay at home and teach the children. These are families who are content to live in a modest home and drive old cars for the sake of right priorities. I'm referring to others who have made wrong choices with what money they have. Often they drive new cars and buy new homes. I want to differentiate between those who make bad choices and those who are truly in need.)

April 1997

For Fathers Only

Moms–PLEASE DO NOT READ THIS!! It is for your husbands only.

Friday I was invited to go to lunch with one of my suppliers. If that were you, would you go? Next, let me tell you it was a saleswoman. Would you still go? Mixed lunches are the accepted norm these days and so are close working relationships. Might someone who didn't participate be looked on as an "old prude"?

Let each one of us ask ourselves whether we believe we have been faithful to our wives. Now let's imagine our wives asking themselves if they feel we have been faithful to them. Do you think our wives' answers would match our answers? What if they knew our thoughts; would they change their decision?

Jesus defined adultery as lusting for another woman. So a definition of faithfulness would likely be even narrower than just that of adultery. We can be sure that our wives would rather they are the ones we are spending time with, no matter what the reason. (Shouldn't that be our feeling as well?) After many observations, I believe that individual (even small-group) time spent with women other than our wives is like playing with fire. I know this statement can evoke some interesting responses, but I am convinced it is true. Let me illustrate this further.

If David, a man after God's own heart, could fall into the trap of adultery because of being where he shouldn't have been, then why do we, who are less spiritual, feel we couldn't fall into a similar trap? Homes are broken and lives damaged all because of what reason? Could it ever be worth that? The idea that we can't become attached to someone else is a lie from hell, with history bearing witness. It is like playing Russian roulette with six rounds loaded!

Let's assume we are all moral giants and totally impervious to physical temptations. (I know it's impossible, but for the sake of my example please stay with me.) In 1 Thessalonians 5:22, we are instructed to abstain from even the appearance of evil. I told the saleswoman I couldn't go as I have determined not to go to lunch with other women. Before I could continue, she laughed and said she wouldn't bite and could even bring a male sales engineer along. I explained that with that aside, what if someone who knew Teri and me saw us together? What might they think? She exclaimed, "Wow, do you really mean that?" I said I did. She understood and thought that was great.

I believe God will honor our commitment to taking no chances. Another example. If heroin were legal, would you try it? Why not? Well, one reason is because we know how addicting it can be, and we don't know how much we have to take to get hooked. So we would be crazy to try it. In that light, how did we fall in love with our wives? For me, I spent time with Teri, she became my friend (and still is), and then I fell in love with her. So why would we expect not to be in danger of becoming attracted to ANY other woman we spent much time with? From David until now, men daily are trapped. Could you be next?

Our wives are home caring for our children. We know they are as bright as, if not brighter than, the women we meet in our vocation. Shouldn't they be the ones we go to lunch with? If childcare is a problem, then we could go home and let them go out with another homeschooling mom to show them how much we appreciate their ministry to our children.

Men, we must not delight in the company of any woman other than our own wives. Not only are our wives worth our faithfulness and adoration, but also, we are commanded to love them. "Husbands, love your wives, even as Christ also loved the church, and gave himself for it" (Ephesians 5:25). Let us be men of God, committed to our wives.

May 1997

Encouragement for Dads

I wonder how many of you dads might actually look at this article. If you are like me, you have a stack of items that you need to take time to read, and this would be one more on "the heap." However, it is my sincere desire to challenge and benefit you in ways that the other items crying for your time likely will not.

One reason this content will be different is that I truly care about your success as a home-educating father. It is a fact that how well or how poorly you do your job as a home-educating father will have impact on many future generations (assuming normal progression). Either your children will be well educated, responsible, Christian men and women or . . . they won't! I believe that the primary reason for success or failure of the children is the father. That is why we all need encouragement!

Where do men usually get this type of encouragement? From their parents? Well, maybe sometimes. From their friends? Hopefully, but often not. From their pastor? Occasionally if you are really blessed, as I am, but not usually. From our wives? Sometimes, but unfortunately, that is extremely difficult for them to do without sounding like they are nagging.

Families today need a father who is a leader—not a boss, but a leader. A father leader is more concerned about the members of his family than himself. He is someone who has deep biblical convictions. He is a man who has passion behind his convictions and knows why he chooses a course for his family. Yes, in fact, he is a man who would lay down his life for his family.

I believe one of the most crucial questions a father must answer is, "Do I own total responsibility for raising my children?" It isn't my wife's job; she is my helpmeet. She is there to help implement the goals and direction I set for the family. Do we feel the awesome weight of that responsibility? I'm not trying to lay guilt on you, just openly discuss the reality of our responsibility as God designed it. The CEO of a company has others who help him, but all of the responsibility is his. He is the one who answers for the success or failure of the company.

The most popular route for fathers is to become engrossed in our jobs and leave our wives with the "little" things. However, which one will matter on the other side of eternity, whether we got the promotion or raised men and women of God?

God wants men who feel the weight of their responsibility and, therefore, realize the incredible blessing in a wife who will pour out herself into her children. Our wives are one in a million; may we be one-in-a-million fathers!

August 1997

Waiting on God

During our evening family devotion, we are currently reading about God freeing Israel from Egyptian bondage. One main question was brought to mind the other night. Why did God take so long to free His people? Couldn't He have sent Moses to Pharaoh and said, "We are out of here tomorrow, Pharaoh," and then had the Israelites march right out?

He could have made Pharaoh powerless to stop them as they left the very next day, no plagues, no miracles, and not a single death. Surely, we have all wondered at times why God chooses to do things in a particular way.

In January, I told my boss I could not do what they were asking me to do. It would violate my conscience as a Christian. I fully expected to be let go. There have been many interactions since then, over this, but nothing has happened yet. I have continued to stand my ground. Two weeks ago, I met with the company president and told him I thought my position ought to be eliminated. No one should be asked to do the things they were requiring of me. The company president gave my boss until the end of the month to resolve the situation. So will it be resolved by then? Only the Lord knows.

However, don't we all have situations that are similar? They just drag on longer than we feel they ought to, or the final outcome isn't what we think it should be. Maybe you have chosen a direction for the family, and the "troops" are murmuring and complaining. Certainly Moses knew how that felt!

As we read the account of Moses, it seems there was an important lesson God had for him to learn. The same would be true for each of us as we lead our families. When God gave Moses instructions in the desert, Moses revealed his problem. He said he couldn't do what God asked because of not being well spoken. Think how ridiculous that is. Moses was telling the sovereign God of the universe that he was unable to do what God asked of him. God, Who knew Moses' every strength and weakness, and Who knew Moses better than he knew himself, knew Moses could do the task.

I don't think Moses was just making excuses. If this had been the case, he would have kept coming up with fresh excuses when the first one was eliminated. I also believe God would have dealt with him differently if he had been simply making an excuse. Therefore, it was possible that Moses was telling God about a true shortcoming in his life. However, this reveals whom Moses was trusting. Himself! At this point in this new relationship with the Lord, Moses had not learned to trust that God would work in his life and use His power to accomplish His will.

I believe one of the reasons for the long, drawn-out process of delivering His people from Pharaoh was to teach Moses to rely on God. Moses—and we, as well—must see that God will enable to be accomplished what He instructs to be done. God will never tell us to do something that we are unable to do.

After the Israelite leaders accused Moses and Aaron of making "our savour to be abhorred in the eyes of Pharaoh" (Exodus 5:21), Moses demonstrated the key to our success as fathers. Immediately after he spoke with the leaders of the people, in Exodus 5:22 we see, "And Moses returned unto the LORD, and said. . . ." Our response must be the same as his response; we must first cry out to our Lord.

When we don't understand, when we need direction, when we lack the means to accomplish our responsibilities (i.e., to raise up godly children), we must go to Him in prayer. We must pour out our hearts to Him Who enables, Who strengthens, Who gives peace. Moses was transformed into a man who knew God and relied on Him. May that be true for each of us.

September 1997

A Dad's Right

Have you ever had someone owe you something that they refused to give you? It can be pretty frustrating. Perhaps it is even something you really need! Moreover, it is ten times worse if that someone is close enough that you encounter them frequently. This is true, in varying degrees, for every one of us right now. What is it?

I marvel at how the creative genius of God designed the institution of marriage. God placed two opposites together in a lifelong covenant that is designed to represent the relationship of Christ and His bride, the church. The purpose of that union is to bring God glory and raise up godly seed (Malachi 2:15).

Into the man and woman, He placed intense inner needs, which can never be circumvented. Women marry for love and companionship. Men need respect. However, what is the husband to do if he isn't receiving the respect he needs (Ephesians 5:22-33)?

Have you ever noticed a situation in the news or maybe at work, where either a group of people or an individual feels their/his rights are being violated? They will demand, get angry, petition for new laws, and do just about anything in trying to get this injustice resolved. The end of this militant campaign is that they are the targets of contempt by the others whom they expected to right the wrong. They appear to be a bunch of whiners and complainers.

So, dads, what do we do if we are not receiving the respect we deserve? First off, we obviously don't turn to another woman. After a while, that other person would realize why our wives don't respect us, not to mention we would be breaking a covenant. I believe the first thing would be to cry out to God and ask Him why we aren't being respected. I think the answer will surprise us. We are receiving more than the respect we deserve! It's true in my life.

Let God show us our failings, bad decisions, and tasks left undone. If He doesn't show us enough, then we can ask our wives, as I'm sure they can give us some more ideas. The result—we will realize that we don't deserve the respect God says our wives are to provide. Yes, it is humbling, but it will take the wind out of our sails and the fight out of our speech.

Of the groups or people we observe, the ones who are determined to fulfill their responsibilities and act according to the respect they desire are the ones who will begin to receive it. Maybe this respect is not fully the amount they think they deserve, but who among us is paid what we feel we deserve!

Now what does that have to do with home education? Everything! With our wives taking so much time and emotional energy to teach our children at home for us, they are under great stress. We will have additional responsibilities when we take on home education. Our wives become very discouraged when we neglect our responsibilities. Trust me, I know from personal experience!

Specifically, I believe we should first apply ourselves to what our wives need most, and that is love. Just as we often don't deserve respect, they won't deserve the full amount of love God has commanded us to give them. However, that is what is needed. It is ironic that with the additional responsibilities home education brings, our wives could be even less lovable. However, we will never love our wives if we allow ourselves to think about their perceived faults; they will never respect us if they think about ours. We are to give them what God says they need and expect nothing in return.

I believe when we concentrate on our responsibilities, of which the primary one is loving our wife, God is free to open her eyes to respecting us like she never has before. The result: peace at home, mama feeling loved, dad being respected, and the children learning and growing in a healthy environment.

October 1997

Raising Teens

I expect most have heard that a child will go through a rebellious stage in their teen years. If that is true, have you ever wondered how God could require in 1 Timothy 3:4 that a church elder, "ruleth well his own house, having his children in subjection with all gravity"? It hardly seems fair for God to require this as a qualification, and then put in human nature the flaw that causes all teenagers to go through rebellion.

It is just like God to require a man to know how to shepherd his family well in order to be entrusted with a position of authority in the church. Since it is a requirement for serving in the church, we can be sure that a rebellious teen is the responsibility of the parent.

How can we avoid rebellion from happening in our families? Most of us know someone we respect who has had a rebellious child. They seem to be a good parent; they seem to love and serve the Lord, yet the child is a rebel. How can this be?

As we read that section in 1 Timothy 3, we see many tests for the would-be elder. What sort of reputation does he have? Is he the husband of one wife? Does he keep himself from alcohol? Does he know the Scriptures? Is he hospitable? Is he gentle and not quarrelsome? Does he love money? These all address his character. He is to be above reproach in his private life, and that is a qualification for church leadership. As listed earlier, even the behavior of his children are part of his credentials. So we see that his example in the home is critical and a litmus test of whether he is good for the church.

I believe the father's example and leadership are the first two legs of a three-legged stool that are necessary in raising children who will not rebel. They are vital in the home. Interestingly, I think these two legs are easier than the third leg, even though the third leg is unbelievably easy. However, that third essential aspect is often neglected and left on the shelf. It is available to every Christian and will not cost us a cent. When a crisis comes, it is one of the first things used. Unfortunately, due to it not being used consistently, it is often quite ineffective. It is possibly the greatest true measure of a Christian. Do you know what it is? It's prayer.

You see, Jesus Christ changes lives. Prayer will, somehow, bring the power of the Lord Jesus into a person's life to change his heart, as nothing else can. We read in Matthew 17 that when the disciples could not cast out a demon, Jesus said, "Howbeit this kind goeth not out but by prayer and fasting" (Matthew 17:21). I'm not saying that a rebel has a demon, but I believe this verse teaches that prayer and fasting must be used when the heart is not changing. Whether it is our children or our spouse, Jesus Christ works in hearts.

Years ago I was very troubled over how our sons' participation in team sports was stealing our family time. I finally told Teri we needed to quit team sports after the season was over. Teri and I both loved to watch the boys play ball, as they were very good. She just couldn't agree to it. I decided that I would begin to cry out to the Lord to change her heart. Notice I wasn't asking God to change her heart due to a selfish motive. I wanted to allow more time so we could be in the Bible in the evenings. In a very short amount of time, God changed her heart and the rest is history!

Earnest, intense, ongoing, sincere prayer is, I believe, the missing weapon of many fathers. I think that if our prayer life is what it should be, God will likely reveal problems early enough that they may be "nipped in the bud."

Dads, do we pray? Do we cry out to the Lord on behalf of our children and wives? Do we know how to pray? Do we love prayer? Can we afford not to?

I believe this "three-legged stool" is why God justly requires obedient children as a qualification for being an elder.

November 1997

Faults?

It is quite interesting how additional time with the family, such as may happen around holiday time, can reveal some rough edges. I love having more time with the children, but when I do I find I become more aware of particular areas of need in each family member's life. This year it was one person's faults, in particular. Unfortunately, once that happens, it can almost be a distraction as you zero in on him.

The person I was most aware of, unfortunately, was me. Don't you just hate it when it is your problem? I would much rather it was someone else's problem and not mine. The question always before me is, have I demonstrated the character of Christ in my home as God has called me to? "And, ye fathers, provoke not your children to wrath: but bring them up in the nurture and admonition of the Lord" (Ephesians 6:4).

Picture in your mind the Lord Jesus having a family. I see Him being patient and gentle, while training and maintaining order in the home. I don't think He would raise His voice when correcting, even if there was repeated disobedience. He would not have a "tone" in His voice. Oh, how I yearn to be like Christ!

Have you ever noticed that when a person deeply loves someone or something, certain things happen? It is very easy to illustrate. Look at the average person who "loves" the Kansas City Chiefs football team. They dress in red and know everything about the team.

They talk about the Chiefs and even long to be "with" them at the next game.

Honestly, as I think back over the last several weeks, I feel that other things have crowded out my love of the Lord. The symptoms are there. I haven't been as careful to have quality devotions as before. My Scripture memorization has slipped, and my focus on Christ has lessened. I'm fooling myself if I think there won't be an impact to my ability to be Christ-like in the home. So what do I do?

The third chapter of Colossians is the perfect prescription for my ailments, especially verse 12. "Put on therefore, as the elect of God, holy and beloved, bowels of mercies, kindness, humbleness of mind, meekness, longsuffering." Wow! Just to apply that one verse alone would be incredible. Unfortunately, even if I could obediently do all that, my heart is the problem. However, that is what Christ does; He changes my heart. It is Christ dwelling in me that enables this verse to become alive and active in my life. I must love my Lord with all my heart and clothe myself as He would (the armor of God in Ephesians 6). I should talk about Jesus more, and not only long to be with Him, but choose to spend more time with Him each day.

The whole section in Colossians from verse 12 to 17 is so good. It is the "tune-up" I need for my walk with my Lord. How about you? Are you demonstrating Christ in your home? If not, you will be discouraged trying to do it in your own strength. It just doesn't work! Jesus Christ changes lives. He is the One Who enables us to be the dads our families need us to be.

January 1998

Standing for What Is Right

It is hard to believe I'm actually awake! After twenty years of going away to work, I now have my office in our home. Often I will hear a quiet knocking on the door. I open it, and a little one will come in. After a hug and updating me on the latest news, the child is gone.

Years ago, God put the desire in my heart to work, vocationally, out of our home, but I saw no further direction. So we waited and waited. We would pray, "Lord, we believe You are giving us this desire. We will wait until You show us clearly what to do." Then, all of a sudden three years ago, we were given the leading to launch a business. What was strange was that I was working full time. I sure didn't have time to do any real work in a business we would start. There was barely time to put together the paperwork to set it up.

After our oldest son graduated from high school, we were able to have him contract out through our new business. God had us put our business in place prior to our needing it. It was the perfect vehicle for his contracting. However, we felt that wasn't going to be the only purpose for the business. I still wanted to be home working full time for the business, but I clearly believed God was saying "not now."

On the twenty-first of January 1997, God led me to take a stand at my job that we thought might cost me that job. Unfortunately, we were not prepared to be without an income, but we knew God would provide if that was His will. To our total amazement, the potential of losing the job dragged on all year. One day I would think I was going to be fired, and the next it would quiet down!

It was such a wonderful time of learning to rest and trust in my Lord Jesus' care. I can't remember one night of losing sleep over it. Don't get me wrong. It wasn't that I didn't care, or that I had my head in the clouds. There was just peace about it and thankfulness that Christ was dealing with the situation.

The next thing we knew, they were no longer talking about firing me. Now there was talk of laying me off. The funny thing was that this was great news since there would be some financial consideration with a layoff as opposed to being fired. We had been praying, "Lord, just make it clear to us that You really want me to leave." What could be clearer than to have your employer lay you off? Right?

Then my employer decided to give me a choice between another job and a layoff. This was not according to our plan at all! God was supposed to make it absolutely clear by not giving us any room for a decision. This new twist brought some real earnestness to our prayers. Finally, God gave Teri and me full peace that I was to leave and come home.

I stand in awe of how the Lord has directed over the last year. It would be very easy to laugh as I look up the road ahead. I have told some that I feel like I'm "out of the boat" right now. I find my competitors and other challenges to be the "waves." However, as long as I keep my eyes on the Lord Jesus, I have real joy and peace.

I know some of you may face similar challenges. My encouragement to you is: don't be concerned with your perceived consequences to a decision, but look only to the Lord for His direction. That is the only thing that matters and will enable you to be calm in the midst of a storm. If I did not have the clear assurance I'm here because God wants me here, I would be troubled indeed. Our prayer has been and will continue to be, "Lord, what do You want us to do that will bring You the most glory?"

February 1998

Living with No Regrets

What if tonight, in a dream, God tells you He is giving you one more year to live? How would that affect the way you interact with your family? How would you spend your time? Is there anything you would do differently? It is my desire that I would live each day as if it were my last.

It seems one area of deathbed remorse is sorrow over things a person wishes they had done differently. I have teenage memories of a great desire to live my life with no regrets. I'm sure that watching my parents divorce after twenty years of marriage might have had something to do with that. Can you imagine facing death without any major regrets? I know we can't change what has already happened, but we can attempt to make restitution for the past and live from now on with renewed purpose.

What if each of us were to live the next year as if it was our last? How would we live it? I know some non-Christians who would try to pack all of the pleasure they could into the time they had left. Hopefully, none of us would do that, but it can be the desire of the flesh. I know a teenager who had cancer, and his parents were letting him fly many places so he could experience as much as possible before he died. Is that the meaning of life, to see as much as possible and have wonderful experiences? If that were true, we would not hear of so many people with great wealth being miserable, and eventually taking their life physically, or by drugs and alcohol.

Frankly, I know quite a few dads who live their lives seeking all the pleasure and recreation they can. The highlight of their week is the football game, or some other sports event on TV. You can quickly tell what is most important to someone by what they will most readily talk about. When compared to the father's pleasure, children are often regarded no higher than pets; they're okay to have around as long as they don't get in the way of the dad's other interests. I love the attitude of a homeschooling family who has moved on. One night after a meeting, while the mom was patiently putting what seemed like the child's seventeenth layer of winter dress on, she exclaimed with deep sincerity, "I feel so unworthy of the honor of serving these children!"

I'm not saying our life is to revolve around our children. However, we do need to die to our own selfish pleasures and center our life on the Lord Jesus Christ. Instead of the law, which the following verse refers to, let us substitute Jesus Christ, Who is the fulfillment of the law, and see how we need to live. "And thou shalt teach Jesus diligently unto thy children, and shalt talk of Jesus when thou sittest in thine house, and when thou walkest by the way, and when thou liest down, and when thou risest up" (Deuteronomy 6:7 modified).

We share with our children what is important to us. If sports are important, then they will be important to our children. They will likely become couch potatoes and neglectors of their families. If pleasure and recreation take prominence, our children will likely be slothful and gluttons. If we are "religious" only on Sunday morning, live for ourselves, and don't demonstrate our love and excitement for Jesus, then our children will likely consider us hypocrites and reject Christ.

Do we look at our children as inconveniences or as blessed opportunities? Are we thinking that they are our heritage, and we only have a very limited amount of time to leave an impression on them? We are leaving an impression on them now, but what kind of impression is it? Do we like what we see in our children's lives? They resemble us. Today is the first day of the rest of our lives, however long or short that may be. Let us live each day as if it were our last. NO REGRETS!

March 1998

Dwelling on Imperfections?

Sit back, close your eyes, and daydream for a minute. I know you can't read with your eyes closed! However, think for a moment about your wife. What thoughts are going through your mind? No one else can truly know what you are thinking, but let's take a few minutes and be completely honest.

Here are the pictures that come to my mind. I see a wife with a child on each side and one sprawled across her lap, as she reads stories to them each afternoon. I see her on a "search and destroy mission" as she crisscrosses the living room, picking up a few remaining toys and socks after the children are in bed. I see her lying down with her back flat for a few minutes to ease the pain so she can get back up and keep going. I see a wife who delights to give her husband a backrub every night when we are in bed on time. The pictures whirl by as God brings to mind the gift He has given me in my wife.

Now what emotions do we experience as a result of the pictures? Peace? Love? Tenderness? Joy? Gratefulness? Are there any negative feelings? There can be, as most wives are not perfect. How do we deal with this? Do we let ourselves ever dwell on something negative about our spouse? The answer should be a resounding, NO!!!!!!!

About six months ago, I did just that. There was a trivial imperfection in my sweet wife, and I allowed myself to dwell on it. Whenever I saw her, I would take up that thought. I began to feel sorry for myself and be judgmental of her. I knew it was wrong, but

I continued to do it anyway. Soon she knew something was wrong and asked me about it. I told her it was my problem, and she could pray for me. Sharing the details with her would have been hurtful and not helped in any way. Her prayers were what I needed.

By God's timing, our church's men's meeting came, and I was eager to go. During a time of sharing, I confessed to the men that my heart was wrong toward Teri, and I needed prayer. I was allowing wrong thoughts, but had not been able to break out of it. As is the custom during these fellowship times, the men gathered around me and prayed for me. The result–God totally freed me from my thoughts, and I had wonderful peace on the way home that night. When caught in a trap, if we are unable to break loose, we ask for help.

If we aren't willing to ask for help, our marriage and family security are in grave danger. "Perfect" marriages have been broken due to that very weakness in the husband (or wife, for that matter). Yes, it is a weakness. Had I been stronger, I would have chosen not to think about a slight fault in my wife, but instead thought of all her wonderful qualities. Think about it. What good could ever be accomplished by dwelling on some fault in a spouse? Hebrews 12:15 warns us that a root of bitterness grows up into evil. "Looking diligently lest any man fail of the grace of God; lest any root of bitterness springing up trouble *you*, and thereby many be defiled." If we allow even a small amount of bitterness to be in our mind, it will always grow. It can be over nothing (mine was). However, it soon won't be small, and we will begin to look at everything our spouse does in a very negative light. It will kill a marriage.

So what is the point? Let us be on guard to not fall into the trap that has shipwrecked many a marriage. We made a vow before God to love and cherish our wives, not to dwell on any shortcomings. We should be crying out to God to work on our own failures. We don't want to be a stumbling block for our wives and give them opportunity to dwell on our faults. Ugh, now that is a scary thought!

April 1998

Dad, Where Is Your Heart?

In school, I preferred fill-in-the-blank questions to essay questions. I think that might be true for most of us. Consider for a minute a special fill-in-the-blank that could save your children from abandoning the faith. Are you game?

What if our children were to fill in the following statements about us?

_____ is most important to my father.

My father talks most about _____.

I don't know about you, but I find these rather heavy. I believe that if my children answered them candidly, I might get a picture of who I really am. Unfortunately, I may not want to know the answers!

In Judges 6:13, the Lord is speaking with Gideon. The Lord has just told Gideon he is a mighty warrior, and He is with him in spite of the fact that Gideon is acting in a very cowardly way. Then we read, "And Gideon said unto him, Oh my Lord, if the LORD be with us, why then is all this befallen us? and where *be* all his miracles which our fathers told us of, saying, Did not the LORD bring us up from Egypt? but now the LORD hath forsaken us, and delivered us into the hands of the Midianites." Now what does this verse have to do with the fill-in-the-blank statements above? I think there are several points worth considering.

If the fathers had been living God-fearing lives, Israel would not have been in the mess they were. God was chastening the nation because the fathers were not living as God had called them to. "And the children of Israel did evil in the sight of the LORD: and the LORD delivered them into the hand of Midian seven years" (Judges 6:1). The fathers were not telling the children that all of this oppression was a result of the fathers' sin. Instead, they seemed to blame the Lord for having abandoned them, as if He didn't love them anymore. Actually, the truth was the Lord did love them and wanted to punish them so they would cry out and return to Him. Dads, are we experiencing hardship or chastening that is a result of our lack of devotion and love of our Lord?

The fathers were actually telling their children about the wonders the Lord had performed. Many dads have felt they were doing all they needed to do by telling their children about the Lord. Maybe they were even going so far as to read to them from a Bible picture storybook at bedtime. Even though that is good, it isn't enough. You see, our deeds speak for us. During the day, we will automatically talk about what really is important to us, and we will live out our values. These fathers were telling their children about what God used to do. However, all children need to see fathers living their lives dedicated to serving a living, loving God. Our children should have fathers who love the Lord so much that they can't help but talk to their children about the tender mercies and goodness of the Lord Jesus. Our children will grow up like we really are, not who we tell them they should become.

Instead of the Lord receiving the blame for difficult circumstances, He should be praised for His goodness when He is disciplining us or leading us through times of trial. Do we only love Him when times are good? Do we want to teach our children to love us only when they think we are being kind to them?

I pray this, "Oh, Father, may we demonstrate our love for You constantly to our children. May we be quick to confess our failures and not blame the consequences of our sin on You. May our children see their father praising You, Lord, and being quick to pray to You. May You be the first and most frequent topic on our lips. May my children know by my actions that You are the One I love more than anyone or anything."

May 1998

Directed by God

Are there any men whom you look up to and respect? What qualities about other men do you admire? Is it because they have great wealth, talents, or intelligence? Someone I respect immensely is Jeremiah the prophet. I just love reading that book because I see a man for whom God had a mission. Jeremiah was willing to be obedient, no matter what the cost. He was clearly not thrilled about it at times, but he was obedient.

In Jeremiah 27:2-7 the prophet describes the Lord's instructions: "Thus saith the LORD to me; Make thee bonds and yokes, and put them upon thy neck, And send them to the king of Edom, and to the king of Moab, and to the king of the Ammonites, and to the king of Tyrus, and to the king of Zidon, by the hand of the messengers which come to Jerusalem unto Zedekiah king of Judah; And command them to say unto their masters, Thus saith the LORD of hosts, the God of Israel; Thus shall ye say unto your masters; I have made the earth, the man and the beast that *are* upon the ground, by my great power and by my outstretched arm, and have given it unto whom it seemed meet unto me. And now have I given all these lands into the hand of Nebuchadnezzar the king of Babylon, my servant; and the beasts of the field have I given him also to serve him. And all nations shall serve him, and his son, and his son's son, until the very time of his land come: and then many nations and great kings shall serve themselves of him."

First, consider how foolish Jeremiah was going to look wearing this yoke around. Can you imagine how his "friends" and neighbors would laugh at him? "There goes that crazy Jeremiah. Ha, ha, ha!" No doubt, he would have looked somewhat strange!

Next, think about Jeremiah sending messages to the king of Judah and neighboring kings. These were not just Christmas cards to his friends. Here is a "nobody" telling kings that they were going to be conquered and that (verses 8-11) they should not resist, but rather serve Nebuchadnezzar. Zedekiah, Judah's king, could have been sufficiently angered to have replaced Jeremiah's head with a basket. Now, not only do his "friends" think he is crazy, but he risks his life by possibly angering many in authority.

So, what does that have to do with Christian fathers of home-schooling children? In Jeremiah 1, we see God told Jeremiah clearly that He had a purpose for him. Jeremiah was to obey and not be fearful. Fathers, do we see ourselves as directed by God to lead our families? Are we fully committed to obeying God's Word and setting an example for our families, even if it is not popular with them, our friends, or our neighbors? Do we cave in when they begin to apply pressure? Maybe you have a child who wants to be in school with "friends." Will you be strong and do what is best for the child?

We see in this passage that God uses plain "ole" people like you and me. What is important is that we are obedient to His Word. He has clearly called us to train our children. That involves character, knowledge of the Bible and the Lord Jesus, skills necessary to earn a livelihood, and information about health and government. This is our responsibility, and it is not easily handed off to another. Are we committed to doing what is best for our children versus what everyone else does? It is so easy for us to be consumed with earning a living that we don't own this responsibility ourselves. May God give us grace to be men of God, dedicated to knowing Him and serving Him, by being the husbands and fathers He intends us to be.

August 1998

Men of Faith

I delight in associating with and investing in men hungry to know and serve God. Sadly, men of God are quite rare these days. The church and families are in great want of men committed to following the Lord Jesus. So who were men of God in the Bible, and what were some of their qualities?

Moses, Elijah, Elisha, Daniel, Shadrach, Meshach, Abednego, prophets, and certainly the Apostles were all men of God, just to name a few. What qualities can we observe in their lives?

1. Men committed to obedience and holiness.

   Even as a young man, when confronted with having to compromise his convictions, we are told, "But Daniel purposed in his heart that he would not defile himself with the portion of the king's meat, nor with the wine which he drank. . ." (Daniel 1:8). (I believe Daniel would have faced death, if necessary, to remain obedient to God's direction for his life.) He could have said, "I'm in another country now and everyone else is . . . ," or, "I'm being commanded by my authority to . . . ," or, "I sure don't want to make trouble." He could have justified it by any number of "reasons." However, as fathers we are to be committed to following through on what God shows us is His will for our family.

2. Men of courage who are committed to prayer.

"Now when Daniel knew that the writing was signed, he went into his house; and his windows being open in his chamber toward Jerusalem, he kneeled upon his knees three times a day, and prayed, and gave thanks before his God, as he did aforetime" (Daniel 6:10). Even when Daniel knew he would face the lion's den, he went to the Lord in prayer.

3. Men of faith ready to face death.

"If it be *so*, our God whom we serve is able to deliver us from the burning fiery furnace, and he will deliver *us* out of thine hand, O king. But if not, be it known unto thee, O king, that we will not serve thy gods, nor worship the golden image which thou hast set up" (Daniel 3:17-18). Even when the three faced the furnace, they knew God could rescue them. They were willing to die if God chose not to deliver them. YEAH! Can you imagine what our families would be like if we men had this same faith and dedication? Are we willing to die daily to ourselves for our families? Our Lord Jesus set the example.

4. Men who speak only the truth.

"And he said unto him, Behold now, *there is* in this city a man of God, and *he is* an honourable man; all that he saith cometh surely to pass. . ." (1 Samuel 9:6).

"And the woman said to Elijah, Now by this I know that thou *art* a man of God, *and* that the word of the LORD in thy mouth *is* truth" (1 Kings 17:24). Every word out of our mouth must be true.

5. A man of God results in God being praised.

"And he returned to the man of God, he and all his company, and came, and stood before him: and he said, Behold, now I know that *there is* no God in all the earth, but in Israel: now therefore, I pray thee, take a blessing of thy servant" (2 Kings 5:15).

6. Men who are able to see God's protection.

"And when the servant of the man of God was risen early, and gone forth, behold, a host compassed the city both with horses and chariots. And his servants said unto him, Alas, my master! how shall we do? And he answered, Fear not: for they that *be* with us *are* more than they that *be* with them" (2 Kings 6:15-16).

7. Men of God are ever improving their skill and knowledge of the Bible.

"All scripture *is* given by inspiration of God, and *is* profitable for doctrine, for reproof, for correction, for instruction in righteousness: That the man of God may be perfect, throughly furnished unto all good works" (2 Timothy 3:16-17). If this verse is true, and I believe it is, we must study God's Word to know how to live and confirm God's direction for our family. I once knew a man who said he was praying about divorcing his faithful wife. If he had known God's Word, he would have known that wasn't an option for him.

There is so much more that could be said, but Jesus Christ is the perfect example. "Dear Father, help us to be like Jesus."

September 1998

God's Warnings

In Matthew 9:13, Jesus responded to the Pharisees' question about His associating with tax collectors and sinners with, "But go ye and learn what *that* meaneth, I will have mercy, and not sacrifice. . . ." I believe this provides great insight into the way our Lord deals with us. I see in Scripture that He will orchestrate events in our lives to bring us to a point of repentance and asking for mercy.

Lot is probably an example of all of us at some point in our Christian walk. There has likely been a time when each of us has chosen some degree of compromise, or lack of obedience. I know I prefer to think that my sin is my sin and does not have an effect on my family. Obviously, that is a convenient and incorrect myth!

The reality is that my walk, or lack of it, with Christ has a definite impact on my family. There is no such thing as a private sin that does not have an effect in some way on those I'm called to shepherd. However, God in His grace will try to gently get our attention.

You've heard the naval expression "a shot over the bow." In naval terms, a shot is fired in front of another vessel to warn them they had better change course, or stop for boarding. God works in much the same manner.

Lot's "shot over the bow" was when God destroyed Sodom and Gomorrah. It was a sinful, wicked place, and he knew it. That is why he didn't want the angels spending the night in the square. Lot was wrong in choosing to live there. Some might argue he was trying to win the city. However, if you pay attention to what the mob and his sons-in-law said to him, it is obvious he was not winning them to his God, but losing his family.

His compromise cost him his wife, when she longingly looked back. It almost cost him his daughters as he offered them to appease an angry mob. It did cost him his daughters' virtue as they demonstrated later with their father in the mountains.

Notice that Lot learned something from his warning. He first wanted to go to Zoar, even though he was instructed to flee to the mountains. The angels knew his physical abilities and were not telling him to do something he was not capable of doing. However, for the same reasons he was living in Sodom, he wanted to go to Zoar. It is likely that after seeing the wickedness of the city, he realized he was at risk. He then chose to be obedient and go to the mountains.

God wants us to keep our families out of evil environments. From my observations, it is often the father who places the family at risk. Praise God that He doesn't immediately chasten us when we disobey. Our Lord desires mercy, not sacrifice. However, to offer us mercy, we have to be repentant and seek His forgiveness.

Several years ago, I was convicted that I had said something unkind to a relative. The Lord was telling me to ask forgiveness, but I resisted. One day as Nathan and I were preparing to leave for work, I decided to let the car roll backwards out of the garage while Nathan went back into the house for something. Unfortunately, I did not see that the rear car door was fully open.

As you can image, our garage doors are not wide enough to accommodate a Honda Civic, with a door open, passing through without some degree of trauma. The car lurched to a stop, and I looked back to see the door bent backwards. UGH! Even though the furthest thing from my mind was needing to ask forgiveness of the relative, that was the thought that instantly filled my mind.

God has a way of warning and chastening us when He needs to. I believe there was not twenty-four hours' passage of time before that relationship issue was dealt with. My gracious Lord had said it was time to take care of it!

My own father inadvertently exposed me to wicked things that have cost me greatly. Eventually, it cost him his family. God had sent him a "shot over the bow," but he ignored it.

How about you? Is there some area of your life that is a compromise God is not pleased with? Is there something that God has warned you about that cries for your repentance and needs a change? If so, don't delay and take the chance of grave consequences; repent of it today. Your family and the Lord will bless you for it.

October 1998

Dad, the Spiritual Leader

How comfortable are you with your role as the spiritual leader of your home? Is this something you willingly own as your responsibility? How do you view it compared to your calling to provide for the physical needs of your family?

We can be wonderful providers for our families and yet, after a full life, have each of our children end up in hell or as worldly, lukewarm Christians. That seems to put the issues into perspective, doesn't it? Have we spiritually reproduced death and carnality, or vibrant offspring of the Lord Jesus?

I remember at one point in my life smugly thinking, "I'm doing what I should as the spiritual leader of my home." We were homeschooling, the children were in Sunday School, and I was having bedtime devotions (a pretty shallow one, but it counted, didn't it?) with the children. What else was there?

Think about Moses for a minute, and God's calling him to lead His people. Moses kept telling the Lord he was not equipped to properly lead the Israelites. Even after God said He would enable Moses for this job, Moses still back-peddled. Finally, in Exodus 4:14-16, "And the anger of the LORD was kindled against Moses," and God agreed to use Aaron. "And he shall be thy spokesman unto the people: and he shall be, *even* he shall be to thee instead of a mouth, and thou shalt be to him instead of God."

I'm grieved by how few fathers really take the role of being the spiritual leader of their homes seriously. There are either excuses about capabilities and gifts or no real effort beyond going through the basics. God equips those He calls. We must believe that God will equip us to do the job He has given us. He gave Moses signs of his authority, and said Moses was to "be to him instead of God." Isn't that an incredible statement? Moses' actions were to be a picture of God in the flesh.

Is it any wonder so many have poor concepts of God when their fathers were terrible examples? What an awesome responsibility we have as fathers. God intended that we dads help form the God image in the minds of our children. That is one reason the Lord's Prayer begins, "Our Father which art in heaven. . . ."

We have no greater responsibility than, as far as we are enabled by the grace of our Lord Jesus Christ, to demonstrate Christ to our families. Christ said if you have seen Me you have seen the Father. His purpose in coming to earth was to reveal the Father. Are we able to fully grasp the seriousness of this calling? Our desire needs to be to live as Christ in full view of our families. We must be crying out to the Lord on behalf of our families, dying to self daily, and if necessary, giving our life for them.

Moses was a wonderful picture of that as he cried out to the Lord for the Israelites. I was greatly challenged by Moses' response to the Israelites making the golden calf while he was on the mountain. God was ready to kill them all and make Moses into a mighty nation. Yet what did Moses say? In Exodus 32:32 he said, "Yet now, if thou wilt forgive their sin–; and if not, blot me, I pray thee, out of thy book which thou hast written."

I believe that is referring to the Book of Life where the names of the saved are recorded. I think Moses was demonstrating his willingness to go to hell if it meant the rest of the Israelites might live.

Here we have the picture of Christ's atonement for our sin made as an offering to the Lord. When that sank in, I was challenged to the depth of my heart. Moses was willing to make the ultimate sacrifice for those he was called to serve.

May we bring our families before the Lord constantly as Moses did in the Tent of Meeting. May our families see us going to the Lord in prayer as the Israelites saw Moses. May we take our calling as a serious matter of life and death.

November 1998

God's Direction Through the Dad

What are your goals for your family? Have you written them down? Are they your goals or the Lord's goals? Without a rudder and compass, not many boats would ever reach the harbor. I think a reasonable analogy would be that our compass should be the Lord's direction. A good example of this is found with Noah.

In Genesis 6:22, "Thus did Noah; according to all that God commanded him, so did he." Now look at Genesis 7:5, "And Noah did according unto all that the LORD commanded him." First, we see that Noah had to have a relationship with God to receive instruction from Him. Do you know the Lord Jesus as your Lord and Savior? The initial step is having Jesus as Savior and, unfortunately, many men never go beyond this point. The second step is for Christ to be our Lord. He must be our boss and commander. His precious blood has bought us, and we are His. That means we do what He tells us to. He will instruct us in how to lead our family.

God gave instruction prior to the flood on how Noah could save his family. God did not tell Noah's family, but He told Noah what to do. Think about the absurdity of what God said to Noah, and then Noah had to tell his family. They were going to build a boat, and it was going to rain and drown everyone. Does your family love and respect you enough to follow your leadership even when they don't understand? Noah had many years to prove himself to his family prior to this unique direction from the Lord. Dads, are we leading our family in ways of righteousness, as God would have us? "But Noah found grace in the eyes of the LORD" (Genesis 6:8). We can't walk in the ways of the world and expect our family to follow us when, all of the sudden, we interject an occasional righteous direction.

In Genesis 8:13-14, we see that Noah waited for almost sixty days, from the time he saw dry ground, before he left the ark. They had been in the ark roughly ten months when they first saw the ground was dry, and it is incredible that he waited another two months. WHY?

It is the secret of Noah's success, and it shall be the key to ours as well. Such a simple thing, really, and our success as parents depends on it. It isn't a matter of how much money we have or how smart we are. The key is revealed in verses 15 and 16, "And God spake unto Noah, saying, Go forth of the ark. . . ."

After being cooped up, under less than optimum circumstances, Noah was waiting on God to tell him when to leave. I expect Noah's family might have had many suggestions as to when the proper time was to leave! However, he waited on the Lord. Dads, that is exactly what we must do! We should get a word from the Lord for every aspect of raising our children. Dads are the rudders. There will be much pressure, from within and without the family, for the father to change course. The father must know what the heading is and stay true, or there are great possibilities for shipwreck.

Dads must be sure that what the family does is consistent with his goals for them, goals given by the Lord. If God has given you the goal of:

Serving–Do your children know what it is like to serve others? How are you demonstrating serving and training them to serve?

Working–Are they learning how to enjoy working, or do they only know how to be entertained? Must everything be fun, or are they learning some real skills? Are sports, friends, and activities the focus? If so, isn't that teaching them that life must always be fun, and can't we expect a generation of couch potatoes and thrill seekers? Was Jesus a "Man of Sorrows" because there was nothing fun to do, or because there were more important things to do?

Worship–Do they know how to worship, or must our children be sent away to Children's Church? Often Children's Church is just entertainment with a few Bible stories thrown in. Children aren't expected to sit still and listen to God's Word being preached. At what special age does preaching automatically become interesting?

We need to examine where God has called us to go and weed out those things that are distractions from the course. There is great joy in working, ministering, and serving together, and our family will be prepared to face life as God has intended.

January 1999

The First Priority

Have you ever wondered how Samson could turn out so poorly when he had seemingly great parents? How could this be? We see a father who desires to raise a child who is pleasing to God, and yet something goes wrong. When grown, this child will be a slave to immorality, which will lead to his being a slave grinding grain for the Philistines. Maybe there are a few morsels of wisdom we fathers can glean from this section of Scripture.

An angel appeared to Manoah's wife, Samson's mother. He gave her instructions on how she was to live and how Samson was to be set apart as a Nazirite. A Nazirite was someone who had such a great love for the Lord that he showed his devotion to God in a special way. Then, when Manoah was told about the angel's message, he prayed and asked God to send the angel back, ". . . teach us what we shall do unto the child that shall be born" (Judges 13:8).

In verse 9, we read that God hears Manoah's prayer and sends the angel back. When Manoah speaks to the angel in verse 12, he asks, "How shall we order the child, and *how* shall we do unto him?" What training should he receive and what will be his vocation? Good question, but the angel totally ignores it. Amazing! God sends the angel back as a result of Manoah's prayer, and then the angel doesn't answer his prayer. Or does he?

What a disappointment! Here he wants to know about the boy, and God (via the angel) is telling Manoah about his and his wife's responsibility. We have another example of this in the third chapter of John. Nicodemus makes an opening comment to Jesus, but Jesus totally ignores the comments and speaks to him about what He wants Nicodemus to hear.

The angel begins and ends by saying Manoah's wife must do everything that she has been instructed to do. The overwhelming emphasis of the angel's message to the parents is–obedience. Note that this is not the child's obedience, but the parents'. Manoah was to see that his wife obeyed the word from God.

As fathers, just what is our highest priority? Is it our children's education, socialization, future vocation, or is it our own responsibilities? I believe God's Word teaches that a father's primary responsibility is to love the Lord more than anything or anyone else. "Jesus said unto him, Thou shalt love the Lord thy God with all thy heart, and with all thy soul, and with all thy mind. This is the first and great commandment" (Matthew 22:37-38).

That means we are to be sure we are in fellowship with Him and living for Him. Our example of being sold-out to Christ is far more important than giving our children hours of instruction on how to live the Christian life. Loving our Lord, and walking in obedience to His Word, is our primary responsibility. I believe that is why the Lord instructed Manoah to be sure his wife did what the angel had told her to. Manoah was to be the leader of the home.

So why did Samson fail in achieving God's best for his life? Certainly, Samson's choices had a lot to do with it, but I wonder if it was avoidable. There are even hints in Scripture that the parents might have had outward conformity, but I wonder about their relationship with the Lord and Samson. Why do I say that?

In chapter fourteen Samson was interested in a Philistine woman, and he told his parents to get her for his wife. His father protested, but then proceeded to do what Samson wanted, even though Moses had told the Israelites not to intermarry. "Neither shalt thou make marriages with them; thy daughter thou shalt not give unto his son, nor his daughter shalt thou take unto thy son. For they will turn away thy son from following me, that they may serve other gods: so will the anger of the LORD be kindled against you, and destroy thee suddenly" (Deuteronomy 7:3-4). Here the father was more concerned that his son not be angry with him than about whether the Lord would be angry. He should have said, "Son, I will die before I willingly do what is wrong."

Don't be distracted by Judges 14:4 where it says the Lord was using this as an occasion to confront the Philistines. God will even use our sin for His purposes. He chose to use Samson's problem with lust and lack of obedience to his parents to fulfill his plan. That does not mean that there wasn't a better way if Samson had not had these problems.

Look at Samson's response to his father. ". . . Get her for me; for she pleaseth me well" (Judges 14:3). We see that Samson did not love and respect his parents, or he would have said, "Father, you are right. God would not be pleased if I was to marry her."

Dads, we need first of all to be concerned about our relationship with the Lord and pleasing Him. That begins in our hearts and is visible to those around us. It can't be mere outward conformity. It must be a walk that comes from a deep love of our Lord, not wanting to displease Him. When our relationship is right with Him, we will be able to win and retain the hearts of our children. If we have our children's hearts, then they will receive the concerns we share with them. They will be grieved when their path is straying from our example.

In verses 14:6 and 14:9, we are told Samson did something he shouldn't have as a Nazirite and chose not to tell his parents about it. Our children must feel the freedom, and need, to share with us their failures and wrong desires. How else can God use us in their lives? Samson's father neglected what was most important and lost his son. Dads, may we not fail in a similar way.

February 1999

An Unloved Wife

Teri and I have been sharing what we believe God's Word teaches on how to avoid having rebellious children. In our pastor's sermon recently, he touched on another cause that I had not considered before. I wish it weren't so, but all that we have shared points back to the father, and this one is no exception.

It is a very heavy matter to lay so much responsibility on the back of the father, but I believe that is where Scripture puts it. As God would have it, we should each do our own study and prayerfully come to our own conclusions. So I encourage you to open your heart and your Bible, and see if this is another warning about rebellion.

Colossians 3:19 says, "Husbands, love your wives, and be not bitter against them."

Most would say they are familiar with that verse as a part of being a good husband. However, our dear pastor developed the point that an unloved wife's bitterness will lead the children into rebellion. It is true, men—unfortunate, but true!

In Proverbs 30:21-23 we read, "For three *things* the earth is disquieted, and for four *which* it cannot bear: For a servant when he reigneth; and a fool when he is filled with meat; For an odious *woman* when she is married; and a handmaid that is heir to her mistress." An unloved wife who does not forgive will become bitter.

I still remember a woman I met roughly ten years ago who had been mistreated and left by her husband. Acrid bitterness dripped from every word she spoke. It had eaten her up and was etched into her jagged-lined face. The encounter was most unpleasant, and it moved me to compassion and sorrow for the pain she was putting herself through.

This woman was an extreme example. However, an unloved wife who has not received God's grace to forgive her husband for the wrongs he has committed will be bitter toward her husband. Just like the woman I mentioned, bitterness toward a husband cannot be hidden, and those around will sense it. Even worse, it will also infect her children with bitterness toward their father, and that could turn into rebellion.

1 Samuel 20:30 says, "Then Saul's anger was kindled against Jonathan, and he said unto him, Thou son of the perverse rebellious *woman*, do not I know that thou hast chosen the son of Jesse to thine own confusion, and unto the confusion of thy mother's nakedness?"

Have you noticed that Jonathan had a rebellious attitude toward his father? Saul felt that Jonathan's mother had hard feelings toward him. Now he is accusing Jonathan of it as well. Look at 1 Samuel 14:29 where Jonathan said, ". . . My father hath troubled the land: see, I pray you, how mine eyes have been enlightened, because I tasted a little of this honey."

The correct response would have been repentance, but Jonathan had a rebellious attitude toward his father, and it came out here. This rebellion wasn't so severe that Jonathan abandoned his father, but it was there. Jonathan was a "good kid" in many ways, because generally he complied with his father's orders. However, he did not respect Saul and demonstrated a rebellious attitude.

We are called to love the wife God has given us. If we don't, we can be sure there will be consequences.

March 1999

Guarding Hearts—A Real-Life Situation

"According as he hath chosen us in him before the foundation of the world, that we should be holy and without blame before him in love" (Ephesians 1:4).

Last week we went to our favorite zoo, which is located in Omaha. It is a special day for everyone, and even our young adults will take a day off work to go with us. This trip was especially a close time as we were in the process of losing our ninth child to miscarriage.

At the end of a wonderful day, we were dropping off the wheelchair that I borrowed to push Teri around. I noticed two documentary videos on Mount Everest in the gift shop. I have a special interest in mountain climbing and thought this would be an excellent addition to our educational video library. It also turned out that one of them was the same footage as was being shown in the Imax Theater. After a little hesitation, I decided to go ahead and purchase them.

When the little ones were in bed, I chose to preview the videos, so we carried the TV and VCR out of the downstairs closet. To my amazement, the opening scene began in a temple where one of the climbers was lighting candles. Ugh! My heart then began to twinge a bit under conviction, and that should have been enough to stop it right there. However, the mental excuses and gymnastics began as I thought of the thirty dollars I had paid for this one. Besides, there probably wouldn't be any more problems with the video (Sure!).

The story unfolded with occasional remarks about his god, temple footage, and other Eastern religion information. To my shame, I didn't turn it off, but continued watching it with the three oldest children. I failed those children! I should have stopped it right then and said, "No more, we must turn it off. This isn't worth compromising our hearts." However, I wanted to watch it! Therefore, we finished the first video, and we started the second tape. This one was about high-altitude effects on the body. By this time I was feeling quite convicted. Then, out of the blue, the guy being interviewed cursed. That was enough to push me over the edge and turn it off. Why hadn't I chosen to stop watching it earlier?

In the last few Dad's Corners, I emphasized the fact that God places all the responsibility for everything that goes on in the home on "dear ole Dad." The sad thing is that I am often the cause of the problems. When I'm struggling with self-control, I can expect to see lack of self-control in my children. We are the shepherds guarding the access to the sheep pen. It is true that every evil imagination, which is similar to improper appetites, does come from the heart. However, we then can guard whether these appetites are fed or not.

The sad fact was, if I had chosen to stop watching the video earlier, my older children would have seen that their father was very careful to guard his heart and their hearts. They would have seen that, even in a situation where Dad wants to continue, he is man enough to deny himself. That was one of those rare opportunities that don't come around often. We are teaching our children in everything we do. I showed them that if it is something that interests you, it is okay to continue. I failed!

Life is so full of opportunities to train our children in the way of righteousness. We must see that as our responsibility. We should protect our heart first, and then our children's. Otherwise we teach them that once you are old enough to be in control, you can use that control for selfish purposes and choose to "enjoy" evil at the expense of righteousness. "But as he which hath called you is holy, so be ye holy in all manner of conversation; Because it is written, Be ye holy; for I am holy" (1 Peter 1:15-16).

April 1999

Dads—Are You the Head of a Christian Home? (Part One)

"Therefore whosoever heareth these sayings of mine, and doeth them, I will liken him unto a wise man, which built his house upon a rock: And the rain descended, and the floods came, and the winds blew, and beat upon that house; and it fell not: for it was founded upon a rock. And every one that heareth these sayings of mine, and doeth them not, shall be likened unto a foolish man, which built his house upon the sand: And the rain descended, and the floods came, and the winds blew, and beat upon that house; and it fell: and great was the fall of it" (Matthew 7:24-27).

Have you noticed how there are so many Christian "this" and Christian "that's"? There are Christian radio stations, Christian music, Christian businesses, Christian schools, Christian curricula, and Christian you name it! Would you agree there are many things labeled Christian that it becomes an increasing stretch of the imagination as to whether they are any more Christian than the "world"? For example, many so-called Christian songs on the radio sound just like the world's music. If you doubt it, turn the volume down until you can't hear the words, and compare it to a secular song. Christians have welcomed the world so much there is little distinction between what most consider Christian and what they would consider the "world." We must bear in mind that the Lord's standard for judging is not as fuzzy.

Most of us have known Christian families where the older children have rebelled. People will then say, "I just don't understand it as he/she was raised in a good Christian home." Usually, the observation is based on a superficial judgment, and indirectly the Lord is being blamed in that situation. It is almost as if the Lord failed in some way. May it never even be thought! We can be sure that is not the case at all. God is always faithful.

I wonder if you have ever asked yourself just what is a Christian home. "Christian home" isn't directly mentioned in the Bible, but the Bible does have plenty to say about what a Christian home is. Before we proceed, what do you say? Is your home Christian, yes or no (no lukewarm voting)?

How exciting to see that God's Word is definitive on every aspect of our lives. Even though our concordance might not list "Christian home" as a selection, the concept is very clearly dealt with.

In 1 Chronicles 17, David is telling Nathan, the prophet, about his concern that God should have a fitting "house." Then in verse 10, God said through Nathan the prophet, ". . . I tell thee that the LORD will build thee an house." Here God ties David's loving concern for his God to God's blessing of David. God draws a parallel between His house and David's house (family). If we want to learn what the basis is for a Christian home, we need only study God's home on earth–the temple.

We will continue this for the next several months' Dad's Corners as there is much practical direction for our homes. Each step of the way I will encourage you to evaluate your home to see if it is really a Christian home or not. There is no middle ground. It is either a home where the Lord Jesus is glorified, or it isn't. If it is in the middle, it is lukewarm. "So then because thou art lukewarm, and neither cold nor hot, I will spew thee out of my mouth" (Revelation 3:16).

Dads, may we provide a loving, nurturing environment, which is conducive for children becoming mature, equipped, dedicated Christians serving the Lord Jesus Christ.

May 1999

Dads—Are You the Head of a Christian Home? (Part Two)

A word of caution before reading on! This month's Corner is a tough one to share. It is possible there will be some reaction to it. Please don't shoot the messenger! Take this before the Lord, and if you then feel God has intended this for you, receive it. If, after praying about it, you are convinced it isn't of the Lord, just ignore it.

I laid a foundation last month by suggesting that God gave families the blueprint for a Christian home. That blueprint was His home on earth—the temple. The temple is a beautiful picture of what a Christian home should be like; we can model our home after His. Of course not literally, but God often uses "types" and "pictures" to help teach us. We can learn much from His home on earth.

First, think about what made God's temple different from any other building. The temple was just stone, wood, and gold until the glorious Spirit of the living, holy, mighty God came down and filled it. So our house is just another earthly house until God's Spirit is able to dwell there. (I understand that our body is God's temple now, but this is just a discussion of types.)

Our homes (and our bodies), as the temple, are to be holy and set apart to the Lord. Isaiah 64:11 says, "Our holy and our beautiful house, where our fathers praised thee. . . ." In 2 Chronicles 3:8

we find, "And he made the most holy house. . . ." I think none would argue that the temple was a holy place.

I have been in many homes where I sensed God's spirit. My pastor's home is like that. I also remember an unbeliever from Holland resting comfortably in our living room and saying he felt such a sense of peace, as he had never experienced before.

Now notice Psalms 79:1, which says, "O God, the heathen are come into thine inheritance; thy holy temple have they defiled. . . ." Note the temple was defiled by the nations invading it. When the world enters the temple, it is no longer holy; it is defiled, and the Lord will not be there.

We defile our homes by bringing the world and its idols in. So the million-dollar question is, "What are the idols of the world that we shouldn't bring in?" First, admittedly, anything can become an idol by usurping the supreme place in our heart that belongs to our Lord Jesus. There are necessary "things" such as jobs, food, and sleep that we can't avoid, but must learn to control them lest they too become idols. However, there are other "things" that the American male has clearly made into idols, but as Christians, we don't have to have anything to do with them. What are they? I suspect the top four are: team sports (participating or viewing), watching TV, entertainment, and alcohol. You may come up with more, but few would argue that these are very high on the list.

Dads, may we never allow the idols of the world in our homes. The Holy Spirit had some very strong words, which He spoke through James. "Ye adulterers and adulteresses, know ye not that the friendship of the world is enmity with God? whosoever therefore will be a friend of the world is the enemy of God" (James 4:4). Friendship, in the Greek, is defined as only a fondness/friendship. That is far less strong than the word "fan" which many men use to describe themselves. The term "fan" is short for fanatic. God's Word is really very decisive in this passage. We can't serve two masters. To evaluate just what we value, we might ask our wives and children to list the top ten things that they see are important to us.

It has been over ten years now since we stopped watching TV. However, I can still remember the conflict the TV presented for me. Just having it upstairs dulled my desire for the Word of God. When we quit watching it, I felt a sense of freedom and renewed desire for His Word.

Dads, we need to live the life we want our children to model. I want my children to see each minute as a precious gift from God, to be used for His glory. That means when I am not working or sleeping, I want to be ministering inside or outside of the home. I want my children to enjoy serving others. If they learn to take joy in blessing others, they will never lack for joy. I can't tell you the delight it gives me to go to the City Union Mission with my sons and have them all say they really enjoyed going.

May we never settle for second best. Let us always seek God's best. A Christian home will be different from the world's homes. Is yours a Christian home?

June 1999

Dads–Are You the Head of a Christian Home? (Part Three) – Jesus Must Be Lord –

Is your home a Christian home? Do you desire to raise godly children? If so, why and how important is it to you? Would we say that it is the burning desire of our hearts? If someone were to ask you what God's primary purpose for marriage is, what would you tell him? I believe how we answer these questions is key to whether we have a Christian home or not.

"And did not he make one? Yet had he the residue of the spirit. And wherefore one? That he might seek a godly seed. Therefore take heed to your spirit, and let none deal treacherously against the wife of his youth" (Malachi 2:15). We read in Malachi that God's purpose for marriage was to raise up godly seed, which means children who will bring God honor and glory. So raising godly children is not just a good idea, not just a popular discussion topic at home-school meetings, not just for the pastor or elders, but it is what God intends to be fruit from every marriage. A Christian home is the necessary environment for such precious fruit.

Last month we saw that when the idols of the world invaded God's home, the temple, it was no longer a place where His Spirit would dwell. We applied that figuratively to our homes. The next reasonable question is, when does God's Spirit dwell in our homes? 1 Corinthians 3:11 tells us, "For other foundation can no man lay than that is laid, which is Jesus Christ." And then in verse 16 we read, "Know ye not that ye are the temple of God, and *that* the Spirit of God dwelleth in you?" Jesus Christ is to live in us and to be the foundation for our homes. This is not a matter of simple preference or religious practice. This is the question for fathers to answer: "Is Jesus Christ my Savior and the Lord of my life?" Jesus Christ is the foundation of our life and our home.

We can't expect godly offspring if we aren't a child of God ourselves. Becoming a child of God happens when we repent of our sins and place our trust in Christ's shedding of His blood for the remission of our sins. That takes care of the first part. Unfortunately, many never go beyond and make Christ the Lord of their life. That is often where idols enter. If Jesus Christ isn't Lord of a man's life, the man himself will reign over his life. When we are reigning on the throne of our heart, we will fill our life with the "things/idols" of this world. The love for our Lord will not be there.

Our focus, our joy, and our passion is to be the Lord Jesus. "Whether therefore ye eat, or drink, or whatsoever ye do, do all to the glory of God. Give none offence, neither to the Jews, nor to the Gentiles, nor to the church of God: Even as I please all *men* in all *things*, not seeking mine own profit, but the *profit* of many, that they may be saved" (1 Corinthians 10:31-33). Then in 1 Corinthians 11:1, "Be ye followers of me, even as I also *am* of Christ." Also, read in Colossians 3:17, "And whatsoever ye do in word or deed, *do* all in the name of the Lord Jesus, giving thanks to God and the Father by him."

This is a perfect picture of our homes built on the foundation of Jesus Christ, and we, as fathers, walking as our Lord Jesus did. This is not talking about outward religious conformity, but a man deeply in love with his Lord and seeking to please Him in every way. It becomes clear that selling out to his Lord is not for the cowardly. It takes a real man!

However, some might say, "Why try? That is impossible. Jesus was perfect, and I'm far from perfect." Yes, that is true, Jesus was perfect, but He lived His life in submission to the Father. I marvel that even though Jesus is God, He chose to do only what the Father told Him to do or say. ". . . The Son can do nothing of himself, but what he seeth the Father do: for what things soever he doeth, these also doeth the Son likewise" (John 5:19). Then in John 12:49, "For I have not spoken of myself; but the Father which sent me, he gave me a commandment, what I should say, and what I should speak." Jesus gave us the perfect example of Lordship–surrendering one's will.

Men, we can't lead our family until we learn to follow our Lord. We have no hope of a Christian home, and resulting godly off-spring, unless Jesus Christ dwells in us and is our foundation. He must be our Lord in practice, not just speech. We should seek the best always, and never settle for anything less. When we choose anything but God's best for our family, we are leading our family astray. Christ chose to follow the Father's every decision. May we choose what Christ says is best for our family. May we be men of God and provide our children with a Christian home.

P.S. One additional thought. In Malachi 2:15-16 we read, "And did not he make one? Yet had he the residue of the spirit. And wherefore one? That he might seek a godly seed. Therefore take heed to your spirit, and let none deal treacherously against the wife of his youth. For the LORD, the God of Israel, saith that he hateth putting away: for *one* covereth violence with his garment, saith the LORD of hosts: therefore take heed to your spirit, that ye deal not treacherously." Note in particular where God warns men about divorce. It is a very stern warning about breaking the covenant we made with our wives. God holds us accountable for how we treat our wives. Admittedly these men were divorcing their wives, but we are held to a much higher standard. We are to treat our wives as Christ treated the church. He died for her.

July 1999

Dads—Are You the Head of a Christian Home? (Part Four)

I am amazed at all of the fantastic, fun things there are on this earth for our pleasure. I loved the challenge and sensations of flying small planes. I loved the wind and salt spray in my face as I would tack a small sailboat into the wind. I loved the rush of acceleration and breeze as the motorcycle gained speed on the highway. I loved canoeing down a spring rain-swollen stream with the sound of rushing water in my ears. It has been many years since I enjoyed those activities, because I know how easily my heart is drawn into them. Are any of those things sin? Most would say, "No, of course not! God gave us this world to enjoy."

Am I saying that these things are bad? No, they are not inherently bad. I know many missionaries rely on small planes for supplies and might use canoes or motorcycles in their travels. However, they are not good if they are getting in the way of something better the Lord has to offer. You see, I know my own heart, how easily it is distracted from my Lord Jesus and what He has called me to do. Fun activities of self-indulgence get in the way of raising godly children and serving our Lord by stealing away the time God would want me to use for His work. So, what is the point of all of this?

As we continue our discussion on God's blueprint for a Christian home, we see another aspect of God's earthly home, the temple; it was a place of sacrifice. It was where a vivid picture of our Lord Jesus' final sacrifice was presented repeatedly before the eyes of those present. I say final because His life was a sacrifice day by day and ended with the greatest sacrifice on the cross. The priests were involved in the bloody, messy work of daily sacrificing in the temple. Have you ever wondered why God chose to make blood red? He could have made it so that it didn't stain the clothes of those involved in the sacrifice. However, because it was red, everyone knew who was involved in the sacrifice.

I see a wonderful picture for us dads in all of this. The Lord Jesus calls dads of Christian homes to a life of sacrifice. There are so many wonderfully fun things in this world to spend our time, attention, and money on. However, if we do, we can be sure we will create the same passions in the lives of our children. So, instead of raising children with a zeal for the Lord Jesus and serving Him with their whole heart, body, soul, and strength, we will have produced children with a love for the fun and entertaining things of this world. On the other hand, when our desire is to sacrifice our lives for our Lord, we demonstrate the spirit of God's design for the father of a Christian home, and thereby reproduce children of like mind and heart.

God gives us good gifts so we can give them back to Him. Our family, our time, and our money are all to be laid on the altar for His glory. I desire to lay it all down before my Lord. I truly want God's best for my life. I know that if I give it back to Him, He will make the best of it. If I give Him my right to recreation and having "time for myself," I know that He will pour out such blessings as I cannot imagine. I look at the lives of true men of God such as Hudson Taylor and George Mueller. They wanted God's best and abandoned their own interests. I see them as men filled with joy and a passion for their Lord.

Sadly, I believe that is what makes the distinction between a Christian home and one of the world's. A worldly home is where the father has his attention on the fun things the world has to offer because he knows he has to "get all the gusto" he can now. The attitude that we can do whatever we want as long as we don't "cross the line of sin" is wrong. The father of a Christian home is working here now, with the anticipation of eternity with his Lord.

Jesus did and said only what His Father told Him to. ". . . The Son can do nothing of himself, but what he seeth the Father do: for what things soever he doeth, these also doeth the Son likewise" (John 5:19). As we read about Jesus' life, we see no mention of His having His own time for fun. His was a life of sacrifice!

I'm humbled when I look at my Lord's life and feel that I'm still holding on to so much of my own pleasures. I pray God would continue to work in my life as He reveals the joy of sacrifice. May we dads never settle for anything less than God's best.

August 1999

Dads—Are You the Head of a Christian Home? (Part Five)

It is much better to ask ourselves this question now than when our children are years older and set in their ways. There are many aspects of a true Christian home that we have "discussed" for several months now. Something important to remember is that these are merely outward evidences of the fact that Jesus Christ is indwelling, and the Lord of Dad's and Mom's hearts. It is not enough to just demonstrate these outward characteristics. It all must begin with a changed heart when Jesus Christ comes into our lives.

Most of us would agree that one of the major reasons we homeschool our children is to raise up godly seed. "And did not he make one? Yet had he the residue of the spirit. And wherefore one? That he might seek a godly seed" (Malachi 2:15).

We expend much effort in setting the right example, and in consistent training, in our desire to teach children to be ambassadors of Christ. A great danger, though, is that the focus often tends toward outward exhibition of Christ-like character. If we dress them up and they act right, we have succeeded, right? Wrong! We know that God looks on the heart and man looks on the outer appearance. We don't want to neglect the former because it truly is our hearts that God desires. "But the LORD said unto Samuel, Look not on his countenance, or on the height of his stature; because I have refused him: *for the LORD seeth* not as man seeth; for man looketh on the outward appearance, but the LORD looketh on the heart" (1 Samuel 16:7).

It is interesting to listen to preaching on child training on the radio. Some would indicate godly character is caught and not taught. Others suggest it is the technique we use to train our children that produces the results. Yes, those two aspects are important, but probably the most critical aspect of raising children is often overlooked. I like to refer to the three aspects of raising children as the legs on a three-legged stool. Each one is dependent on the other two. But which leg of a three-legged stool is the most important? Obviously, it is whichever one is missing.

The first leg is the righteous, set apart, God loving/fearing lives of the parents. The second is a biblical-based, consistent approach to parenting. The third is faithful, fervent, intercessory prayer, asking a holy, righteous God to work in the hearts of the children as they grow. "Create in me a clean heart, O God; and renew a right spirit within me" (Psalms 51:10). "O LORD God of Abraham, Isaac, and of Israel, our fathers, keep this for ever in the imagination of the thoughts of the heart of thy people, and prepare their heart unto thee: And give unto Solomon my son a perfect heart, to keep thy commandments, thy testimonies, and thy statutes, and to do all *these things . . .*" (1 Chronicles 29:18-19). You see, it is God who works in the hearts of men, and we must cry out to Him to work in our children's hearts.

I admit that prayer is the easiest for me to omit, and that reveals an area of character weakness in my life. It is pride that leads us to believe that, if we are a good enough example and train our children properly, they will become mighty men and women of God. I strongly believe that is why so many fail. The children look and act good, but their hearts really haven't been changed. The same pride in the parent's lives has reproduced itself into the life of the child. Our prayer for God to work in our children's hearts is that hidden labor that only an omniscient God sees and hears. To the rest of the world, we may appear to have a wonderful Christian home, raising wonderful Christians. However, if the children eventually rebel or, just as bad, come to love the world and are effectively neutered as Christians, we see the real outcome of children raised without intercessory prayer.

Yes, God's temple was a place of prayer. Jesus said that His Father's house was to be called a "House of prayer." In the same way, if we would say a "house of brick" or a "house of wood" or a "house of straw," this implies what the house is built from. Are our homes built on prayer? Christian homes are. Is prayer such an integral part of our lives that we are pleading with our Lord about every aspect of raising our children? If we aren't, sadly, it reveals the pride in our lives: "We can do it without God." We may not think that, but when something is manifested in our actions it indicates the hidden core belief.

Dads, may we honestly evaluate whether or not our homes are homes of prayer–Christian homes.

September 1999

Dads–Are You the Head of a Christian Home? (Part Six)

A bright, blue Saturday a couple months ago as Nathan, Christopher, Joseph, John, and I were leaving City Union Mission, we saw a B-2 bomber making a thundering fly-by. We realized it was the weekend for the Kansas City air show. We had been told the air show had some incredible aircraft on display, and every male in my family would have loved the chance to look over the airplanes.

Unfortunately, the air shows around here always play loud rock music. We will not go to them since I have purposed that I will not trade a few minutes of aircraft excitement for the filling of our souls with the wicked audio influence of our world. On the way home, we decided we would ask a neighbor to record the portion about the air show from the 6 o'clock news. We did this, and there was no little excitement when the videotape arrived later that evening.

I put the tape in the VCR, and hit "play" to an excited crowd of young ones. Before I could get to where I could see, Sarah, who had just entered, exclaimed that the little ones needed to look away quickly. To my incredible disappointment, indignation, and mounting feeling of violation, there was a preview of some TV show with ladies in underwear, right before the 6 o'clock news began.

". . . for what fellowship hath righteousness with unrighteousness? and what communion hath light with darkness?" (2

Corinthians 6:14). A Christian home is a home where the things that are acceptable to the world are not present. It is a place of purity. It is wholesome. It is not defrauding. It does not entice lust. Is it any wonder that "Christian" youth, who have watched TV all of their lives, are as involved in immorality as the youth of the world?

In Acts, chapter 21, when the Jews thought that Paul had defiled the temple by bringing Greeks into it, they closed the temple doors. "And all the city was moved, and the people ran together: and they took Paul, and drew him out of the temple: and forthwith the doors were shut" (Acts 21:30). God's home on earth, the temple, was to be pure, and the things that defile it were to be shut out. They pulled Paul out of the temple, and the doors were slammed shut!

Dads, are we owning this responsibility? Do we zealously guard the purity of our children and ourselves? Homeschooling our children is a worthy accomplishment, but if their souls are drawn away, what really have we gained?

Often I have heard the statement, "We are careful what we allow our family to watch." Simply in light of the six o'clock news, how many believe that is even possible? Please, don't receive this as judgmental; receive it as one brother pleading with another. There have been times when a brother loved my soul and encouraged me in some positive way that challenged me. If you watch any TV at all, would you receive this encouragement from me? Our every activity should be at the direction of the Lord Jesus. Have you asked Him?

Truly, the heart is full of every evil imagination and is the source of evil, but Satan uses vehicles like TV to stir it up. Why would any father ever hand Satan the tools to destroy the purity and innocence of his children, not to mention temptations for the father himself? David said, "I will set no wicked thing before mine eyes: I hate the work of them that turn aside; *it* shall not cleave to me" (Psalms 101:3). Why would a father allow glamorous people into his home selling and promoting (selling through commercials and promoting through unwholesome programs) lewd dress, alcohol, immorality, squandering of time, and a godless worldview?

It was David's lack of control over his eyes that led to the downfall of his family. Men, I see that happen in many "Christian" homes as well; don't let it happen to yours. Like our Shepherd, the Lord Jesus, Who guards His flock, the church, we are to protect our family from evil. "Then said Jesus unto them again, Verily, verily, I say unto you, I am the door of the sheep" (John 10:7). The shepherd was prepared to give his life for the sheep to protect them–are we?

Certainly, many, many other areas require our diligence as well. However, may I encourage you that cutting off the TV is a great place to start. May we all agree with Paul when he said, ". . . I would have you wise unto that which is good, and simple concerning evil" (Romans 16:19). It is not God's way to teach both the good and evil. God's way is for us all to be innocent concerning evil.

As I pointed out earlier, the temple doors were to shut out evil, and we are the "door" that shuts out evil to our home. However, it isn't enough to shut out the darkness. If that is all we have done, it still is dark inside. It is only when we bring in the blessed light of Jesus Christ that we have light. Just as He was the focus in God's home on earth, may the focus in our homes be Jesus Christ, not the TV. My heart breaks at the image of families huddled around the TV in the evenings. Even if there were no evil, what a waste of precious time it is. Again, dads, are we the head of a Christian home?

October 1999

Dads—Are You the Head of a Christian Home? (Part Seven)

"And Noah builded an altar unto the LORD; and took of every clean beast, and of every clean fowl, and offered burnt offerings on the altar. And the LORD smelled a sweet savour; and the LORD said in his heart, I will not again curse the ground any more for man's sake; for the imagination of man's heart *is* evil from his youth; neither will I again smite any more every thing living, as I have done . . . And God blessed Noah and his sons, and said unto them, Be fruitful, and multiply, and replenish the earth. . ." (Genesis 8:20-21, 9:1). Following Noah's exit from the ark, while his family watched, he immediately was led to offer up the first burnt offering recorded in Scripture. God's response was one of compassion, mercy, and blessing.

Dads, do we want to intimately know and commune with the holy, righteous, living God Almighty? Do we love Jesus? Do we want God's blessing on our lives and families? Here is a test to see if our answer is from our heart (a committed way of life) or our head (the way we know it should be, but we don't live it).

What has it taken in the past for us to neglect our personal and family devotions? If the answer was from our heart, it would have taken a crisis, but if it was from the head, it hasn't taken much. Also worth noting, some will confuse the consequences of not having devotions as the crisis causing them to be missed.

Of course we don't have a real "altar" in our home as found in the Old Testament. The altar was the place to meet with and get right with the Lord. It was where sin was dealt with. It was a place of repentance and sacrifice. It was also where Abraham proved that God was first in his life. Just how easy is it for you and me to make something else a higher priority than meeting with our Lord?

This time with the Lord is not an outward religious act of seeking to appease an angry God. Rather, it is a time of meeting and of laying hearts bare before the Living Word. It is an opportunity to "present your bodies a living sacrifice, holy, acceptable unto God" (Romans 12:1). How can I say I love my Lord and want Him to vibrantly live through me, if I don't cherish time with Him? Wouldn't you question my sincerity if I claimed to be a Christian and yet didn't love to spend time with the One I say is my Lord? Wouldn't you doubt that I had a Christian home if I were not daily bringing my family before the "altar" of the Lord to examine Scripture together?

We read in Leviticus 6:12-13 that the altar fire was never to go out. Someone had to cut and carry the wood, then place it on the fire before it went out. It took effort and diligence. One could not wait until he felt like checking on the fire or for a convenient time, but he had to devote willful, constant attention. I see that as a perfect picture that the cleansing, purifying work of the altar is to be a continual process in our lives. It will take diligence on our part to make sure it happens. As my heart is exposed to God's Word each morning, He convicts me of my sin. I'm able to confess it and repent of it. Praise God that He is faithful to forgive us of our sins when we ask.

Some time ago, I had deceived myself in misplacing priorities. I was consistently working so late on Saturday nights that I did not get up on Sunday mornings early enough to have time with my

Lord Jesus. At church one Sunday, a dear brother, who seldom has much "fluff" to say, told me what a glorious time he had during his quiet time that morning. He mentioned his magnificent time of confession and worship in preparation for worship at church. He shared how his Sunday morning quiet time was consistently the best of the week. God used that dear brother to convict me of my wrong priorities. I had believed the lie that my personal devotion time was not all that important prior to church, since I was going to worship anyway.

Also note in Exodus 40:29 that the altar was near the entrance to the tabernacle. The acknowledgement, confession, repentance, and restitution for sin had to occur before one could enter the temple and worship God. Even though I meet with another brother and pray prior to church, it isn't the same as special private time alone with my God while the home is still quiet. My time of corporate worship is much more special when I adequately prepare my heart.

I will also confess that having a Saturday morning quiet time is a constant challenge for me. Since my routine is different every Saturday, it takes extra effort to make sure I have allowed time to meet with my Lord. However, once God convicted me that it was my pride that caused me not to make time with Him the highest priority, I have been able to be consistent in meeting with Him.

Most dads are busy, but if that were used as an excuse to neglect time with our wives, it would lead to an unhealthy relationship. In the same way, if we neglect time with our children, they will quickly seek love and acceptance from others. Truly, how we spend our time reflects our priorities.

If we slight our time with the Lord Jesus, individually or as a family, it reveals the most serious character problem we could have—our pride. It shows whom, deep down in our soul, we are really depending on. If we truly believe God is responsible for every aspect of our lives, we would seek to spend time with Him. We would want to get direction from Him, to lay out the problems we are encountering before Almighty God. Some will wait until they are in the middle of a crisis to call on the Lord, after they have been neglecting Him. He desires to lead us, as His flock, to places of pasture and away from danger.

Frequently, while I'm speaking with a brother, he acknowledges struggles in his Christian walk and does not know God's direction. I will ask if he is having daily personal and family devotions. I'm never surprised to learn he is not having a quiet time with the Lord in the morning. We cannot have fellowship with God, know His direction for us, and bypass the "altar."

May we be zealous for loving, serving, and spending time with the Lord Jesus. May we be the heads of Christian homes.

November 1999

Dads—Are You the Head of a Christian Home? (Part Eight)

What if a dad wants desperately to have personal and family devotions, but does not know where to begin? Since there are few things more important than this in a Christian home, it warrants making the subject as practical as possible.

Due to the critical nature of consistent, quality devotions, I recommend that a dad find another man to hold him accountable if he has difficulty in having a daily, quality time with the Lord. First, pray about whom God would have you ask. He should be someone who cares about your soul and would take the request for an accountability partner very seriously. It can be discouraging to have someone agree to help and then stop asking how you are doing. I suggest that you not ask your wife. This arrangement may work occasionally, but I believe it is more likely to not be successful.

It might be good if your accountability partner would ask you the following questions each week:

How many days did you have devotions last week?

How long were they?

Where are you reading?

Did God reveal any new truths?

Did God show any areas of struggle that I could pray for you on?

JUST AROUND THE CORNER

I suggest that you don't try to do anything else while you have your devotion, such as exercising, driving, or bathing. Would you be pleased if on a date with your wife, she spent her time reading a book? There have been times when I was late for an early morning appointment and decided to have my prayer time in the car, while driving. I can assure you that driving and praying may allow one to check off prayer time technically, but it is not the way to build a relationship! Should we ever give the Lord less than our best?

Here are some suggestions for implementing a personal time with the Lord:

Have a set time each day. The days you are off work may require a different time, but pick one that will work for each day.

Find someplace where you can be alone. Remember this is time for just you and the Lord.

May I encourage you not to use some of the little devotional booklets that are someone else's thoughts, a touching story, and a few verses. Rather, make it just you, your Lord, and His Word.

Concentrate on the application of His Word to your life. Ask yourself how you can apply to your life what you are reading. Learn from the mistakes made by people in the Bible. God recorded those events for our teaching.

Ask yourself many questions about the passage. Why did he do that? What should he have done? What priorities are shown in this person's life? Did he seek God's direction before making this decision? What are the consequences encountered in a wrong choice? And so on.

Don't try to tackle difficult sections until God leads. Read the four Gospels, Joshua, Judges, 1 and 2 Samuel, and 1 and 2 Kings.

Many of these same points are applicable for family devotion. Have no distractions, a set time, accountability, and the Bible as the source. Ask tons of questions of the family and don't worry about having the answers beforehand. One of the most exciting things I do is to ask the family a very difficult question about a passage. I may have wondered about this question for a long time and then have it answered by one of the children, or by God. God gives new insight on the spot! I could not begin to tell you of all the incredible things God has revealed to us during our family altar time. Other books are fine for additional reading, but this is a time to be focused on God and His Word.

It is okay to feel weak and inadequate. God will give His grace and enable you to lead your family. Your children will respect you, and your wife will be thrilled. I have yet to meet a Christian mom who did not yearn to have her husband be the spiritual leader of the home. Dads, do we truly desire to be the head of a Christian home?

December 1999

In Pursuit of Those Things That Matter

As usual, we have received the yearly missives from family and friends across the country. One dear woman handwrites her multiple-page letter to us, and it is a celebration of life in a family serving the Lord Jesus. Others, like ours, are mass produced and get the message out to a large number quite effectively.

As a letter is read, the family is presented through the eyes of the writer, usually Mom or Dad. The family's events and accomplishments of the previous year that are considered important to the parents are condensed down to a page or two. So in just a couple of minutes of reading, we are updated on the noteworthy accomplishments of a family.

However, I'm grieved by most of the letters we receive from Christian families. What is being shared generally shows such a worldly focus in the homes. There is mostly entertainment and trivial pursuits, versus serving and life preparation, that rule. Is the Lord's bride in love with Him or the world? Sadly, the proof is on the paper.

Certainly, these letters reveal the hearts of dads. Let's "talk" Christian "man to man" for a little bit as we reflect back on this year and look forward to a new millennium. The return of our Lord Jesus draws closer each day. Will He find us busy? If so, busy doing what?

Will the Lord Jesus say to us, ". . . Well done, *thou* good and faithful servant: thou hast been faithful over a few things, I will make thee ruler over many things: enter thou into the joy of thy lord" (Matthew 25:21). After reading the majority of the letters we received, I wonder whether it really won't be, ". . . *Thou* wicked and slothful servant. . ." (Matthew 25:26).

How can a family know whether they are spending their time harvesting chaff or spending their time as the Lord desires? As usual, it begins with the father's daily, personal, quiet time with the Lord Jesus. Dad must be "plugged into" the Vine if there is to be a chance of knowing what God wants his family to do. It may even be something that is good, but if the Lord hasn't told us to do it, we must not.

Next, don't seek a ministry, but seek Jesus. Frankly, it may be that the dad and mom with young children do little, if any, "ministry" by themselves outside the home. I've seen churches so hungry for male leadership they will take a father away from the home when the mother desperately needs him. There are seasons in life, and raising little ones may demand the full attention of Mom and Dad for several years. That is how the family strengthens their testimony for future years. Later, when they have succeeded in raising up godly children, the seeds and credentials for a strong ministry have been planted.

Dads, we must understand that a "need" is not a call. Only when the Lord clearly says, "Go!" and it does not impede our responsibilities, should we do it. It may be that the Lord has someone else He wants to fill the position (or if it is unprofitable, He doesn't want it filled at all), and it really wasn't for us. So if you have little children and are asked to do something that requires even an hour away from your family (few things ever really take only an hour anyway), and you can't take your children with you each time, then this might not be the time to say "yes."

A few years back, a friend greatly surprised me by nominating me for a statewide position I should never have accepted. I had a lot of interest in helping the "cause," but it really wasn't the season for me. After limping along under the conviction it wasn't God's will, I finally had to resign. So the need, a friend's counsel, and a hurried prayer led to a wrong action. Something that required my time should have had serious prayer. Since my decision to agree to the nomination was needed right then and time would not allow for sufficient prayer time, it was clearly not God's will for me.

Last evening I heard a radio interview with a retired Navy Blue Angels pilot. He said he felt it was a wonderful career opportunity to show that a Christian could do the job. However, he went on to say he had really struggled with the conviction that he should be home with his children instead of traveling three hundred days a year. I had to turn the radio off! Why wasn't he man enough to quit and do what God had called him to do first?

The pressing need of our day is for fathers to turn their hearts to their children. Even those of us who think we are involved in our children's lives need to constantly be on guard to be sure we are looking to their hearts. Taking children to Boy Scouts, T-Ball, and soccer is not turning our hearts to our children. These may be enter-taining and fun, but they have little, if any, eternal benefit. Do we want to raise up men and women of God, or worldly, pleasure-seek-ing children who never mature? Even if some may argue the above is not chaff, no one should argue that if we are not doing what Jesus wants us to do, it is chaff. That is all that matters.

Most of those letters were such an indictment of the modern "Christian" family. Dads, may we hold each other accountable. May we challenge and exhort each other to good works. Are you willing to pour out your life for your family and your Lord, to cherish your wife and delight in her, to count every activity and commitment as chaff unless the Lord directs you to do it?

I would challenge every one of us in this matter. Why not, as husband and wife, agree to eliminate EVERY activity and pursuit? (This includes TV, books, sports, clubs, etc.) Now, prayerfully add back in only those that the Lord clearly says He wants the family and individual to be involved with. Don't add it back until you can look your wife in the eye and say, "God has told me that we are to do this." May our Lord welcome us with, "Well done my good and faithful servant," on His return.

January 2000

Modesty

A while ago, we had a Christian family over for dinner. It had been a most enjoyable evening. After dinner, we gathered in the living room to sing and listen to Christopher play a few hymns on the piano. I was sitting on the floor by the fireplace, looking across the room to the hallway opening, where the piano was located. The wife of the other family was sitting on the edge of the loveseat, putting her almost directly in my line of sight to see Christopher.

She was rather conservatively dressed except for a loose fitting top with a medium neckline. She was sitting with her baby on her lap, and then she bent over to set the child on the floor in front of her. She was now directly in my line of sight. As she set the child down, she looked across at me. To my horror her top hung open, and it could have appeared to her I was inappropriately looking at her. I immediately closed my eyes and turned away, but I was never so humbled in all my life. I honestly could have wept right there.

After the fall, Adam and Eve immediately were aware that their nakedness was to be covered. "And the eyes of them both were opened, and they knew that they *were* naked; and they sewed fig leaves together, and made themselves aprons" (Genesis 3:7). Adam and Eve had been in close fellowship with God, and even though they had just disobeyed Him, they knew they needed to cover their nakedness. Think about it. There was no one else around other than their God Who created them, and they still felt shame and the need to cover up.

Why don't many Christians feel shame and grasp the need to be modest in dress? Why is it that all seem to have a different idea of what is an acceptable level of dress (or undress)? What influences a person to come to the opinion they have about it? How can someone decide? Who is right? Does anyone have the right to say that someone else's clothing is inappropriate or immodest? Why do some consider it "okay" to wear a revealing swimming suit to the lake or pool, but not to church? Everyone draws the line of modesty somewhere, but why do some draw it where they do? One thing I'm confident of, few if any of those who choose to dress immodestly have ever earnestly sought the Lord for His will in the matter.

Some churches have dress standards that are more or less enforced, whether overtly or through subtle pressure. Forget all of that. I encourage dads to put away all outside factors as you consider the subject of modesty.

Dad, what is your role in this, or is it a personal matter for you and your wife to decide separately? What Scripture would you base your answer on? Unfortunately, my experience has been that the more immersed a family is in the world, the more their values will reflect the world's. If they have a frequent diet of TV, even with the more acceptable shows, the family will still be sitting there for commercials. Fifteen years ago the Diet Coke and yogurt commercials would display scantily clothed women's figures to sell their product. I only shudder to think how things are advertised today.

A frequent exposure to this type of visual conscience-searing will affect how a couple views what is modest. Also, the amount of time spent in God's Word will have a great effect on one's attitude about modesty. What Scripture would a husband use in reference to this whole issue?

What does God say is appropriate? How does He want us to dress? Is there a different set of modesty standards for going to church, shopping, the beach, and elsewhere? Before the fall, there was no shame, but after the fall, the response was shame regarding nakedness. Note, Adam and Eve weren't naked by today's standards; in fact, I expect they would have been considered clothed. Remember, they had sewn fig leaf aprons to cover themselves. However, in Genesis 3:10, Adam said he hid because he was naked. God must have agreed that Adam was naked, because God killed animals and made coats to cover them. The Hebrew word used for coats means to cover. This would appear to be a large covering for their nakedness since Adam's fig leaf apron was insufficient in God's sight. It is possible that the aprons were even more of a covering than many swimsuits worn by Christians today.

The husband is responsible before God for his wife and for her purity. "For the husband is the head of the wife, even as Christ is the head of the church: and he is the saviour of the body. Therefore as the church is subject unto Christ, so *let* the wives *be* to their own husbands in every thing. Husbands, love your wives, even as Christ also loved the church, and gave himself for it; That he might sanctify and cleanse it with the washing of water by the word, That he might present it to himself a glorious church, not having spot, or wrinkle, or any such thing; but that it should be holy and without blemish. So ought men to love their wives as their own bodies. He that loveth his wife loveth himself" (Ephesians 5:23-28). Could Scripture be plainer about the husband's role in guarding the purity of his wife?

We read in Luke 8:27 that the demoniac wore no clothes. Once the demons were cast out, he was clothed and sitting at Jesus' feet. Then in 1 Timothy 2:9 we read, "In like manner also, that women adorn themselves in modest apparel," where modest means "well arranged, seemly, and modest." Remember that the word naked was used to describe Adam and Eve after they had "covered" themselves with fig leaf aprons.

I find this topic similar to tithing. I have known people who will attempt to argue that the Bible does not command Christians to tithe, and others who will argue it does. I find the subject of Christians drinking alcohol in the same light. I believe God has given us a number of topics like these to test the heart. My question regarding these issues is, "Am I looking for the line of sin, or for how close to my Jesus I can draw?" When there is a question whose answer I'm not totally clear on, it is the desire of my heart to choose the side of holiness and the side closest to my Lord.

Have you ever seen something interesting out the side window while you were driving? The tendency is to inadvertently steer in the direction you are looking. If we keep our eyes on Christ, we will move closer to Him. If our focus is on the world, we will be drawn to it and agree with what the world deems as acceptable.

Is anyone in the family wearing clothing that is seductive, tight, revealing, and exposing? Which side do you want to err on? Your Lord's or the world's? The world wants to show as much skin and body parts as possible, whether visibly or through tight clothing. *Vine's Expository Dictionary* lists Matthew 25:36, 38, 43, 44; Acts 19:16; and James 2:15, where "naked" means "scantily, or poorly, clad." This being the case, how many churches on Sunday morning have members fitting this description?

I'm not advocating wearing black trash bags with holes cut out for the eyes. What I am pleading is for dads to be the heads of their Christian homes. Our calling as parents is to raise up godly seed (Malachi 2:15), and that is why many choose to homeschool. We are to carefully guard the purity of our wives and children. Each dad should take this issue before the Lord, and study the Bible until he knows for sure what is pleasing to his Lord. Remember, it is not a matter of what we feel is okay, but what is pleasing to our Lord Jesus. We should never try to see how close to the line of sin we can come without stepping over, but rather how close we can draw to our Lord Jesus.

May we be men of God and lead the way for our family in setting the example of modesty. After having studied the subject, dads may be convicted that not wearing a shirt or wearing cut-offs or shorts is immodest. If so, I encourage you to be strong and courageous and demonstrate to your family that you are more concerned about what God thinks about you than you are about your own personal comfort.

We need to communicate what we have learned to our family and our desire that they dress as the Lord would have them. We could help them evaluate their clothing and retire anything that is deemed unsuitable.

It blesses my heart to have my wife and daughters bring me their new clothing for my opinion. I have not mandated that they must; it is because they want their clothing to be pleasing both to the Lord Jesus and to me. I know this whole subject is a personal and sensitive issue. It is my desire that no one feels judged or condemned by this, but I pray that I may spur each dad to own this area of responsibility, to study the matter, take it before his Lord, and then to present it to his family.

February 2000

Guarding Their Hearts

It was the night of our local homeschool moms' meeting that we had decided to have in our home because of a scheduling difficulty with our normal location. I had been looking forward to taking the five little ones to Wal-Mart to enjoy a fun evening out.

After some shopping, I decided to buy the children a treat at the snack bar. All six of us were crowded into a small booth, while they enjoyed nachos and Icees. My heart was very happy as I was enjoying my little gifts from my Lord and Savior. Unfortunately, in an instant, like a light switch, my joy turned into a heavy, sad heart.

Our booth was on the edge of the nearly deserted eating area. Right next to us, a young woman of maybe seventeen years had pulled her shopping cart up and stopped. She had a wedding ring on her left hand and a baby in the cart. She had short hair, a stud piercing her right nostril, and she was somewhat unattractive. She was just staring into the snack bar area with the most sullen, sad expression I can remember seeing. Her eyes screamed of the hurt that she was experiencing. Her blank stare was periodically interrupted as her hand came to first one eye and then the next, wiping away what appeared to be tears.

When I had purchased the children's snacks, a young man had stood behind me in line buying a hot dog and soda. He was scruffy and unkempt. His clothes were mostly black, and he wore a black ball cap. The cap had caught my eye as the bill was bent so it had a ridge in the center, and was pulled down far enough that I couldn't see his eyes. All I could see was a nose, mouth, and cheeks with a two- or three-day-old beard covering them.

Now I realized that she was standing there waiting for him. "No, God, surely not!" After several minutes of silence, he got up and came out to her. There was no greeting between them, only what appeared to be a few dagger-tipped words exchanged. Then as if the two faced a meal of poison, they reluctantly walked off. It was terrible to watch.

I looked down at my two bright-eyed, happy little girls and thought, "Lord, there goes some daddy's little girl, but where is he now?" How did a father ever let this happen to his little girl?

Some might wonder if the stud protruding from her nose hinted she had a rebellious history, and if she was the one to desert her father. Certainly, children have their own wills, and we cannot force them to be godly, but as long as there is a God in heaven that answers prayers, fathers must not give up.

I love the example Jesus shares with us in John 10. "Then said Jesus unto them again, Verily, verily, I say unto you, I am the door of the sheep" (John 10:7). The shepherd used to sleep in the doorway to the sheepfold. The sheep were in there for their protection and could not walk out without the shepherd letting them go. In the same way, wolves or thieves could not enter without first having to confront the shepherd. This section is a perfect picture of a father's calling. The father is to be the shepherd of the flock that God gives him. This chapter has many wonderful encouragements for us dads.

"I am the good shepherd: the good shepherd giveth his life for the sheep" (John 10:11). Dads, are we so committed to our calling that we will give our life for our family? We are the door to our family. Our children don't go out, and others don't come into their lives unless we allow it. There are no excuses; we are responsible before the Lord in leading and protecting our family.

I don't believe this teaches the father is a dictator; otherwise, Jesus would have used some other example. A shepherd does not drive the sheep like a cowboy drives a herd of cows. The shepherd leads the sheep with love and gentleness.

With the gentleness of our Savior, we are to protect our family. We must, with great tenderness, guide them to safe pastures. If we have chosen certain goals and paths for our family, we must be on guard for those who would draw them away. Often a family is doing many things right, but then they will allow wrong influences to pull their children away. I can't tell you how many times I have seen it, and it always leads to grief unless something drastic is done.

For example, if parents have chosen to homeschool a child who is less than thrilled about it, they have to be careful of other influences that will feed and reinforce the child's dislike of the idea. It might be a close friend who is not homeschooled, a youth group, or an outside activity that prevents the child from coming to peace with the father's decision. If the bond between the father and each child is not stronger than any other outside influence, he will lose his child, or children, to that influence.

These can present very challenging situations, and it may take a tremendous amount of prayer on the father's part to know how best to resolve them. It may be the only solution is to sever an influence, but whatever the Lord reveals, it must be done. If not, the parent will lose the child.

No one can serve two masters. They will either be drawn to you or to someone/something else. Obviously, dads, we need to be sure we are following the path of God's calling. At all costs, the father must maintain that bond of love and respect with his children. Once the other influence "wins," it is then only a matter of where it pulls them.

Over the last twenty years, we have had to make three very major decisions to correct the pull of outside influences. None of these influences were "bad" in themselves, but after much prayer, it was clear that the direction was contrary to that of God's leading for our family. They had a different heart thrust and thereby were dangerous to our staying on the course and not raising up discontented hearts in the family. Since making those changes, we have not regretted them at all. Rather, we have praised God that He gave us the grace to persevere and follow through once the decision was made.

The good Shepherd is careful to lead His sheep to safe, healthy pastures, and so must we. However, what if a sheep strays anyway? Do we label that sheep as stubborn and rebellious, and let it go? A hundred times no! "How think ye? if a man have a hundred sheep, and one of them be gone astray, doth he not leave the ninety and nine, and goeth into the mountains, and seeketh that which is gone astray?" (Matthew 18:12).

I find a most interesting reaction in my heart. When I have a child who is struggling with obedience, my flesh wants to pull back from that child. I have even justified this in my mind by telling myself, "When I sin, doesn't that separate me from my Lord? My child's sin is causing a separation between him and me." That sort of rationalization will only result in my losing the child. This is a most crucial time, and it is critical we don't draw away. It is imperative that we build our relationship with the child. Just like the shepherd who has left the ninety-nine on the hills and gone after the lost one, we must as well.

Our world expects us to blame someone else for our troubles. The shepherd didn't blame it on that stubborn, rebellious sheep or perhaps a clever wolf. He knew he was responsible for the life of the sheep and would risk his life to protect it, whether it was from an external threat or the sheep's own doing. "Lord Jesus, please give us the gentle, loving, determined hearts we need to lead, love, and protect our family."

March 2000

Anger (Part One)

Mildred is probably in her seventies and has short, straight, gray hair. Her life is clearly displayed on her face as it is so often with the elderly. Her bottom lip protrudes sharply from her face as a young pouting child's often does. However, hers is fixed there due to many unhappy years. I don't believe I have ever seen her smile.

In spite of all that, I love Mildred. She has been a resident at the County Infirmary for the nine years our family has participated in a church service there on the first and third Saturdays of the month. For years, I asked Mildred if she would come to church. With lip out, she would shake her head back and forth and say, "I don't want to." I would pat her shoulder, maybe speak with her briefly, and go down the hallway.

Then, to my surprise, Mildred, one day a year or so ago, said, "Yes." I couldn't believe it, but not wanting her to change her mind I grabbed the wheelchair handles and whisked her away to the day-room. Since then she faithfully answers, "yes," and I push her down to church, patting her shoulder and talking to her all the way.

There are others I would share about as well, if we had time. By patiently expressing love and encouragement, we have seen God do a wonderful work in their lives. However, I'm convicted that I will often expend greater emotional effort and patience with these elderly friends than I do with my own children! It gets worse than that. I know that there are times when I'm more patient with our golden retriever than with the children! Truly, that is something I have pondered and am not very proud of.

Anger has to be the most damaging emotion a father can pour out on his children, whether I raise my voice or simply have an irritated tone. I know that, and yet I still will choose to let myself get angry. It really is a choice. If we say it isn't, we are lying to ourselves. A good test is if our children do something wrong when someone we want to impress is present (perhaps at church), versus when we are at home by ourselves. Do we respond in the same way? I know I frequently don't. But unless I want to damage my relationship with my children, anger cannot be allowed.

To begin to overcome anger, I have to first acknowledge that my anger is wrong and simply a matter of choice. I will not control my temper unless I see it first as sin. "But I say unto you, That whosoever is angry with his brother without a cause shall be in danger of the judgment. . ." (Matthew 5:22). It is clear that 99.9999% of our anger is sin. I know some will say that Jesus was angry, and the above verse referred to a "cause." However, I believe that seldom, if ever, do we dads really have a just cause that Christ would agree with. I'm not referring to larger issues such as abortion, but matters of the home. Jesus' anger was righteous anger, and I expect if we critically evaluated why we were angry at home we would see it is sin.

Perhaps I will get angry because the child did not obey me. That is pride. It is not out of concern that my child has broken God's command for him or her to obey me. I want the child to obey me. Simple. If one child hurts another, and I am angry, is my anger because they sinned against God by not showing brotherly love? No. My anger would be due to my desire for peace in the home and it has been disturbed. Yes, it is possible that it could be righteous anger but ever so unlikely. We would be far better off to allow the Lord Jesus to be the One to demonstrate righteous anger.

"Be ye angry, and sin not: let not the sun go down upon your wrath" (Ephesians 4:26). Even if it was righteous anger, the question is whether I will sin or not when I'm angry. We would not be commanded in Scripture to "sin not" if we couldn't control it. I believe that even when I have an irritated tone in my voice, that is sin. I'm not being loving and patient, and God has called me to serve my family, not my own selfish pleasures.

Last weekend our family was returning from Teri's grandmother's funeral in Iowa, and I had a wonderful opportunity to be kind and patient. The children had had no naps for two days previously, and it was their naptime. They were all quite tired, and soon the situation was definitely not Christ-like. Complaining, crying, and other less admirable activities were taking place in the back of the van.

I was content to drive and did not want to have to pull off the side of the road to deal with it. It was laziness on my part, and as a result, I became angry. After a while, I was tired and wanted Nathan to drive while I got some rest. An amazing thing happened! As soon as I was in the back with the children, they settled down and there were no more problems. Had I been willing to stop earlier when it was needful, it would have been a far more pleasant trip, and I would not have gotten angry.

We have worked hard to teach our children proper table etiquette, but that had become a real source of frustration and anger for me. This may sound stupid to you, but it is true. I had one child in particular who would not chew with his lips together and others who would either eat with their elbows on the table or not sit up nicely. I would remind them and remind them, and eventually I would get angry. You can imagine that did not make for pleasant meals. God is so gracious though. When we desire to please Him and if we cry out for wisdom, He is faithful in answering our prayers.

I asked the Lord to help me train them without getting angry. The idea came to me that if a child is demonstrating poor manners I could catch their attention and then raise my pointer finger indicating the first mark. If I see another problem with the same child, I will raise two fingers indicating two marks. If I see a third occurrence, they are excused from the meal. I have found this very freeing. I have a way of communicating the problem without getting angry, and there are consequences that the children will work hard to avoid. Seldom has anyone had to be excused from the table, and I now have children who are striving to demonstrate proper manners. The best part of it is I don't get angry any longer over training the children at the table.

I have found that if I confess my anger as sin, repent of it, and cry out to the Lord for ways to avoid it, He will meet me at my point of need. Anger and love will not coexist. I have to be willing to die to my own agenda to get a grip on anger. I know that I cannot go wrong by grieving and repenting over every occurrence of it. May we be men of God and turn our hearts to our children by choosing not to get angry. Christ will be glorified and our children will flourish in our love.

April 2000

Anger (Part Two)

Last month I shared how I have struggled with anger. Not fits of rage, yelling, or other demonstrations of anger usually considered forbidden for Christians, but at times a spirit of irritation was heard in my voice.

How I hate that tone. I had heard it for most of my childhood years, and now, as a parent, I had the same irritated tone. If something displeased me, I would have an edge on my voice that my family knew all too well.

Have you noticed that certain levels of anger seem to be acceptable in the church? Nearly any Sunday you can observe a parent "communicating" with their child. The face is tight, and the eyes are boring holes in the child. Even if you can't hear the threatening tone, it is obvious the parent is not happy and is doing their best to evoke a change in the child's behavior.

However, if a parent were to raise their voice at the child, it would generally be frowned upon, and others would feel they had "crossed the line." That characterizes my experience with anger. As long as I avoided raising my voice, I could accept my response and not feel the need to confess it.

Last month after my Dad's Corner, we received an e-mail from someone who said they had struggled with anger and that a tape by Dr. S. M. Davis called "Freedom from the Spirit of Anger" had really helped them. We had listened to another tape by Pastor Davis on anger, and it was excellent. Since we had heard the one, I felt no urgency in ordering a tape and listening to it. After all, I didn't have a problem with anger, just an irritated tone.

The next week Teri and I were in Peoria, Illinois, giving workshops at the APACHE homeschool conference. Pastor Davis was also giving some workshops at the conference and had a table with audio and videotapes. It was wonderful; I was able to visit with him and purchase a number of tapes.

Soon after Teri and I arrived home, I popped the cassette called "Freedom from the Spirit of Anger" into the player. Within fifteen minutes, God had broken my heart and convicted me that my "tone" was really a spirit of anger, and I knew it had to be dealt with. To my relief, Pastor Davis shared, during the remainder of the tape, how I could have victory . Isn't the Lord Jesus so merciful? He will deal with sin in my life if I let Him. I have been rejoicing over finally having some relief from my spirit of anger. It is such a new experience for me. When something has been a way of life for years, a period of adjustment is necessary to overcome it. First, I've found that there are times when I am not aware of it. Then there are times when I'm correcting a child, and I'm not even sure how to speak to them. I feel like a child having to learn new behavior, but it is wonderful.

Today as I was pulling the van out of the garage, I had an opportunity to respond peacefully. Without thinking, one of the children picked up the garage door opener (yes, the opener is actually a closer as well) and pushed the button before we were all the way out of the garage. We managed to clear the door in time before it came down on the van, but it was close. Then, I began hearing a torrid of reasons why it wasn't her fault. What makes it worse is, I have told the children never to pick the opener up while we are in the garage. I was trying to get her to stop and listen to me when I heard an angry tone in my voice. As soon as I recognized it, God gave me peace. I was able to calmly explain again, they are not to touch the "closer." Later, she told her mother she thought I was really going to be angry and was surprised to find I wasn't. Isn't God good?

Unfortunately, I realize I have quite a long road ahead as I will have daily opportunities to yield my anger to the Lord. If He wants to get angry over something, then that is His business.

What about you? Have you been a "good Christian father" and attempted to control the angry outbursts and throttled your anger back to angry tones and searing looks? Praise God there is hope in the Lord Jesus. I will not attempt to share here what dear Brother Davis has done so powerfully. Maybe I am the only one on the Corner list who has struggled with this. If not, you may be interested in knowing how to obtain a copy of the audio.

To order your copy, you may go to www.SolveFamilyProblems.com (Dr. Davis' site), or www.Titus2.com, or call 913-772-0392.

My spirit of anger had infected our family just as any father's spirit of anger will infect his family. If a spirit of anger is a problem in your life, you might give them a call. May God bless and enable us to be the gentle, meek fathers He desires us to be.

May 2000

The Shepherd Was Asleep

I have been reminded again how critical it is for the father to be the shepherd at the gate of the sheep pen. In the same way that the pastor is responsible for protecting the flock, the father must always be on the lookout to protect those God has given him.

A number of months ago my two adult sons told me about a new fiction novel they had read about the end-times, and they thought it was great. It sounded interesting and even a little tempting, but for quite a few years now, I've been able to avoid recreational reading. The issue is not whether the books are bad (some are and some aren't), but whether there is a better use of my time.

My heart's desire is that I would spend my time as the Lord Jesus would have me spend it. I know there is a world of fun things out there that might not be classified as sin, but the question is, are they profitable? I truly want to use my time obediently, doing God's best and not settling for anything less. I don't share that arrogantly, but as the sincere desire of my heart.

Paul said, "All things are lawful unto me, but all things are not expedient: all things are lawful for me, but I will not be brought under the power of any" (1 Corinthians 6:12). The word expedient means profitable. Even if something was not sin to Paul, it might not have been profitable for him and his walk with the Lord Jesus. That is what I want for my life, to discern what is chaff and avoid it. Even if something is not technically sin, if it is not profitable for my walk, then I might as well consider it sin. So, if it isn't profitable, I really don't want to spend my time and attention on it.

As I share about this experience, please understand that my intention is not to be critical of someone else's writing. However, as I write of my failure in this area and what Scripture has to say about it, I don't know how else to explain without some reference to the books.

When Teri and I were leaving on our twenty-fifth anniversary trip last fall, one of the children sent along a CD version of the book. That was all it took. We were "hooked," and over time, Teri and I read the series. (This is the man who doesn't take time for recreational reading!) Did we have cautions? Yes. Did I rationalize ignoring them? Obviously.

The first book begins with a man's adulterous thoughts. That was a red flag to Teri and me. We felt that if a compromise like that were used to get the audience's attention, there would be other areas we would have difficulty with as well. Did we stop reading? No. When I read the detail about the anti-Christ and focus on him, that was another red flag. Comparing what the Bible has to say about the anti-Christ, we do not see the detail and glorifying of the man that is to be everything "anti" to what we believe. In Scripture, Jesus Christ is always preeminent.

I am greatly humbled by admitting this to you, brothers, but I feel God compelling me to share this. Unfortunately, it goes on. In each book we read, there were the red flags and promptings of the Spirit that it was not edifying, although greatly entertaining. Next, there was increasing gory and violent detail that, again, I knew was not profitable.

I once discussed the subject of graphic detail with the head of a Christian missionary organization. His newsletters would describe in detail the terrible things that were perpetrated on Christians around the world. He defended his writing style by referring me to

Hebrews 11 that describes how many Christians have been mar-tyred. "Women received their dead raised to life again: and others were tortured, not accepting deliverance; that they might obtain a better resurrection: And others had trial of *cruel* mockings and scourgings, yea, moreover of bonds and imprisonment: They were stoned, they were sawn asunder, were tempted, were slain with the sword: they wandered about in sheepskins and goatskins; being des-titute, afflicted, tormented" (Hebrews 11:35-37). However, notice the total lack of detail in those verses. Even when reading the Old Testament about violent things taking place, the degree of detail is slight compared to what I was reading in his newsletter. Paul exhorts us in Romans 16:19 to be wise unto that which is good, and simple in regard to our knowledge of evil. Finally, in Ephesians 5:12 we are told not even to speak of the evil deeds done in secret.

Reading accounts such as Ehud in Judges 3 still do not hold a candle to the graphic descriptions the presses are turning out these days. Have you noticed how little detail God gives when it comes to the suffering of His saints in the New Testament? Is this possibly an omission by God, or maybe He didn't have the details to include? Certainly not! No one but God could explain the minute details of what someone suffered as they were being sawn in two, stoned, or crucified. Yet, He did not choose to tell us. Why? There may be many reasons, but I believe one reason is that "man" struggles with fear, and He did not want to hand Satan any instruments to use in tormenting us. It is so easy for men, women, and children to be fear-ful, and the more detail used in describing the atrocities that happen to mankind, the easier it is to be concerned that they will happen to our wives, our children, and us. In God's mercy, He is sparing us, even though our sinful, depraved nature cries out for the detail.

Think about how much detail God gave us about the crucifix-ion of the Lord Jesus. Most of us have heard descriptions of what Christ suffered, but we didn't "hear" that from the Bible. Rather, it came from sermons or articles. God does not want us to fill our mind with the details of a person's suffering. Some justify the details as being necessary to move people to prayer and involvement. Unfortunately, wrong methods never justify the means, as there will always be consequences.

Finally, I could not ignore God's promptings any longer when we began reading another book in the series. The whole focus was on Satan's man. The last straw was when it related the words of praise that little children were singing of the anti-Christ. Teri and I were in a motel room in a city where we were giving workshops and had a little time before bed. We would take turns reading. Teri happened to be reading and came to those words. My heart ached when she started to read them and quickly said she would skip that part. But it was too late. She had already read enough of it to know it was not healthy. Here God has called me to protect my wife, and I let her fill her mind with words of praise to the anti-Christ. There is certainly no profit to our walk with Christ in that.

Can you see the absolute absurdity of the whole situation? Here were two believers, bought with the precious blood of the Lord Jesus, being entertained reading about the anti-Christ. I knew it was not profitable from the first book, yet I was weak and continued reading. Teri and I take great joy in praying together, and that would have been a joyful, profitable use of our time.

Remember it isn't that I don't enjoy recreational reading; in fact, I do enjoy it very much. The problem is that at the very least, it isn't profitable, and in this case, I believe harmful to my walk with the Lord.

A short time ago, Teri and I had a couple days away at a bed and breakfast, and that time was spent wisely. We discussed goals for the children, evaluated their progress, prayed, and watched five wonderful preaching videos. We came away filled with love for the

Lord Jesus, each other, and a renewed vision for our family. What a stark contrast to how we spent that other time.

I have repented of my attitude of compromise and slothfulness, and as a family we have committed not to read any more of these books (which were written for the lost anyway). Even after all of this, it will no doubt be tempting. It was hard to share this with you, but it is my prayer that God may use my failure for good in your life.

June 2000

We've Reversed a Bad Decision

Before you read any Dad's Corner, may I share a caution? Dad's Corners are from a father's heart to another father's heart. It is our desire that these Corners would build the family up and never create a controversy between a husband and wife. It is possible to undermine our goal if a mom read and agreed with a Dad's Corner and the husband didn't. Never would we want to undermine respect for Dad in the direction he has chosen for the family. Therefore, we would encourage moms not to read Dad's Corners first, unless as a couple, you have discussed and agreed who should read the Dad's Corner first.

Recently I loaded the five younger children into the van so we could be off for Kansas City. The children's big toy (backyard climbing playhouse) was in need of some repair. After about seven years in the Kansas sun, dry rotting had weakened some of the dowels and boards. Our mission was to buy the necessary replacement parts.

Each Saturday I try to spend some time with the younger children by running errands or on building projects. It is a special joy for me to spend time with them. Understand, I'm not saying that they are perfect every minute as we do have opportunities for growth (either on their part or mine). However, in general, I love being with my children, and next to Teri, there is no one I would prefer to spend time with. In between conversations in the van, I thought back to the early eighties when we only had three of the eight children we now have.

We lived in Clearwater, Florida, and had some very difficult times. I'm hesitant to share such a level of personal trial, but it might be an encouragement to some. Teri and I loved the Lord Jesus and were growing in knowledge and our relationship with Him. However, due to her body's inability to regulate progesterone, Teri was suffering with extreme depression.

In addition, the three children we had were presenting significant challenges for Teri to cope with. The medical community, and even a Christian counselor, had no solutions for us. It became clear to us that three children were all that Teri could manage, so we looked to ways of eliminating further pregnancies. Members of our conservative church accepted surgically cutting off more children through sterilization as a practical way of doing this. I sought counsel from her dad and others, and all were supportive that it was the wise thing to do. So, around 1984 we cut off the possibility of more children. We were content with our decision. We enjoyed our three greatly, and I spent all my free time with my family. However, we truly felt it was necessary to prevent future pregnancies.

In 1985 we moved to the state of Washington, and we continued to grow in the Lord Jesus. We still had some very difficult times, but it was getting better. One thing began to trouble us, though. We started to feel that we were wrong in cutting off more children. We would frequently re-evaluate the decision even though we "knew" that it was imperative that we did it for Teri's well being. This continued to be a subject of discussion and prayer until one day I was home from work, ill.

I told Teri that I was going to find out what the Lord had to say about children and settle the matter right then. I spread my Bible and reference books out on the bed. I began looking up each verse about children to see what God had to say. I started in Genesis and continued through the Bible. After a while I had tears running down my face, and my heart was broken. I cried out to the Lord, "God, I was wrong in cutting off additional children. I can now see that children are our heritage from You. They are our reward and, next to salvation, the most precious gift You could give us on earth." I will share what God has shown me regarding children.

"Lo, children *are* a heritage of the LORD: *and* the fruit of the womb *is his* reward. As arrows *are* in the hand of a mighty man; so *are* children of the youth. Happy *is* the man that hath his quiver full of them: they shall not be ashamed, but they shall speak with the enemies in the gate" (Psalms 127:3-5). I thought about the issue of inheritance and how happy most people are to be informed they are in someone's will. Imagine someone being told that they would inherit a tremendous amount of gold and saying, "No thank you. I have enough and am very content with what I have." No one would refuse the inheritance because of the value that is placed on gold. Frankly, had I truly valued children we would not have had them surgically cut off.

The word "heritage" also draws our thoughts toward the One giving the inheritance. Usually, when parents leave an inheritance it is out of a desire to bless their children with something they will cherish as a token of the parents' love. Had we understood the preciousness of the gift of children from the Father we would not have rejected more children.

Malachi 2:15 reads, "And did not he make one? Yet had he the residue of the spirit. And wherefore one? That he might seek a godly seed. . . ." God's purpose in marriage is to produce godly seed. "And God blessed them, and God said unto them, Be fruitful, and multiply, and replenish the earth. . ." (Genesis 1:28). God never took the command back. In His Word, He never told Teri and I that we were to decide how many children to have. Had I understood His purpose and command for marriage, we would not have cut them off.

As I reflected on the physics of intimacy, it was clear that God intended to be the One in control of the family size. Truly God gave man an ongoing desire for intimacy. However, He did not give man the natural ability to control whether there was conception during times of intimacy. This was no mistake, but clearly God's plan. God's creation of the body is so incredibly perfect. Had He intended us to be in control of whether children were conceived, He would have designed that control into our bodies. As science has progressed, modern man has figured out ways of preventing pregnancy. If that had been God's intent, however, He would have designed that into the "system" at creation.

Some might have said we were foolish and "not counting the cost" in considering reversal surgery and risking another pregnancy. "For which of you, intending to build a tower, sitteth not down first, and counteth the cost, whether he have *sufficient* to finish *it?*" (Luke 14:28). However, this verse speaks of commitment. It does not say we must consider whether we can afford more children. Jesus was challenging the disciples to evaluate their level of commitment. If Jesus meant this verse to be applied to whether we have the funds for raising children, He would have been contradicting His own teaching.

Jesus says in Matthew 6:25-27, "Therefore I say unto you, Take no thought for your life, what ye shall eat, or what ye shall drink; nor yet for your body, what ye shall put on. Is not the life more than meat, and the body than raiment? Behold the fowls of the air: for they sow not, neither do they reap, nor gather into barns; yet your heavenly Father feedeth them. Are ye not much better than they? Which of you by taking thought can add one cubit unto his stature?" By feeding the birds of the air, Jesus meant their offspring would be fed as well. Jesus continues and compares those who would worry about such things with the Gentiles. They had no god who would provide for them and therefore had reason to worry.

That is why I believe this issue strikes at the very heart of our walk with Christ. If I choose to let Him be in control of my family size, then I must trust the Lord to provide. That can be a scary thing. Not until I began writing this did I notice the "therefore" at the beginning of Matthew 6:25. It refers back to Matthew 6:24, which reads, "No man can serve two masters: for either he will hate the one, and love the other; or else he will hold to the one, and despise the other. Ye cannot serve God and mammon."

The fact is if I let the Lord choose the size of my family, He might not let me have the standard of living that I'm accustomed to, or I might have to sacrifice for my children. Even if I were called to sacrifice for my children, isn't that the essence of Christianity? Are we not to die to self for the sake of someone else? The servant says, "Lord, I am yours, and You tell me what You want me to do." That is why I have come to believe that this is one of the greatest issues within the family and church today.

I was convicted that we were wrong in taking matters into our own hands and determined to set it right. Almost immediately, we sought out a doctor and prayed that God would provide the funds to reverse the previous surgery. Within a short amount of time, God provided a doctor and the funds for the surgery.

Once the decision was made, a funny thing began happening in my heart. Even though I knew the decision was right and children were a blessing from God, I was still a little apprehensive about more children. However, the closer the surgery came, the more excited I became about more children. The Lord took our small step of obedience and replaced our fear with joy and trust.

Frequently, when I look at my family seated at the dinner table, I can't help but wonder how many more there would be if I hadn't made a poor decision. Even now with self-employment, RH factor complication, Teri's age, and miscarriages, I know we can trust a mighty God.

This seems to be a forbidden subject in the church, but in Dad's Corners, I'm able to share my heart and experience. Most men have never sat down with another brother and heard him share about such things privately. If this strikes a chord in your heart, praise God, but if not, forget it. May God bless you as you strive to be the man God wants you to be.

July 2000

A Husband's Perspective on His Wife's Depression

We have had so many e-mail us to ask about how we dealt with the depression Teri suffered from years ago, we decided to write this month's Corners on it. It is important to remember that we are not doctors giving advice but believers sharing our experience. What I am writing in this Dad's Corner is a result of what the Lord taught me through the years Teri struggled with times of depression. Depression was a part of her life off and on for about fifteen years. It was the worst when I worked long hours and traveled a great deal. Only in the last eight years has the Lord brought Teri out of those dark times. Not only was the depression something Teri had to cope with, but it obviously had an impact on the children and me as well.

When a wife is suffering with depression, it can be very difficult for the family. Depending on the age of the children, they may be aware of it and asking questions as to why Mommy is crying or sad. There don't seem to be any easy answers. However, everyone is in agreement that they want Mommy happy again.

Working through issues in my mind was critical to developing a godly perspective on Teri's depression. It was very easy to think about myself and not the pain Teri was suffering. I believe that was absolutely the first and most important step: that I would get my mind off of myself and focus on my wife's and children's needs. Isn't that what we are really called to do as husbands and fathers? Isn't that a perfect picture of the shepherd who is tenderly caring for an injured sheep?

I had to realize that God was not surprised by the situation. He had a plan for it. "And we know that all things work together for good to them that love God, to them who are the called according to *his* purpose. For whom he did foreknow, he also did predestinate *to be* conformed to the image of his Son, that he might be the first-born among many brethren" (Romans 8:28-29). God desired to use my wife's depression to conform me into the image of His Son Jesus Christ. It is interesting to note that the word "conform" is from the Greek word "morphe," from which we get the word morph. His desire is to morph us into the image of Christ. Are we willing?

It may mean that there are "things" in my life that are hindering God's conforming me into the image of Christ. I believe that God uses problems in a wife's (and children's) life to bring serious pressure to bear on a husband. As long as things are smooth sailing, we might not be willing to deal with areas that may be displeasing to the Lord. However, as the pain grows in my family, I become increasingly more willing to surrender what I might not previously have let go. I have now learned to use every serious difficulty that our family faces as motivation to cry out to God to examine my life and for Him to point out sin that He wants to eliminate. Pain in the family can become a wonderful stimulus to seek God's will for change in my life.

I also saw my wife's struggles as opportunities to show her my love. It is easy to love someone when she is pleasant and meeting my needs, but what about when her eyes are swollen from crying, and she isn't much fun to be around? Maybe it isn't too difficult for one or two days, but what about when it is longer than that? Truly, I could demonstrate that I meant my wedding vows by choosing to love Teri through better or worse. Whether my wife is discouraged all the time or just a few days a month, I must be understanding and love her as Christ loved the church. "Husbands, love your wives, even as Christ also loved the church, and gave himself for it" (Ephesians 5:25). Those are not just nice-sounding words used to fill up an empty page; God commanded us husbands to live them out. I must choose to give of myself in whatever way God tells me to. "Likewise, ye husbands, dwell with *them* according to knowledge, giving honour unto the wife, as unto the weaker vessel, and as being heirs together of the grace of life; that your prayers be not hindered" (1 Peter 3:7). So what does "according to knowledge" mean? *Vine's Expository Dictionary* amplifies it as "to come to understand." I needed to understand the struggles my wife was having. I needed to shoulder the load she was stumbling under.

When Teri was depressed, I had to learn how to listen. As I prayerfully listened I heard about things that I had not adequately dealt with, things that produce bitterness and hurt. Unresolved offenses are fertile ground for Satan to sow seeds of doubt and discouragement in a wife's heart.

As I listened, I heard about areas of intense struggle with the children that she did not have answers for and that led to frustration. Again, they had to be dealt with as well. A dad may hear that his wife is discouraged because she is too busy while accomplishing too little. Dads often can be the cause of encouraging lots of activities for the children. This can be terribly draining to Mom of both energy and time, not to mention introducing many additional character problems with the children. We need to be prepared to encourage the elimination of unproductive use of time and be willing to help. It might mean doing the grocery shopping or cleaning house; whatever it takes, we should be prepared to do it as long as necessary. Although one caution is that I don't believe it would have been good for Teri if she'd had nothing to do. Idleness gives Satan much opportunity for working in a person's mind. A certain balance of work and rest is good, but having nothing to do is harmful.

One thing I learned was that doing the family budget was stressful for Teri. She had begun doing it to free up some of my time. However, it was adding to the pressure she was under and was actually hindering me from being financially responsible. I have found, and now believe, that it is good for the husband to manage the finances so he feels the financial pressure. I am freer with money than Teri is, and when she tracked the spending, it caused her to worry. However, if I have to manage it and see the bills, I'm more likely to be careful. I now handle the finances–not as efficiently as she did, but adequately and without her having the pressure.

There could be other areas of responsibility that a wife has taken on that really should be her husband's. When a wife is shouldering any extra load that God did not intend for her to, it can clearly lead to depression. Unfortunately, most wives will quickly step in to take over an area when the husband is not doing the job.

There are many things I don't understand about women, and one in particular is the effect clutter has on them. I can be content with a closet so full it takes a week to find something in it! As long as the door is closed, I'm fine. Not so with most women. There is something about clutter that nags at a woman's heart and will bring her down. I know that when I help Teri by building storage areas and weeding things out, she is unbelievably grateful. It is as if a big weight is lifted from her shoulders.

When she was struggling, I needed to understand that her choice of words might be less gracious than normal. I had to be prepared to be loving and accepting anyway. The situation would not have been improved if I became insensitive and offended because she was more direct now than at other times. Truly, we need to be men of understanding. Next, I believe that the husband needs to take full responsibility for his wife's depression. "For the husband is the head of the wife, even as Christ is the head of the church: and he is the saviour of the body" (Ephesians 5:23). It was not my wife's problem, but it was my problem. We are one, and if part of the union is hurting, we are both hurting. Unless I took full responsibility for my wife's depression, I was not going to have the compassion that God desired for me to have, and I would not have been crying out to Him for direction. I believe that most of what Teri is sharing in her Mom's Corner is a result of God answering our prayers. It was not a pamphlet we picked up somewhere, but our Lord hearing our cries to Him and slowly showing us new things.

Just after moving to Florida in 1980, I was extremely troubled and concerned for her. I was led to fast and pray about the situation. God is so good! In my heart, I felt strongly that He told me not to worry, but to be loving, patient, and supportive. I would have preferred a quick solution, but God had as much for me to learn as He did for Teri. One of the most critical things I did was closely maintain my walk with the Lord and do everything I could to encourage Teri in her walk. "The LORD *is* my strength and my shield; my heart trusted in him, and I am helped: therefore my heart greatly rejoiceth; and with my song will I praise him" (Psalms 28:7). Oh, how great our pride to ever think that we can get along without a close walk with the Lord. During times of depression the mind can play all sorts of games, and to focus on God and His truth is imperative. If we have neglected the Lord, we must repent and turn to Him. "If we confess our sins, he is faithful and just to forgive us *our* sins, and to cleanse us from all unrighteousness" (1 John 1:9).

Taking responsibility also will ensure that I am not being judgmental. It was easy to become impatient and critical. However, Teri would have given anything to be herself, and it was not a wrong choice she was making. If anyone could have just willed it differently she would have, but she couldn't. "Charity suffereth long, *and* is kind; charity envieth not; charity vaunteth not itself, is not puffed up, Doth not behave itself unseemly, seeketh not her own, is not easily provoked, thinketh no evil; Rejoiceth not in iniquity, but rejoiceth in the truth; Beareth all things, believeth all things, hopeth all things, endureth all things" (1 Corinthians 13:4-7). Again, God commanded me to love my wife as Christ loved the church.

Don't be distracted by "non-issues." Often when Teri felt bad, she would think some circumstance must be the cause. Most things were not really the cause of her feelings, but they would seem very monumental at the time. We would discuss it, and I, in typical male fashion, would come in and tell her how to fix it. Finally, it dawned on me that what she needed was someone to listen to her. I didn't have to fix it, just listen! There were times when I would ask her, as she would begin to share a problem, "Honey, do you want me to listen or fix it?" That helped so much as I finally understood, at that moment, that all I needed to do was be sympathetic and listen to her. I think this was one of the most challenging lessons God had for me. To my shame, there are times now when I really just need to listen and not jump ahead to a solution. So much still to learn and so little time.

In our experience and that of people I've spoken to, there just doesn't seem to be a "silver bullet." Unfortunately, that is what we usually want. We need to be very cautious if one is proposed—a quick fix so we can get back on track and things can be normal again. Husbands, we must get our heart fixed on Christ, and be prepared that it could take a while. How long before our sovereign God says it is enough? Obviously, no one knows, but we need to set our expectations such that if it takes years, then we will minister in whatever way God calls us to during that time.

That is about all I could think of that God might have me share. Truly, it can be such an awful time for husbands and wives. I think the easiest to deal with was when the depression was mostly caused by my failures. Then, if I'm willing to humble myself, God is able to resolve the situation fairly quickly. However, God designed women the way they are for a purpose. Hormones are not a design flaw; our wives are perfect according to His plan. When the depression is physiological in nature, it might last a while, and we need to be the strong, faithful shepherd that God desires us to be. This won't happen in our own strength, but it can happen when we are in full, complete dependence on the Lord Jesus Christ. He is our strength and our shield. All praise to Him.

September 2000

A Man and His Dawg

Our children are similar to most in that they love pets, especially dogs. When we visited someone's home and they had a dog, the poor thing would be smothered by our children's love and attention. Inevitably, on our way home one or more would ask if we could get a dog. My answer was always, "We raise children in our home, not pets. However, you may certainly pray about it." You can be sure they did!

About two years ago the strangest thing happened–I would often find myself thinking about buying the children a dog. It was the funniest thing; it wasn't just to be a dog but was to be a golden retriever. I knew the thought was crazy, as I didn't even know what one looked like; I knew it would be lots of trouble; I knew Teri would be against it because everyone already had many responsibilities; and I knew my in-laws would think I'd gone off the deep end. But–I just couldn't shake it. In fact, I began to believe the Lord was the One behind it. Once I realized it might be of the Lord, I began to look for confirmation.

One day, during my regular walk with my father-in-law, I broached the subject to him. He has a heart for his "little girl" (as you would expect), and I was sure he would advise against anything that would increase her responsibilities in keeping the house clean. If I remember right, there were two words out of his mouth, "Great idea!" I was shocked.

After such a positive response from Grandad, I reasoned that if the Lord was in it, Teri would likely be in favor of it as well. Boy, was I surprised by her response. Not only was she in favor of it, but also she said, "Why don't we get two, a boy and a girl?" Since I was feeling God's leading, and Teri was in favor, the decision to purchase the pup was quickly made. So, what have I learned through the process of introducing a dog into the Maxwells' home?

First, some might think (with a light chuckle) that I no longer encourage the children to pray about something I'm against. Quite the opposite, I'm very much in favor of it. It is excellent for the family to see that God rules in the heart of their father, and the Lord can easily change Dad's heart if He chooses to. They were able to see God turn their daddy's heart. They have seen God answer other prayer requests, but this one was extra special to them.

Next, God has shown me how patient I can be with an animal that is not always obedient. You know how it is. Haven't we all secretly been amused to watch a neighbor frantically calling out to a totally deaf, unresponsive dog, "Maverick, come here. Come here now. Hurry up and get in here. Right now. I mean it." On and on it goes. The dog is having a great time and the owner looks and sounds quite silly. And yes, I have "been there, done that" during those early training months. In spite of the pup's initial obedience struggles, I generally remained quite calm. The Holy Spirit has prompted me with this question, "Am I just as calm and patient with my children?" I am ashamed to say that I have actually been more longsuffering with a silly dog (just an expression) than with God's precious heritage. That lesson continues to weigh heavy on my heart.

Sarah, my oldest daughter, will occasionally tease me by saying, "Come on Daddy, admit it, you love that dog." What is there to admit? How could I say I love a dog? I love my children and Teri, but I can't see "loving" a dog (please, no e-mails from anyone who does). Without playing word games, isn't love really a choice that is demonstrated by actions? So, if Sarah watches the way I patiently interact with the dog, scratch its neck, and offer to let the dog ride along in the car when I'm going somewhere, she might draw the conclusion that I love that dog!

Sarah's question was used by the Holy Spirit to teach me the greatest lesson, and it is worth dwelling on. By observing my inter-action with the dog, Sarah was reasoning that I loved the dog. The question that came to my heart was, "If someone observes the way I interact with Teri, the way I hold her hand, stroke her neck, help her, and whether I want to be with her, will they conclude that I greatly love my wife?" I can have wonderful discussions with my children as we talk about how we treat those we love, but do they actually observe their father acting that way? Am I a hypocrite liv-ing for my own pleasure or a man of God demonstrating true love for his wife?

Have you ever thought about how easily a family could fill the roll of a jury if the father's love was on trial? (Not just a guilty or innocent verdict, but evaluating it on a scale such as a jury might award damages.) My family observes how I act toward Teri. They know if I'm demonstrating true love to their mother. We may be able to put on nice faces when we go to church, but there is no fool-ing the children. My example, whether good or bad, is making a deep impression on their lives.

A worthy question each father could consider asking himself is, "Am I choosing to exercise true love toward my wife, or is my love a pretense?" Jeremiah 3:10-11 is great for showing us what God thinks of pretense: "And yet for all this her treacherous sister Judah hath not turned unto me with her whole heart, but feignedly, saith the LORD. And the LORD said unto me, The backsliding Israel hath justified herself more than treacherous Judah." God calls living a life based on outward show treacherous and unfaithful. He said that backsliding Israel was better than Judah who was not sincere. That is a very heavy indictment for any dad whose love for his wife is a pretense.

I don't know about you, but I struggle greatly with selfishness. It is so easy for me to focus on my needs and myself. As long as my needs are being met, I can be very satisfied with how things are going at home. Something tells me that this is true for most dads. We will go on our merry way while our wives struggle under the burden of keeping house, homeschooling, and being wife and mother (all the while feeling unappreciated and maybe defeated). I think that if we had as "full a plate" as our wives we would often feel like quitting. Most men I know leave a job long before it gets that bad.

However, when I lavish my love on Teri, both verbally and by my actions, she is better able to face the challenges each day brings, knowing how much I love her and appreciate all she does.

I believe that Christian homeschooling dads are blessed with the most wonderful wives on the face of this earth. Our wives are walking down a road that requires great personal sacrifice. They would have so much more time on their hands, and far less challenges, if they weren't teaching the children. Think about the character your wife demonstrates and how fortunate you are to have a wife like that! Truly, may our children see a father who loves their mother with a deep, genuine, and true love.

October 2000

A Precious Relationship

Special Note: Steve has asked that moms please not read the Dad's Corner unless your husband has read it first.

Sometimes I marvel at God's plan for marriage when I think that He chose two opposites and brought them together to make them one. "Therefore shall a man leave his father and his mother, and shall cleave unto his wife: and they shall be one flesh" (Genesis 2:24). God provides us a beautiful picture of taking two objects and combining them into one new object that cannot again be divided without doing damage to those who were joined.

We recently had to strip wallpaper off the bathroom walls as it had suffered at the hands of little children for many years. In addition to that, there were quite a few late nights running a steaming hot shower so a croupy little one could breath. That room full of steam had soaked the seams of the wallpaper to where they were opening up and peeling back. I was confident it would be quick work to remove as it looked like it was already falling off the walls. Unfortunately, when the original owners had hung the wallpaper, they had chosen to apply it directly to unprimered sheetrock. The glue had soaked into the sheetrock in many places, providing a great example of two becoming one. It was impossible to separate them without doing considerable damage to both. (In the same way, some marriages that are coming apart at the seams would appear to be easily dissolved in divorce, but severely damaged lives result.)

Imagine for a minute that your wife came to you with a special request. "Honey, I know this may sound a little funny to you, but you will never guess who called me today! Jack Howard. You know, he was the one I told you about who was the boy next door when I was growing up. I couldn't believe it! It has been so many years since I saw him, and just the other day I was wondering what ever happened to him. We were neighbors for ten years; he was like a brother to me. There were no other playmates near us, so we were best friends and did everything together. We had such great times together. Well, he is going to be coming back to town once a year for a conference of some sort, and he wondered if I might be able to spend some time with him—for memories' sake. He said we could go out for a nice dinner, and then he would bring me home before it got late. What do you think? I can hardly believe it. I'm so glad you know I love you and aren't jealous in any way. I told him it would be okay as I was sure that you wouldn't mind. It is so wonderful to be married to you. I feel such freedom in our marriage and I knew it would be fine with you."

God gave us the marriage relationship to give us an earthly example of our relationship with Christ. That is why, when Israel sought other gods, God called them adulterers. "And I saw, when for all the causes whereby backsliding Israel committed adultery I had put her away, and given her a bill of divorce; yet her treacherous sister Judah feared not, but went and played the harlot also" (Jeremiah 3:8).

God wanted the Israelites to understand the pain that He felt when they did not give Him their complete love and affection. That is why He had Hosea marry Gomer, so that Hosea would know how God felt when the Israelites left Him for "someone" else. ". . . And the LORD said to Hosea, Go, take unto thee a wife of whoredoms and children of whoredoms: for the land hath committed great whoredom, *departing* from the LORD" (Hosea 1:2).

Why don't we think of God as being jealous over us? We know how He was provoked to jealousy by the Israelites following after other gods. Why don't we think that our attitudes and actions also cause Him to be jealous of us? "Thou shalt not bow down thyself to them, nor serve them: for I the LORD thy God *am* a jealous God, visiting the iniquity of the fathers upon the children unto the third and fourth *generation* of them that hate me; And showing mercy unto thousands of them that love me, and keep my commandments" (Exodus 20:5-6). I have come to believe that for my family to participate in Halloween would be committing spiritual adultery. I have come to believe that to participate in the high, holy day of evil (from a Christian perspective) would be the equivalent of my wife going out with another man for dinner.

Just because Teri and I had pleasant youthful memories of going through the neighborhood on Halloween is no justification for us to participate in this holiday. I don't want to teach my children that there can ever be sufficient rationale to forsake our Lord. Just because my wife is confident of my love, I do not want her spending time alone with another man. (Please don't e-mail me and say you would have no problem with your wife spending time with another man in the above situation. It isn't that I don't trust her, but I prize my relationship so highly that I don't want to take any chances. Also, one would have to consider the issue of the appearance of evil for a wife to be seen having dinner with another man.) I believe my Lord does not want my family spending time in a wicked celebration regardless of whether our intentions are good or evil. It would not matter how innocent a wife's intentions could be in having dinner, or ours in participating in Halloween—it does not change the fact that we would be spending time with "another."

I know some will say, "Steve, don't worry about it, you are now free in Christ." Many don't understand the purpose of our freedom. Yes, we are free in Christ, but free to serve Him only—we are not free to do whatever we want. "For I am jealous over you with godly jealousy: for I have espoused you to one husband, that I may present *you as* a chaste virgin to Christ" (2 Corinthians 11:2). God desires that we are pure and set apart to Him only. "For ye are bought with a price: therefore glorify God in your body, and in your spirit, which are God's" (1 Corinthians 6:20). In good conscience I cannot let my family participate in a "holiday" where the dead, wicked, and evil are glorified. Some might encourage our family to participate in the neighborhood activities to better relate to them and possibly win them to the Lord. I would consider it if I saw in Scripture Jesus participating in evil activities to win the lost. He was with sinners, but He did not join in their evil practices. "Be ye not unequally yoked together with unbelievers: for what fellowship hath righteousness with unrighteousness? and what communion hath light with darkness?" (2 Corinthians 6:14). Regardless of how Teri and I wanted to justify the children's participation in Halloween, it was clear that we could not. It does not take much thought to see how wickedness is glorified and darkness triumphs. (If we want to win our neighbors to the Lord, we should serve them.)

Others might encourage me not to worry about "eating meat sacrificed at the temple." I believe this analogy is often misused. To purchase Halloween candy at the store and eat it with a clear conscience is how I believe that verse could properly be applied. I don't believe for a minute that Paul would participate in a pagan sacrifice at the temple. That is how I would feel if my family were to participate in Halloween.

Just how much attention would your wife have to give another man before you were jealous? What if she only went to dinner once a year? What if it was something that she looked forward to? What if he did nothing more than hold her hand as she got out of the car? What if she said the other man wasn't special to her, but she wanted to use the dinner opportunity to witness to him? I want Teri to love me with her whole heart and want to spend time with me–not someone else. I would not be comforted if she told me the other man meant nothing to her, but she just wanted to relive those wonderful old times together.

My good intentions to let the children have fun and be a part of the neighborhood do not change the fact that my family would be participating in a wicked event. Halloween stands for absolutely nothing good! I can easily picture the Lord Jesus Christ being jealous and hurt when those He has bought with His own precious blood are participating in such a "celebration."

What is there to "gain" by it? Wouldn't I be teaching my children that participating in evil is acceptable as long as there is some sweet reward? Rather, shouldn't I teach them to avoid evil? "And this I pray, that your love may abound yet more and more in knowledge and *in* all judgment; That ye may approve things that are excellent; that ye may be sincere and without offence till the day of Christ" (Philippians 1:9-10). Let's not quibble about where the line of sin is but use good judgment and choose things that are excellent. May God give each of us wisdom to lead our family in righteousness.

November 2000

In the Way He Should Go

Several months ago, while studying in preparation for a workshop, I came to a new understanding of the well-known verse Proverbs 22:6: "Train up a child in the way he should go: and when he is old, he will not depart from it." I believe this is one of the most commonly quoted verses but least appropriately applied.

How can it be misapplied when the verse is so straightforward? Doesn't it teach us that if we raise our children in the way we want them to go, they will live like that as adults? I have observed "good" Christian parents raising their children–families who go to church, espouse to love the Lord Jesus, and even homeschool their children. Aren't they training their children in the way they should go? Let's find out.

Sadly, even within the Christian homeschooling community, I'm seeing children who are being raised to be children all of their lives. They are trained, but is it really in the way they should go? Does it match the goals these parents have for their children? In another twenty years, will the entertainment-focused Christian youth of today all of a sudden change their ways? A turnaround in focus didn't happen as my generation grew up, nor do I honestly believe that Proverbs 22:6 teaches it will.

If the years of one's youth mean one fun activity or sport after another, when do children learn to enjoy work? Must our children always have great fun while homeschooling? If this is their training, how will they respond as adults to jobs that aren't always fun? In Genesis 2:15 we read that God put man on the earth to keep the garden. Our lot in life as men is to work and serve.

It is as if we believe there is some magic switch on the back of our children's heads that, when flipped, will instantly turn a child-like youth into a mature, Christ-serving adult. Unfortunately, a child who has been fed a constant diet of fun and games is not going to have an appetite for work and the things of the Lord. What happens when church is the place of boy-girl relationships and pizza parties? It will likely mean that church must have a great social calendar, potlucks, and sports leagues to keep our adult children coming back. Hmmm. If it isn't the intention of parents to raise perpetual children, why are so many doing just that?

We must search our souls over this. How will our sons ever grow up to be responsible, Christ-serving men of God if we don't truly "train them in the way they should go"? If our young men are fed a diet of fun activities and sports in their youth, won't they grow into adults with an appetite for ongoing recreation and couch-potato-type viewing? I've met very few men who began life with an entertainment focus and were able to break the training (actually, I can only think of two).

Christ is our example and our Lord. We see no hint of the Lord Jesus spending His time on what is the norm for Christian youth and men today. Why didn't He? Was it because there wasn't entertainment back then? No! It was because Jesus knew the clock was counting down, and He was not going to waste precious time on activities of no eternal value. I think that may be at the heart of the parent's problem. Our focus today is on how to spend as much time as possible doing what is the most pleasurable. We do not believe that time is precious, and that we need to be about the Master's business. "Redeeming the time, because the days are evil"

(Ephesians 5:16). "But this I say, brethren, the time *is* short. . ." (1 Corinthians 7:29).

Most Christian parents will say they want their children to grow up to be good Christians. Sadly, what our generation has come to accept as "good" Christians is, I believe, very different from being dynamic followers of the Lord Jesus Christ. "Then said Jesus unto his disciples, If any *man* will come after me, let him deny himself, and take up his cross, and follow me" (Matthew 16:24).

This leads to the first step we parents should take to train our children in the way they should go. May we bow before the Lord and ask Him to evaluate our lives. What is my relationship like with Jesus? What is the focus of my heart? What do I enjoy doing the most? Who do I want to be with the most? What priority does my daily quiet time with the Lord Jesus hold? I think we will agree the answers to these questions reveal whether we are carnally or spiritually minded. I join you in bringing these questions before the Lord.

Generally, our children will follow in our footsteps. Are those footsteps leading them in the way they should go? If we are setting a good example, then the fruit will be good. If, however, our example is of following the world, then the fruit will be bad. We must approach Proverbs 22:6 with stark honesty. We should realize that what we are creating now is ultimately what our children will be. Certainly, God can perform a miracle as He did with Paul, but He is holding us responsible for how we lead our children. The issue goes beyond whether or not we are satisfied with the example we are setting for our children. Rather the question would be, "Is the Lord Jesus pleased with our example?"

May we be fathers who will critically evaluate whether we are leading our children in the way they should go. If not, may we seek the Lord for a change of direction and then be obedient to it.

December 2000

Dad's and Mom's Corners Via E-mail

If you enjoy what you read in this book, you may want to sign up for the monthly Dad's and Mom's Corners e-mail. To be on the Dad's and Mom's Corners list (which is never given away or sold—all addresses are kept strictly confidential), stop by our website, www.Titus2.com, or call us (913) 772-0392.

Index

A

B

C

devotions
dad's 248, 309, 313
family's 166, 271, 309, 313
mom's 58, 139, 147, 223
discipline
children's 19, 63-64, 65, 81, 107, 111, 113, 117, 143, 188, 190, 198
consequences 61, 114-115
consistent 129
prayer for child's 82
discouragement
mom's 18, 28, 49-50, 59, 61, 74, 83, 106, 135, 189
wife's 353

E

encouragement
children's 23, 30, 78
dad's 210, 233, 250, 306, 328, 346
mom's 25, 67, 74-75, 183
entertainment 317
children's 91, 96-97, 277
dad's 204, 218, 222, 252, 290, 370
teens' 96, 369
example
character training 129

Christ's 222, 264, 295, 364, 370
dad's 219, 228, 244, 262, 267, 272, 275, 281, 301, 302, 325, 361, 371
discipline 113-114
mom's 18, 84, 149
protecting children 103
wife's 69
exercise
children's 162
mom's 179
expectations
mom's 81, 83, 143, 181

F

faith
children's 102, 257
dad's 263-264
homeschooling 135
husband's 103
mom's 17, 19, 46, 67
regarding children 15
teens' 102
wife's 158
faithful
dad 222, 357
devotions 178

moms 42, 50, 58, 134, 135, 147, 184, 196

planning 13-14, 32

prayer 173

preparations 173

reasons to 301, 324

summer 109

teens 89-90

I

identity 207

idols 290, 293-294

J

job

dad's 207, 233, 272

husband's 354

L

leader

dad 92, 219, 221, 225-226, 233, 244, 271, 275, 315, 318

husband 19, 45-46, 71, 91, 138, 315

love

children, for God 18, 40, 218

children's 83, 298, 303

dad's 227, 243, 248, 252, 255, 258-259, 280-281, 294-295,

310-311, 329-330, 334, 342, 345, 360, 369

family's 275

husband's 71, 199, 230, 240, 256, 283-284, 323, 352-353, 356, 361, 365

mom's 25, 30, 35-36, 50, 131, 144, 147, 182

wife's 239

M

marriage 16, 239, 293, 347, 363

minister

adult children 89, 98-99, 103-104

dad 206, 222

family 97, 122, 193, 356

mom 26, 107, 136, 220, 231

teens 98

O

obedience

child's 330

dad's 262-263, 267, 280

mom's 149, 154-155, 160

mom's thoughts 83, 150, 157, 171, 180

parents, to God 16, 280, 349

wife's 160

organizing 109-110

P

R

Additional Resources

Books (pages 382-390)
Audios (pages 391-398)
Websites (see below)

www.Titus2.com—Titus2.com provides information and resources to encourage, exhort, and equip homeschooling parents. On the site you will find articles, information about the Maxwells' books, audios, and other resources. Steve and Teri Maxwell write free monthly e-mail articles for Christian parents. The Dad's and Mom's Corners address issues that are at the heart of Christian families. You may sign up on the website.

www.ChorePacks.com—Ancillary to *Managers of Their Chores*. Book owners can download chore forms and make pre-reader chore cards. Also, check out ChoreWare, which greatly facilitates ChorePack development, on www.ChorePacks.com. ChoreWare is available for a small yearly subscription fee to owners of *Managers of Their Chores*.

www.FamiliesforJesus.com—A website dedicated to building up and challenging Christian families as they share Jesus with a lost and dying world.

www.HomeschooleCards.com—eCards designed to encourage homeschoolers and Christians in the Lord Jesus Christ!

www.PreparingSons.com—Work project center, messageboard, and more!

www.PreparingDaughters.com—A website especially for daughters who are striving to be women of God.

Managers of Their Homes
A Practical Guide to Daily Scheduling for Christian Homeschool Families

by Steven and Teri Maxwell

A homeschool mother's greatest challenge may be "getting it all done." *Managers of Their Homes* offers solutions! Responses by families who have read *Managers of Their Homes* and utilized the Scheduling Kit indicate the almost unbelievable improvements they have realized.

Step-by-step instructions and a unique Scheduling Kit make the setting up of a daily schedule easily achievable for any homeschooling family. *"People have told me for years that I need a schedule, but every time I tried I couldn't get one to work. I always had problems fitting everything that needed to be done into one day. With your system, I am actually accomplishing more, and I have more time left over! The key to it is the great worksheets. They are invaluable."* Who wouldn't like to accomplish more and have time left over?

How does one schedule school time? Are you struggling with keeping up in areas such as laundry, dishes, or housekeeping? Does it seem like there is no time for you in the day? Do you feel stressed over the busyness of your days or not accomplishing all you want? It doesn't matter whether you have one child or twelve, this book will help you to plan your daily schedule.

Managers of Their Homes: A Practical Guide to Daily Scheduling for Christian Homeschool Families sets a firm biblical foundation for scheduling, in addition to discussing scheduling's numerous benefits. Chapter after chapter is filled with practical suggestions for efficient, workable ways to schedule a homeschooling family's days.

Thirty real-life schedules in the Appendix give valuable insight into creating a personalized schedule. Also included is a special chapter by Steve for homeschool dads.

"My schedule has given me back my sanity!! I can't believe the way my life has changed since implementing a schedule." Tracy L.

"I had read almost every organizational book there was, and I still couldn't get to where I wanted to be until I applied this method!" Corrie

"In retrospect, having used the book, I would have paid $100 for it, if I could have know beforehand the tremendous benefits I would gain: peace in my busy home, and the ability my schedule gives me to accomplish the things I feel God wants me to do in my family." Tracy

"Your book helped to make our second year of homeschooling much smoother than the first! My three boys (8, 6, 6) have learned to be very helpful around the house and much more independent with their assignments for school. God has used your book to help prepare us for His plans! I feel totally confident and able to handle mothering and homeschooling and the new baby that will be arriving in January." Julie

"The advice and easy-to-apply information in the book are a must for large and small families alike. It is flexible and anyone can do it; I love that. Even those who normally wouldn't be that structured are saying they love it, and it's so much fun. It's not just adding structure—it's advancing confidence!" Tina

Moms who have applied these methods have gained new hope from MOTH *(Managers of Their Homes)*. They have moved from chaos, stress, and disorganization to peace, contentment, and productivity. You can as well!

To order or for information visit: www.Titus2.com

Or call: (913) 772-0392.

You may also e-mail: managers@Titus2.com

Managers of Their Chores
A Practical Guide to Children's Chores

by Steven & Teri Maxwell

In the same way that *Managers of Their Homes* helped tens of thousands of moms "get it all done," *Managers of Their Chores* helps families conquer the chore battle. The book and included ChorePack system have the potential to revolutionize the way your family accomplishes chores. Whether you are chore challenged or a seasoned chore warrior, you will gain motivation and loads of practical advice on implementing a stress-free chore system.

Before writing this book, we took a chore survey, and hundreds of families responded to our request for information on their experience with chores. Response after response revealed the lifelong benefits of chores or the long-term consequences of not having chores. Most would view the question of whether their children do chores or not as a simple parental-preference decision. However, when we saw how the vast majority of those surveyed indicated that chores were crucial to their preparation for being a parent, a chore book took on a whole new urgency for us.

Many questions arise as families look at the issue of chores: Should children be expected to do chores? How many chores should they have? What age do we begin assigning chores? How do we encourage our children to accomplish their work? Is there a biblical basis for chores? Do chores bring benefits or burdens to our children? *Managers of Their Chores* tackles these questions, giving answers and direction.

Written by parents of eight, *Managers of Their Chores* begins with the biblical foundation for chores and the many benefits chores will bring to a child—both now and in the future. It moves into key factors in parents' lives that will affect a chore system. The book gives pertinent information about what kinds of chores should reasonably be done in a home with children.

One chapter is devoted to helping moms work with their preschoolers on chores. For those moms who say they have no idea where to even begin, the book develops various pieces of a chore system and how it can be set up. Aspects of accountability, rewards, and consequences are addressed. Finally, *Managers of Their Chores* provides step-by-step directions for setting up a ChorePack chore system.

Managers of Their Chores comes with all the ChorePack materials typically needed for four children, including ChorePacks, chore card paper, and a ChorePack holder. In the appendix of the book, you will find a chore library with more than 180 chores listed, forms for use and future photocopying, and sample chore assignments from eight families. Help prepare your children—from preschoolers to teens—for life by teaching them to do chores.

"I can't believe how much time we have gained in our days now that we have our ChorePack system in place." A mom

"Its simplicity and ease of use encouraged independence and accountability at a young age." A mom

"I have just implemented Managers of Their Chores. *Wow! My children are consistently doing their chores and I am free from the daily burden of trying to do it all. Now I know it will get done at a certain time, and my children are growing in responsibility and independence and obedience. Thank you for such a wonderful resource." Heather*

"It enabled the girls to do their own chores well, to not have to argue about whose turn it was or what they were going to do, and I didn't have to nag." A mom

To order or for information visit: www.Titus2.com

Or call: (913) 772-0392.

You may also e-mail: managers@Titus2.com

Keeping Our Children's Hearts
Our Vital Priority
by Steven & Teri Maxwell

Written for parents of young children to teenagers, this book shares the joys and outcomes of our vital priority—keeping our children's hearts. Rebellion and immorality are common among teens even within the Christian community. Does Scripture offer any path of hope for more than this for our children? What can parents do to direct their children toward godliness rather than worldliness? When does this process begin? What is the cost?

Steve and Teri Maxwell believe the key factors in raising children in the nurture and admonition of the Lord (Ephesians 6:4) are whether or not the parents have their children's hearts and what they are doing with those hearts. *Keeping Our Children's Hearts* offers direction and encouragement on this critically important topic.

Included in this book is a chapter co-authored by the three adult Maxwell children concerning their thoughts, feelings, experiences, and outcomes of growing up in a home where their parents wanted to keep their hearts. There are also questions at the end of each chapter, which are thought provoking and helpful.

"The most complete and most balanced book I have read on how to raise children who won't rebel!" Dr. S. M. Davis

"This book is making me rethink what my purpose as a Christian, mother, and homeschooler should be." A mom

"The Scripture and its experiential application was encouraging and refreshing." A dad

To order or for information visit: www.Titus2.com
Or call: (913) 772-0392.

Homeschooling with a Meek and Quiet Spirit
by Teri Maxwell

The desire of a homeschooling mother's heart is to have a meek and quiet spirit instead of discouragement, fear, and anger.

Because Teri Maxwell, a mother of eight, has walked the homeschooling path since 1985, she knows first-hand the struggle for a meek and quiet spirit. The memories from her early homeschooling years of often being worried and angry rather than having a meek and quiet spirit are not what she would like them to be. Her prayer is that as she shares the work the Lord has done in her heart, through homeschooling, you would be encouraged that He can do the same for you. She also desires that you could learn from the lessons He has taught her so that you would begin to have a meek and quiet spirit long before she did.

Will your journey toward a meek and quiet spirit be completed upon finding the perfect spelling curriculum or deciding which chores your child should be doing? Perhaps the answer lies on a different path.

In these pages, Teri offers practical insights into gaining a meek and quiet spirit that any mom can apply to her individual circumstances. She transparently shares the struggles God has brought her through and what He has shown her during these many homeschooling years.

In *Homeschooling with a Meek and Quiet Spirit*, you will discover the heart issues that will gently lead you to a meek and quiet spirit. Come along and join Teri as you seek the Lord to homeschool with a meek and quiet spirit!

"This is one of the best, most helpful, encouraging, and empathetic books I've read during my 5 years of homeschooling." A mom

To order or for information visit: www.Titus2.com
Or call: (913) 772-0392.

Preparing Sons to Provide for a Single-Income Family

by Steven Maxwell

In today's world of two-income families, preparing a son to provide for a single-income family seems an overwhelming task. Christian parents will find it helpful to have a purpose and plan as they raise sons who will one day be responsible for supporting a family.

Steve Maxwell presents the groundwork for preparing your son to be a wage-earning adult. He gives practical suggestions and direction to parents for working with their sons from preschool age all the way through to adult-hood. You will be challenged to evaluate your own life and the example you are setting for your son.

As the father of eight children, four of them now wage-earning adults, Steve has gained valuable experience he openly shares with other parents. Learn these principles from a dad whose twenty-four-year-old homeschooled son purchased a home debt free a year before his marriage, and whose second son has done the same. Steve explains how it is possible for parents, with a willing commitment, to properly prepare their sons to provide for a single-income family.

"You are dealing with topics that no one I know of has dealt with as thoroughly and practically as you have." Dr. S. M. Davis

"Preparing Sons was a big blessing to my husband. All you ladies should get a copy for your husband and every church library needs one." Shelly

Preparing Sons is available in paperback or unabridged audio-book.

To order or for information visit: www.Titus2.com
Or call: (913) 772-0392.

Just Around the Corner: Encouragement and Challenge for Christian Dads and Moms, Volume 2

by Steven & Teri Maxwell

Just Around the Corner, Volume 2 is a compilation of Steve and Teri Maxwell's monthly Dad's and Mom's Corners. Steve's writing will challenge dads in their role as the spiritual head of the family. Teri's writing addresses many aspects of daily life that often frustrate or discourage a mom.

You will find the Mom's Corners grouped together in the front of the book and the Dad's Corners in the back. The Corners are all indexed so that you can read the ones relating to a specific topic you are interested in, if you so choose.

Topics addressed in *Just Around the Corner,* Volume 2 include anger, the importance of prayer, contentment, dads as the leaders of their families, influencing children's spiritual outcome, parenting, homeschooling, husband/wife relationships and much more!

With four of the Maxwell children now adults, Steve and Teri write from the perspective of having seen the truth of God's Word put into practice. At the same time, they are still in the trenches homeschooling four children.

"The Maxwells are so encouraging and down to earth." Michelle

"It always seems as though the Mom's Corner is exactly what I need to hear at that particular time. I am so glad that Teri can be an 'older' Titus 2 woman in my life, although, somewhat indirectly." A mom

To order or for information visit: www.Titus2.com
Or call: (913) 772-0392.

The Moody Family Series
Summer with the Moodys
Autumn with the Moodys
Winter with the Moodys
Spring with the Moodys

Often parents are concerned about negative examples and role models in books their children are reading. One goal in writing the Moody Series was to eliminate those kinds of examples replacing them with positive, godly ones.

In the four books, you'll find the Moodys helping a widowed neighbor, starting small businesses for the children, enjoying a family fun night, training their new puppy, homeschooling, Mom experiencing morning sickness, and much more! Woven throughout the books is the Moodys' love for the Lord and their enjoyment of time together. Children (parents too!) will enjoy Mr. and Mrs. Moody, Max, Mollie, Mitch, and Maddie—they'll come away challenged and encouraged.

"My six-year-old son asked Jesus into his heart while we were read-ing Autumn with the Moodys. *These books are wonderful, heart-warming Christian reading. The Moodys will always have a special place in our hearts!" A mom*

"At last, a Christian book series that is engaging and encourages my children to love Jesus more and bless their family and friends." A mom

To order or for information visit: www.Titus2.com
Or call: (913) 772-0392.

Audio Resources
Encouragement for the Homeschool Family

by the Maxwell Family

Encouragement for the Homeschool Family is an eight-session audio seminar which will encourage, exhort, and equip homeschooling families. Included in the album: *The Homeschooling Family—Building a Vision, Managers of Their Homes, Manager of His Home, Loving Your Husband, Sports—Friend or Foe, Anger—Relationship Poison, Experiencing the Joy of Young Womanhood,* and *Success or Failure* (for young men).

To order or for information visit: www.Titus2.com. Or call: (913) 772-0392.

Feed My Sheep
A Practical Guide to Daily Family Devotions

by Steve Maxwell

Tried them and failed? Never tried because you knew it would be too big of a battle? No time for them even if you wanted to? Do any of these questions describe your experience with family devotions? This two CD set is highly motivational and practical.

In the first CD, Steve Maxwell gives realistic advice for achieving success with family devotions. He reveals the secret that he guarantees will work. He also explains common problems causing many families to fail with daily family devotions and then gives solutions to these difficulties.

The second CD contains two of the Maxwells' family devotions recorded live. You'll feel like you're right at home with Steve as you listen to him lead his family in their time in the Word. You will see how easy it is to lead your family in the most important time of the day.

Join Steve, father of eight, as he shares about the Maxwells' favorite part of their day. We pray you'll come away with an excitement for the daily feeding of your family from God's Word!

To order or for information visit: www.Titus2.com
Or call: (913) 772-0392.

Manager of His Home
Helping Your Wife Succeed
As She Manages Your Home

by Steve Maxwell

Most dads truly desire to lead their families in a way that is pleasing to the Lord. But how is that learned since many men have not had a good role model to follow? How are we to responsibly lead our families without being a dictator or being so soft as not to lead at all?

In this session you will be given practical, biblical suggestions for how you can support and facilitate your wife in her role as a homeschooling mom. Often there is no better way to convey your love for your wife.

"I would recommend this message to others because it provided plenty of practical, daily examples of how to lead the family." A dad

To order or for information visit: www.Titus2.com
Or call: (913) 772-0392.

Individual Audio Titles

The Homeschooling Family — Building a Vision

by Steve and Teri Maxwell

Whether new or experienced home-schoolers, this motivational and practical session helps a family attain their heartfelt goals for raising and educating their children. Doubts, discouragement, and burnout can easily shipwreck the family that doesn't know "where they are going." What is it that keeps a family homeschooling through a mom's feelings of being overwhelmed, a child with a rebellious spirit, or a house full of babies and toddlers?

Together, Steve and Teri share in this session how they moved from homeschooling for convenience (we'll try it a year and see how it goes) to homeschooling forever. They will give you concrete examples from homeschooling struggles they have experienced and how they made it through. With four adult children whom they homeschooled and four more children who are currently being homeschooled, they have the experience to know how to keep on while still being in the trenches of day to day homeschooling.

Loving Your Husband

By Teri Maxwell

This is an incredible session every woman should listen to. It is easy for a mom to become consumed with children and day-to-day life. This leaves the opportunity for creating a huge gap in her relationship with the key person in her life—her husband. Don't damage or lose that special relationship with your husband but rather develop and strengthen it.

Sports — Friend or Foe?

By Steve Maxwell

Homeschooling families are heavily involved in sports. What are the parents' goals in having their children participate in organized sports? Are these goals being met? Are the children better or worse by being one of the team? Steve shares data from a large on-line survey that he conducted regarding Christian families and sports.

Anger — Relationship Poison

By Steve and Teri Maxwell

Homeschooling families have a heart's desire to raise godly children. However, it seems that anger is found in many homeschooling parents, and it can undermine all the hours invested in positive teaching. It can destroy our most precious relationships. Have you noticed how certain levels of anger are accepted and justified? Is a little anger beneficial? Do you have difficulty controlling your anger? Is a harsh tone in your voice anger? Are you discouraged by the anger in your life and in your home? Steve and Teri will encourage you on this universally needed topic as they share from God's Word and personal testimonies.

Experiencing the Joy of Young Womanhood

By Sarah Maxwell

Sarah explores aspects of a young woman's life that lead to true joy. It all starts with the foundation—your relationship with Jesus Christ. She delves into hindrances to joy as well as practical aspects of it. Plenty of personal testimonies from Sarah's life are sprinkled into the session.

Success or Failure — Where Are You Headed?

By Christopher Maxwell

Homeschooled young men have incredible potential for success in their lives—both spiritually and vocationally. There are tragic pitfalls that might appear innocuous on the surface to be avoided. In addition there are basic elements crucial for success in the spiritual world and in the business world. This session explores how the different aspects of a young man's life will affect his future.

To order any of the audio titles or for more information: www.Titus2.com Or call: (913) 772-0392.

Dr. S. M. Davis Audio Titles

Freedom from the Spirit of Anger
by Dr. S. M. Davis

We feel this to be the most important audio message you could hear to help you overcome the spirit of anger. Dr. Davis will grip your heart as he shares about this life-changing issue. Even if you just have a "tone" in your voice, it is still anger. Dr. Davis gives ten key steps to find freedom from the spirit of anger. It has helped us make tremendous positive change in our family as we seek to overcome anger.

Changing the Heart of a Rebel
by Dr. S. M. Davis

We recommend this audio message for parents only. We feel it is a very important topic and ties in with the theme of *Keeping Our Children's Hearts.* Even if your child is not rebelling, you will glean great insight from listening to this sermon. You'll discover warning signs for which to watch plus a strong resolve to keep your child from rebelling.

The Attitude No Lady Should Have
by Dr. S. M. Davis

Do you struggle with submission to your husband or wrong attitudes toward him? We believe this message holds the key to many areas of struggle Christian women face concerning their husbands. Dr. Davis contrasts the Mary versus Martha attitude, making it applicable to a husband/wife relationship.

How a Wife Can Use Reverence to Build or Save Her Marriage

by Dr. S. M. Davis

Dr. Davis shares principles and keys to how a wife can build her marriage through reverence. Oftentimes, wives will tear their husbands down, unknowingly and sometimes knowingly, through correcting, criticizing, complaining, and many other things. Listening to this sermon has the potential of totally changing your marriage. We highly recommend this audio to any wife or single woman (many of the principles could apply to your father).

What Pride Does

by Dr. S. M. Davis

Pride hides, something Dr. Davis emphasizes throughout this very important message. You may be surprised to hear there are several different types of pride, which Dr. Davis explains. It's easy to think you don't struggle with pride, but after listening to this incredible audio, you'll likely discover a hidden area of pride. Don't let pride destroy your Christian walk and testimony!

To order any of the audio titles or for more information: www.Titus2.com
Or call: (913) 772-0392.

How to Humble Yourself
by Dr. S. M. Davis

A great sequel to *What Pride Does*. If you have realized the destructiveness of pride, that is a good start. But what are you going to do about it? Repentance is one of the keys to humbling our selves. Dr. Davis provides practical advice on what steps a person, who wants to be humble, should take. The big question is: will we put forth the effort? Dr. Davis encourages us in the blessings that await us if only we choose to.

God's Viewpoint on Having Babies
by Dr. S. M. Davis

We recommend this message for parents only. It's a great message from Dr. Davis that deals with family size from a Biblical perspective.

The Language of The Christian's Clothing
by Dr. S. M. Davis

This is an excellent message on the important topic of modesty. *The Language of the Christian's Clothing* covers such a crucial issue that often stirs up division in Christian circles. We feel that Dr. Davis has dealt with the issue of a Christian's modesty from a very biblical and sound perspective.

To order or for information visit: www.Titus2.com
Or call: (913) 772-0392.